The Dancing Goddess

THE *Dancing*

Goddess

PRINCIPLES OF A MATRIARCHAL AESTHETIC

Heide Göttner-Abendroth

TRANSLATED BY MAUREEN T. KRAUSE

BEACON PRESS · BOSTON

Beacon Press
25 Beacon Street
Boston, Massachusetts 02108

Beacon Press books
are published under the auspices of
the Unitarian Universalist Association of Congregations.

First English edition
published by arrangement with
Verlag Frauenoffensive.

98 97 96 95 94 93 92 91   8 7 6 5 4 3 2 1

Text design by Linda Koegel

Library of Congress Cataloging-in-Publication Data
Göttner-Abendroth, Heide, 1941–
[Tanzende Göttin. English]
The dancing goddess: principles of a matriarchal aesthetic /
Heide Göttner-Abendroth; translated by Maureen T. Krause.—
1st English ed.
p. cm.
Translation of: Die Tanzende Göttin.
Includes bibliographical references.
ISBN 0-8070-6753-9
1. Feminism and the arts.   2. Women and spiritualism.
I. Title.
NX180.F4G613   1991
700'.1'03—dc20   90-24769
CIP

For Helen
my youngest daughter
who is filled with music
and whom I almost lost
but recovered in a wondrous way

Contents

Preface

The continuing interest of my women and men readers has resulted in a second edition of my book. I am happy about that and would like to express my thanks in two ways: first, through this preface, which addresses very briefly the basic ideas of the book; and second, through a longer afterword, in which I come to terms with critical opinions and views concerning the theme "matriarchal art and spirituality." I am indebted to those critiques for the clarification of many arguments in my book; they also form the basis of my response in the afterword.

My book consists of four essays. The first offers a critical analysis of the history of art in patriarchy. The second lays the theoretical groundwork for a matriarchal art; and, as a theory of art, it is an aesthetic. The third essay interprets the tendencies in contemporary women's art that seem to correspond to the criteria of matriarchal art. Drawing on those results, the fourth essay establishes the connection between matriarchal art and matriarchal spirituality—which are merely two aspects of the same phenomenon. The fourth essay concludes with suggestions on how this complex art-spirituality can be realized.

These suggestions are not mere utopian speculation but the description of a concrete process in which I am creating this new matriarchal *Gesamtkunstwerk,* or "comprehensive artwork" (an entirely inadequate term) in cooperation with other women.

From this experience I have gained the gratifying recognition that matriarchal art really is as I conceived of it several years ago. Moreover, I have also rediscovered myself as an "artist" in the radical sense of art formulated here—whereas I was formerly merely a "philosopher" or a "writer."

My definition of *matriarchal art* is radical because it neutralizes the conventional separation of the artistic genres; the division of the traditional domains of "art," "science," "religion," "economics," and "politics"; and the dichotomy between the spheres of "art" and "life." All such divisions are typical characteristics of the *patriarchal* mentality and social organization, in which art appears only as "beautiful semblance," in contrast to life as "hard reality."

In patriarchal societies all social spheres are strictly separated and isolated in various institutions. That in turn creates elite groups and serves to enforce power interests. All of society is hierarchically ordered according to those power interests. The result is domination and oppression—not only *within* but *among* the individual institutions. For example, "science" is at the top of the scale today and "religion" is at the bottom—in past centuries it was the reverse. In the face of such "hard realities," what possible significance can "art" as "beautiful semblance" have?

I am using quotation marks because these terms designating isolated spheres, purviews, and categories are merely verbal crutches for the development of an all-encompassing view: totality is the theme of this book and the essence of my radical conception of art. My goal is to surmount the patriarchal, power-oriented splintering and artistic hierarchy, which empties our lives of beauty, ignores our complex experiences, and denies our concrete, multifarious being of any force.

I call this radical conception of art *matriarchal art* because, in formulating these new ideas, I have drawn upon my research into matriarchal societies. Matriarchal societies did not recognize such hierarchies and consequently knew neither dominance on the one hand nor oppression and exploitation on the other. Matriarchal societies did not split consciousness into "art," "science," "religion," "economics," and "politics"; nor did they recognize an antagonism between religion and science—neither theory's contempt for life and vice versa, nor morality's hatred of human instincts and vice versa.

All these misanthropic dismemberments were alien to matriarchal societies, since their worldview held that all existing things were embedded in the grand context of life in all its manifestations and expressions. There was no above and below, no good and evil; even death was not a great phantom of anxiety but merely a passageway to a different form of existence. A worldview having no hierarchy of values inspired each individual to view herself/himself as a part of a larger community, and people as a whole to recognize themselves as part of a larger nature.

These relationships and this holistic way of thinking were so self-evident to those earlier, matriarchal peoples that they did not require the divisive concepts imposed later. But *we* need such concepts in *patriarchal* cultures, and these concepts have become so self-evident to *us* that we no longer even notice the alienation of parts from the whole, the inhuman inner strife, and the cynical irrationality they entail. We can learn to think and speak differently, but only with great difficulty, for we simply lack the terms.

But perhaps they can be developed. The concept of "matriarchal art" is one such new term, for it never refers to *art alone* but always to a *societal form* entirely different from those known today. Any discussion of "matriarchal art" always entails everything else simultaneously: matriarchal science, matriarchal spirituality, and the matriarchal way of life. In addition, "matriarchal aesthetics" always connotes matriarchal politics. My discussion of matriarchal aesthetics is limited only by the scope of this book.

To come to terms with the isolating and fragmenting object known as a book, I first wrote about "matriarchal mythology" in *Die Göttin und ihr Heros* (The goddess and her hero), in 1980, and then about "matriarchal aesthetics" in the present work— *an attempt to realize fundamental ideas of matriarchal mythology on the plane of artistic-ritualistic practice.* "Matriarchal mythology" and "matriarchal aesthetics" are merely two aspects of the same phenomenon. Thus, my more rigorous and methodical study on matriarchal mythology represents the scientific core from which my present essays on matriarchal art have evolved. This, by the way, should answer the question put to me many times—namely, whether this second book is "scholarly" or not.

The radicalness of my definition of "art" has alarmed many contemporary women artists who have already obtained with great effort or are still willing to struggle for a place in contemporary art. Their reaction is largely vehement defensiveness against these new ideas and a clinging to traditional forms of art, into which they laboriously attempt to fit their new contents. However, this nascent discrepancy between the constrictive forms of patriarchal art (which have remained essentially unchanged despite any modernistic posturing) and the new, experiential modes that women bring to art (which exceed the scope of patriarchal art) will intensify. The conflict will in turn open the way to matriarchal art: an art that transcends types, genres, and other purviews; an art that no longer has the character of a "work"; an art that is a dynamic *process* and no longer coheres to art *objects* (which are becoming increasingly artificial); an art that is a perpetually fluid, symbolic expression in which the "works" are organically embedded as poetic-energetic symbols.

Of course I understand the ambivalent reaction of women who are still trying to validate themselves in traditional forms of art. Nevertheless, several women artists of my acquaintance are solving the problem in a positive way: with complete openness and the wealth of their artistic talents, they have entered with me into the process of matriarchal art, on which we have been collaborating periodically for a year. By doing so, these artists have ceased to be the sometimes admired, often egocentric, isolated, solitary individuals that the modern-day art world had made them. Instead, they are united in a group of equally original women who together create symbolic expression within a larger framework requiring all our powers.

However, the common interest of the group does not preclude the expression of the artists' individuality but engenders artistic dialogues in which one artist takes up and continues what another began—a fascinating interplay. This cooperative situation is new and unusual but, by its very nature, brings satisfaction and joy to the participants. In addition, these women also continue to work independently as artists, poets, musicians, and dancers. Participation in these cooperative experiments in matriarchal art precludes conventional individual work as artists in *theory* but not necessarily in *practice*. Such a dogmatic exclusionary position would be an unnecessary constraint in view of the present ambivalent situation of women in the sphere of art—and all other social spheres. These artists are free to decide whether to continue to participate in artistic practice that bears the imprint of patriarchy and adheres to patriarchal divisions, differentiations, and hierarchical-sexist criteria of value. One wonders, however, how long women can continue to endure such oppression in the face of their own constantly changing situation.

The association of "art" and "spirituality" may seem problematical to some women, but such a reaction betrays a disjointed way of thinking I no longer share. In archaic matriarchies, matriarchal spirituality permeated *all* social phenomena—including the scientific, artistic, and political—as an all-encompassing interpretation of the world, not as a spiritualistic or clerical superstructure but as a comprehensive view that united all manifestations of life. It was expressed in the rich and profound texture of the seasonal cycle and the ring of recurring festivals, which mirrored the worldview and social order of the matriarchies. Today, matriarchal spirituality contains the nucleus of the same all-encompassing view of things, although no longer on a naïve level but on a philosophical and contemplative plane. Modern matriarchal spirituality strives to discover and decode the remnants and ciphers of the archaic matriarchal way of thinking handed down to us. That is *our* task, since the discovering and decoding have not been done for us by researchers influenced by patriarchy.

The remnants and ciphers of the ancient seasonal cycle are of particular importance, because matriarchal thought was vivified in the cycle as a continuous chain of multifarious, artistically structured festivals. The true mission of "matriarchal art" is to reclaim those festivals and adapt them to our present situation; to enrich them with all our talents in dance, poetry, music, and the visual arts; and to gain a better understanding of ourselves in the process.

NOVEMBER 1983

Acknowledgments

I would like to thank Susanne Kahn-Ackermann for her tireless assistance in obtaining materials on and works by women artists and for her intelligent reading of my manuscript. I would also like to thank Anna Fengel for her support in providing further artistic material, and Margaret Tesch for bringing several folk customs to my attention and for helping to proofread the manuscript.

In the beginning, Eurynome, the Goddess of All Things, rose naked from Chaos, but found nothing substantial for her feet to rest upon, and therefore divided the sea from the sky, dancing lonely upon its waves. She danced towards the south, and the wind set in motion behind her seemed something new and apart with which to begin a work of creation. Wheeling about, she caught hold of this north wind, rubbed it between her hands, and behold! the great serpent Ophion. Eurynome danced to warm herself, wildly and more wildly, until Ophion, grown lustful, coiled about those divine limbs and was moved to couple with her. . . . So Eurynome was likewise got with child.

Next, she assumed the form of a dove, brooding on the waves and, in due process of time, laid the Universal Egg. At her bidding, Ophion coiled seven times about this egg, until it hatched and split in two. Out tumbled all things that exist, her children: sun, moon, planets, stars, the earth with its mountains and rivers, its trees, herbs, and living creatures.

ROBERT GRAVES, *The Greek Myths*

In the beginning, Eurynome, the Goddess of All Things, rose naked from Chaos, but found nothing substantial for her feet to rest upon, and therefore divided the sea from the sky, dancing lonely upon its waves. She danced towards the south, and the wind set in motion behind her seemed something new and apart with which to begin a work of creation. Wheeling about, she caught hold of this north wind, rubbed it between her hands, and behold! the great serpent Ophion. Eurynome danced to warm herself, wildly and more wildly, until Ophion, grown lustful, coiled about those divine limbs and was moved to couple with her. . . . So Eurynome was likewise got with child.

Next, she assumed the form of a dove, brooding on the waves and, in due process of time, laid the Universal Egg. At her bidding, Ophion coiled seven times about this egg, until it hatched and split in two. Out tumbled all things that exist, her children: sun, moon, planets, stars, the earth with its mountains and rivers, its trees, herbs, and living creatures.

ROBERT GRAVES, *The Greek Myths*

ONE

Art as Ghetto

A Critical Examination of the History of Art in the Public Sphere

I would like to develop a new perspective on art and the theory of art against the backdrop of my studies on matriarchal mythology.[1] When I speak of "the history of art in the public sphere," I am already proceeding from an altered conception of history that extends back to very early epochs having only oral traditions.[2] My view of history makes it possible to examine the consciously ideological origins of historiography—which served as the justification for the patriarchal form of society and later became unconsciously ideological—and to rediscover an epoch of humankind that has been suppressed from public knowledge, namely, the matriarchal age.[3] The existence of the matriarchal age is not a matter of a distant, archaic, primitive age, as our history books would have us believe; on the contrary, it encompassed all continents and in many places developed over the millennia from simple agricultural societies into highly cultured civilizations.[4] These matriarchal civilizations—ancient Indus, Sumer, Egypt, and Crete, for example—not only formed the foundation for later patriarchal civilizations but also had an extraordinary, previously unacknowledged impact on them.

I would like to approach the problem of "art and art in the public sphere" from this new historical perspective.[5] In doing so, I am less concerned with the usual linear sequence of epochs than with the comparison of patterns of social structure—that is, the matriarchal pattern and the patriarchal pattern in their variations, into which art was embedded along with its functions. These preliminary remarks bring me to my theme, the Muses and Apollo.

Art and Its Audience in Matriarchal Societies

The story of the Muses and Apollo refers to a prehistoric revolution that upset the balance between feminine and masculine principles, namely, the suppression of matriarchy by patriarchy. In former times, the poetic trance had been an integral part of the ecstatic veneration of the ancient matriarchal Greek Muse, who, as the Triple goddess, ruled heaven, earth, and the underworld.[6] She was worshiped on mountaintops, and her altars stood at the foot of Mount Parnassus, Mount Olympus, and Mount Helicon, where her female devotees danced during festivals of the moon. Among them was a male dancer. He invoked the Muse and sang hexameters to the music of a lyre until, in an ecstatic circle dance, the Muse became incarnate in one of the female dancers. The dancer spoke, sang, and acted upon the command of her Goddess. The frenzy generally culminated in the death of the male singer-dancer, for he was the voluntary sacral victim of the wild Muses, just as Orpheus was of the Maenads.

In Greece, shortly before the eighth century B.C., the patriarchal god Apollo took over the veneration of the Muses and transformed their cult to suit his own religious purposes by electing himself their leader and chief dancer. In this way he personally laid claim to authority over the Goddess. At this stage, the invocation of the Muse gradually turned into a mere formality. When her veneration was dissociated once and for all from the rites of the altar, she never again spoke through a female initiate, because from that moment on it was Apollo who, as leader of the Muses, dictated the poems. Although he rose to become the patron of poetry, Apollo was incapable of including an authentic trance and so prohibited any ecstatic expression—with the exception of his own highly tendentious oracle.[7]

This story of the Muses and Apollo is a myth that in its original form—without Apollo, but with that first dancer, the hero-king as the partner of the goddess of music—was associated with a historically visible ritual. The ancient ritual corresponded to the matriarchal myth of the Great Goddess, who ruled the three-tiered world.

There were other correspondences in the matriarchal ritual festival that reveal the cultural, social, and political reality of the myth, for the myth also mirrored the matriarchal form of society, in which the women dominated. That social order was in turn dependent on an economy in which the very production of food, clothing, shelter, and tools lay in female hands. Goods were distributed according to specific patterns that corresponded to the myth of the Goddess, who provided equally for her earthly children. The mythic ritual festivals, as they recurred in the normal sequence of the seasons, mirrored all the complex practices of matriarchal societies.

As a result, their forms of expression were extraordinarily multifarious: dance, music, song, processions, dramatic scenes, and voluptuous revels coalesced into an indivisible totality. The central dramatic scenes in the course of the seasons—initiation, marriage, sacrificial death, and resurrection—were not merely depicted but actually executed as sacred acts. According to the beliefs of that epoch, those scenes possessed a magical character and safeguarded earthly fertility and the cosmic order as the eternal return of life. The public magical dramas were the culmination and symbolic fulfillment of complex social practice itself. This was art in the matriarchy, although no such category yet existed. Art included everything that happened at the magical ritual festivals. Art symbolically and actually encompassed all the complex activities of those societies. These were the "practical arts," such as the art of agriculture, the art of cultivating plants and breeding animals; the art of toolmaking, of weaving, of potting; the art of herbal medicine, of astronomy and astrology, of music as mirror of the cosmos; the art of the trance, of eroticism, of the oracle, of wisdom; the art of discovering and directing natural, spiritual, and social relationships; the art of ruling without coercion. Art included everything that exerted a positive influence on the community.

Since art was erudition and practical knowledge in the form of public ritual magic, it actively and decisively influenced social life: there was no separation at all of art and audience. The magical festivals were the climax of the fusion of the mythological and the social—the aesthetic dimension in which they moved was not "beautiful semblance" but social and political *reality*. The aesthetic dimension determined social life to such an extent that social structures were ordered according to the conceptions of the myth as it manifested itself in ritual: people tried to harmonize all things because they considered their community to be the earthly image of the cosmic order of the matriarchal goddess, the muse.

The Patriarchalization of the Magical Arts

With the advent of early patriarchal societies, the aesthetic dimension underwent a fundamental change, as evidenced by the relationship of the god Apollo to the Muses: not only did Apollo supplant the matriarchal hero-king—the dancer at the ecstatic rituals—and steal his title; he also subdued the Muses and, in Homer's words, "tamed their wildness."[8] Suddenly, the Goddess was subordinated to the new gods. The myth was distorted, the social order inverted, and the old rites of divine-poetic ecstasy abolished. From then on—as Robert Graves describes in his historical studies—poetry became a matter of form, and the residue of inspiration, which was still tolerated in oracles, received a tendentious character that served the political aims of patriarchy.[9]

The status of the aesthetic dimension changed: it was transformed—to the extent that it could be redefined—into an instrument of power, into ideology. Or, in cases where the aesthetic dimension resisted this spurious redefinition, it was demoralized and banished to the ghetto, the shadowy fringes of society. The earlier magical harmony between society and the external and internal cosmos was shattered. Ritual acts lost their magic and were transmuted into allegory, into representations of the power elite.

The Muse suffered a dual degeneration: first, in the service of the power structure, she became a model of ideological mythology, religion, and art; her acts became contrived utilitarian forms designed to convey meaning. She thus served to legitimate the very powers that subjugated her. In that role she increasingly amplified her histrionic aspect, since she had lost her spontaneous, erotic-ecstatic quality—which henceforth came to be regarded as chaotic and dangerous. As domesticated by Apollo, the Muse was cut off from social reality and became vested with an illusory reality of formal criteria, rules, and prescribed themes and tones.

Her second degeneration assumed other forms: insofar as her female and male devotees evaded domestication, they preserved the old magical forms and their original meaning, but they could do this only secretly, in the subculture of the lower classes and fringe groups. Matriarchal undercurrents thus subsisted within patriarchal societies through the millennia as a reminder of the Golden Age and as utopian hope. In the beginning this took the form of conscious criticism, rejection, protest, political opposition, and political hope—a revolt, if only in fantasy. The constantly seething opposition within the new system increasingly came under pressure, defamation, and persecution.

In the secret cults, however, the old rites degenerated into empty formulas and mere repeated patterns whose original meaning had faded. Those forms soon became incomprehensible to those who transmitted them, and the Muse in the ghetto became the rustic, colorful, trivial entertainment of street singers, conjurers, gypsies, and all migrant groups in general. The Muse developed into folk art, folk festivals, and popular entertainment—from the fiesta to the Mardi Gras. She was surprisingly varied in expression and surprisingly invariable in form. Equally invariable was the disdain with which she was regarded through the millennia by the "true" artists, who made their careers in the service of the power structure.

The splitting of the aesthetic dimension into a domesticated Muse on the one hand and a Muse in the ghetto on the other hand prevailed throughout the patriarchal millennia. Those in power created for their art a predisposed audience consisting of people who shared their privileges. The ghettoized art, which did not even recognize itself as such and was repudiated by others, roved about among the simple folk, where it enjoyed a wide audience but in an enclave of powerlessness. That is my thesis. I shall now elucidate it by means of concrete examples.

CLASSICAL GREECE

The Olympian religion of Hellenic Greece played the role of ideology in this early patriarchal society. As such, its repercussions were still felt in classical Greece and manifested themselves in the monumental state buildings of the time—the great temples to the glory of the Olympians, particularly the father of the gods, Zeus—and in these temples the colossal, flawless statues that documented the perfection of official art, its high degree of technology, and its simultaneous loss of substance. Art was primarily a matter of representing the new patriarchal worldview and supporting the dominion of the new aristocracy. This decorative state art, which comes under the category of the domesticated Muse, later reached its greatest diffusion and greatest vacuity in imperialist Rome, capital of a violently conquered world-empire.

The development of representational state art runs parallel to the defamation of nonofficial art—of older, repressed traditions. Those traditions in no way regarded themselves as "art," in the new sense of the term, but as the symbolic fulfillment of life. It was primarily mythos that became the object of derision and rejection by the highly regarded state philosophers of classical Greece, the theoreticians of the legitimation of the new society. According to Plato, myths are fabricated stories, complete inventions that serve only to deceive and confuse the spirit—for the new philosophical spirit no longer thought in images but in abstractions. Plato thus created a deep chasm between the aristocratic thinkers and the common people, with their mythological "old wives' tales." Those who perpetuated this deception and confusion of the spirit by narrating mythology—namely, the poets—were to be banished from Plato's philosophical state.[10]

The sexist intent of this defamation becomes obvious in Aristotle. For him, the feminine is the incarnation of the dark, the material, the sensual, the nonspiritual—all that is inherent in matter and its confusing manifestations. And everything associated with this sex, including mythology, is tacitly excluded from his logic and science.[11]

Apparently, the difficulties involved in repressing the ritual festivals central to the matriarchal form of society were greater than those involved in repressing the already distorted mythos.

Although the matriarchal goddess-priestess and her hero-king who performed those rites had long since been eliminated, the far-reaching significance of that constellation did not fade as quickly. The notion that the hero experiences his fate—through the agency of the Goddess and as the representative of all people—as rise, fall, and return in transfiguration persisted for a long time. Greek theater, that is, tragedy, which portrayed the heroic in precisely that sense, originated on the foundation of this matriarchal conception of the heroic. But with the loss of the ritual festivals, theater and its complex forms of expression turned into folk festival.

Like the matriarchal festivals, Greek theater drew the audience deeply into the action; but the terror, the catharsis it engendered, was nothing more than an echo of the magical powers of the old rituals, in which the people identified with the hero and suffered with him the entire spiritual-cosmic transformation. Greek theater was only an echo of the matriarchal ritual festivals, for the action in Greek theater was a mere *fiction:* instead of being executed, it was merely enacted. The reality of the action was lost and, with it, the credibility of the aesthetic dimension. That is what characterizes Greek theater as the *Muse in the ghetto,* whose main attribute is social inefficacy.

THE MIDDLE AGES
The European Middle Ages are another epoch with classically patriarchal features. The Middle Ages developed in northern Europe according to processes of social and cultural superimposition similar to those that had occurred much earlier in the Mediterranean region. Medieval Europe, too, had a feudal economy, a patriarchal social structure, and a religion that legitimated the new worldview; it, too, created a sharp opposition between religious and courtly art on the one hand, and folk art on the other hand.

As oral tradition, folk art occupied a broad domain but, as

artistic expression, never penetrated the consciousness of the upper class. Nevertheless, that did not prevent the court poets from drawing directly on folk tradition—legends, fables, and fairy tales, all of mythic-matriarchal origin—to create their most beautiful motifs and epics. The introductions to their works, however, are characteristic of the domesticated Muse of those privileged court poets in that they invariably mention their patrons, who supposedly gave them their subject matter and themes, and their own artistic talent, which set them apart from the uneducated, illiterate masses. The court poets, however, clearly distanced themselves from the true sources of their subject matter: the minstrels and traveling storytellers, the vagabond street players and scholars—all of whom knew the old mythological treasures from memory and narrated them to the people at the marketplaces. But the latter represented the Muse in the ghetto and, as such, were despised. As a result, the definition of "true" poets always had the same gist: the vagabonds and minstrels were thoroughly incapable of narrating the material in the correct sense! In actuality, the vagabonds and minstrels narrated the material in the original magical-matriarchal sense, whereas the court poets distorted it for so long that the ancient narrative pattern changed to mirror the worldview of the new patriarchal Christian Age of Chivalry, including insinuations about the fickleness and worthlessness of women.

BOURGEOIS SOCIETY
With the emergence and strengthening of the bourgeoisie in modern Europe, and its triumph following the bourgeois revolutions, the social picture changed: between a semifeudal, wealthy upper class and a semiagrarian, industrial lower class there evolved an administrative middle class. The patriarchal character of society persisted and, with it, an intensified splitting of the aesthetic dimension, for art was now becoming

increasingly class-specific and artificial, and its audience increasingly problematical.

Art passed through various stages. During the period of the bourgeois revolutions, the principle of artistic autonomy was formulated, a principle originally having a progressive thrust: to free art from the ideological grip of throne and altar, to make the domesticated Muse into a true Muse again. However, the path that was to lead there was contradictory: art itself was elevated to a religion, the Muse to a pseudosacral cult, and the artist to a genius who, in renouncing external influences on art, ostensibly created everything from himself/herself (the principle of originality). The artist and his/her art increasingly became the theme, and the problems expressed became an ersatz mythology for a small class—the educated. That tendency led to an elitist *self-ghettoization:* in its ivory tower, art visibly lost its social function.

Another major trend in modern art seemed to run counter to this self-ghettoization, namely, the psychologicalization of art. Psychic and social connections were now presented in realistic language and turned critically against the prevailing social order. Following its social-critical zenith, however, this art increasingly became the sole arena for libidinal energies no longer tolerated elsewhere—whether it preserved in its representations the repressed and lost erotic and utopian possibilities or provided free territory for the otherwise taboo psychic desires of the artist himself/herself. As a result, the subjectivization of forms, language, and meanings rapidly increased until every work became its own mythos, and every artist his/her own prophet or therapist. Art became an ersatz libido of arbitrary individuals, whose arbitrary experiences and arbitrary views interested the audience less and less. In this way, the social function of art became so individuated that it all but disappeared.

The third major style of modern art, its abstract variation, attempted to solve the problem by exposing the structures of art and refusing to resort to interchangeable and increasingly diffuse meanings. Now art, which in patriarchy had long been a substitute for genuine poetic power—i.e., magical-erotic ecstasy—was itself replaced by the intellectual analysis of its forms, which turned into self-representation. But were those *forms* a more objective category than the *meanings* that had degenerated in the meantime? They were no longer forms of an ancient mythic-poetic pattern from matriarchal times, which, in its very structure, expressed an entire worldview and was acknowledged by all people. On the contrary, the forms were recently accumulated, increasingly artificial formalizations based on systems of the ideological content of rules that changed according to fashion. Without questioning those formalizations themselves, abstract art merely made use of contrived chance, and thus degenerated into pure artistry of the artificial. Not even as meta-art did it achieve what it strove for: an objective category beyond meanings. Art, which had once been the symbolic fulfillment of the complex social practice of an entire society, thus ultimately deteriorated into an empty cipher in the hollow space of social functionlessness.

While bourgeois art degenerated in this way into an artificial gesture of itself, folk art took a no less fatal course. Inexorably separated from the encapsulated elite art, it fossilized as meaningless folk art, which is marketed today as bric-a-brac for tourists. Of course, it did achieve greater influence when it was perverted into trivial art, since it was consumed by the masses, the broadest audience of all. But such "folk art" is not produced by the masses within the framework of folk traditions; it is produced by members of the bourgeois middle class, who produce it for commercial purposes. Thus, an established social class produces art for a nonestablished class by imitating the latter's ancient forms and themes and, at the same time, discrediting them. That is because mass art is merely technically reproducible fairy tales: erotic fairy tales become romance novels; heroic fairy tales, science fiction; and fairy tales depicting contests of cleverness, crime novels. The perverse aspect of this trivialization of art is that the middle class ascribes to the consumer class an intellectual level that corresponds to its own cynical intentions. In the past, one did not write for those whom one despised; today one does so because it is very profitable. I am tempted to call this "the Muse in bankruptcy."

Contemporary Art Theory: The Neo-Marxist Movement

As a result of the degeneration of bourgeois art and folk art, the situation of contemporary art is extremely paradoxical. In her refusal to be domesticated further and in her will for emancipation (but without exactly comprehending from what or why she desired liberation), the Muse became entrapped in an increasingly obscure ghetto and unwittingly hastened her own complete domestication. She became conscious of this problem only when poised on the brink of her own annihilation. But continued naïve poetic dabbling was no longer of any use; clarifying theoretical reflection was the only recourse in the crisis. Hence, theories of art have appeared in unprecedented numbers in recent decades, and the central theme of most is the recovery of the social function of art.

I shall briefly discuss those theories so that we can turn again to contemporary art with clarified knowledge and a newly opened perspective. The two major international movements in modern theory of art are the neo–Marxist and the formalist schools. The neo-Marxist movement is represented by such theoreticians as Bloch, Benjamin, Adorno, and Marcuse.[12] The formalist movement has several subdivisions, which include semiotic-information aesthetics (Eco and Bense), structuralist-linguistic aesthetics (Lotman, Mukarovsky, Jakobson, Levin, and Barthes), and reception aesthetics (Jauss and Iser).[13]

In both the neo-Marxist and formalist movements there is a great awareness of the problem of the gulf between art and the public sphere, and theoretical efforts were made to overcome it. Adorno and Marcuse, for example, developed ideas on a socially engaged, critical-utopian art. The formalists long debated the problem known as the Duchamp paradox— namely, how the communication system of art should be changed so that it could be reintroduced into the communication system of social life.

The social role of art has been developed especially clearly in neo-Marxist aesthetics—which is what distinguishes it from the many bourgeois aesthetic theories. From the outset, Adorno characterizes the social role of art as a dual one: on the one hand, art plays an *affirmative role* by affirming and serving the prevailing system; on the other hand, art plays a *critical-utopian role* by pitting itself against this system as protest and resistance.

Adorno's theory of art is not descriptive but prescriptive in that he uses his concepts of affirmative and critical-utopian art to pass value judgments: he dismisses and ascribes a fundamentally affirmative character to many historical forms of art that were previously highly esteemed as classical-exemplary. According to Adorno, the ideological content of classical art is presented in a particular form: the closed form. Authoritarian instincts, which could no longer be gratified elsewhere, were given full vent in closed art—which was extolled as perfect— and closed culture. Thus, Adorno contends, an affirmative element coheres to all traditional art the richer it is, the denser, the more closed, the more compulsory. Moreover, in these perfect works, their own perfection appears as an instance of force and hence evil.

The situation is different for modern art: it rejects facile perfection and, precisely because of its flaws and transgressions, avoids strengthening the establishment with its own systematizations. According to Adorno, modern art criticizes society and its authoritarian and totalitarian tendencies more through its inner movement against society than through its explicit attitude; and sometimes a utopian element appears like a lightning bolt. In contrast to orthodox Marxist art theory, which prized traditional art and rejected modern art as bourgeois and decadent (Georg Lukács), Adorno's theory defends precisely this devalued avant-garde art.[14] Herein lies the merit of Adorno's theory.

Nevertheless, I must take issue with his basic premise, since he merely *inverts* the judgment of orthodox Marxist theory and thus achieves little more than it did: traditional and modern art still stand in opposition to each other, and one function is attributed to each. Neither theory makes it clear that the historical forms of art themselves fall into an "affirmative" role and a "critical-utopian" role, just as "affirmative" and "critical-utopian" tendencies coexist in modern art. I have already described the nature of the "critical-utopian" aspect of historical art: the imperfect, unacknowledged art of the oppressed classes, the Muse in the ghetto. She definitely had utopian, social-critical elements, but her criticism was inaudible because the power elite did not listen to her. Only the "affirmative" high art, the domesticated Muse, was audible. The significance of the splitting of the aesthetic dimension did not occur to Adorno, because he took for granted the fundamentally patriarchal structure of European society since antiquity. Adorno was incapable of recognizing the connection between patriarchy and the rift in art that led to the loss of its public presence.

The situation is different for Marcuse. In his book *Eros and Civilization,* he traces to their origins the psychosocial patterns of patriarchal society—although he does not expressly designate it as patriarchal.[15] Marcuse proceeds from the assumption that in previous societies a conflict existed between the pleasure principle (Eros) and the performance or reality principle (civilization)—a conflict that was always resolved through the renunciation of pleasure. As a result, happiness was subordinated to the discipline of work, and eroticism to the discipline of monogamous reproduction and the prevailing system of law and order. However, as Marcuse argues against Freud, this conflict is not necessary for the *creation* of civilization; on the contrary, it is the *result* of a very definite historical organization of human culture, namely, patriarchy.

Marcuse's utopian concept thus focuses on a culture having no oppression, a culture based on different experiences of existence and completely different relationships between humanity and nature. For Marcuse, "nature" signifies the extrahuman environment and vital human drives. According to him, there is a power that offers resistance against the established mechanism of oppression, namely, fantasy. Fantasy obeys only the pleasure principle and since the dawn of human cultural evolution has protected the original demands and goals of the pleasure principle from being traumatically repressed. The reemergence of those repressed desires in human history is precisely what disturbs the established culture and feeds the underground countermovement against it. At present, fantasy is increasingly manifesting itself as a force of resistance, as an attempt to recover the memory of the archaic paradise. Fantasy has preserved its truth content in archetypes of a life without oppression and anxiety—archetypes that surface in mythos, fairy tale, poetry, and folk custom—and is once again revealing those archetypes as a possibility for genuine freedom in a mature culture. As two examples of such archetypes, Marcuse mentions Orpheus and Narcissus, two heroes of Eros.

This new type of human being—oriented on the feminine principle, as Marcuse understands it—is in a position to form a new society. Such a society has a decisive relationship to the aesthetic dimension, because the aesthetic in the broadest sense of the term unites these features: it is the inner relationship between pleasure and sensuality, truth and freedom—the unlimited play of possibilities resulting from the unleashing of all erotic forces. Here, order becomes beauty, and work becomes play. The fundamental mode of experience in the aesthetic dimension is intuition, not conception; and Eros reigns in place of the reality principle. Therefore, Marcuse concludes, it is ultimately a question of the aestheticization of the entire society.

While Marcuse's ideas are still fascinating and similar to my own, several are vague: his concept of patriarchy, which he uses allusively, is superficial. Furthermore, Marcuse not only fails to incorporate historical and ethnological knowledge into his social-political concept but follows Freud's abstract notion of the "primal horde," an ostensibly *patriarchically* organized association of tribes. This idea of Freud's is patently false: patriarchy has no such eternal value.[16] Laboring under such presuppositions, Marcuse naturally fails to see that his "archaic paradise" is merely a phantasm and that it was the archaic *matriarchal* societies of early history that possessed precisely the paradisiacal features inherent in the fusion of the pleasure principle and the reality principle. In addition, Marcuse fails to recognize that mythos and fairy tale, poetry and folk custom, are not mere *fantasies* of an archaic paradise but *concrete memories* of very real prepatriarchal societies. His blindness is particularly obvious in his analysis of the mythic figures Orpheus and Narcissus: his interpretation remains a philosophical conceptual game that ignores the social background of those figures. Orpheus and Narcissus, however, are not mere creatures of fantasy but types of matriarchal hero-kings inexorably linked with matriarchy. Separated from their form of society and their cult, they are completely inconceivable as archetypes of matriarchal masculinity. Marcuse indeed senses this, but he does not know it for a fact.

I have clarified precisely these connections in my study on matriarchal mythology.[17] I have also shown that, through the European Middle Ages, fairy tales and poetry were still fundamentally characterized by the structures, figures, and symbols of matriarchal mythology. Hence, if patriarchal fantasy still revolves around those figures, there are extremely real social and political reasons for it. Unfortunately, however, Marcuse rejects any notion of the historical existence of matriarchies.

As a result, his "concrete utopia" is by no means concrete; it floats in the clouds as pure speculation, for it has no mooring in history or ethnology. It is difficult to conceive of a *future* society that reconciles Eros and civilization without drawing upon the *past* forms of such societies realized in early history. Therefore, such concepts as "fantasy offering resistance," "the liberation of the pleasure principle," "universal Eros," "the aestheticization of the entire society" necessarily remain empty notions. Thoughts on the aestheticization of society as a concrete utopia are meaningful—in my view—only when those aesthetic societies, matriarchies, have been studied and their real provisions for a new utopia have been researched. In this context, *utopia* does not signify a simple projection of a historical form of society into the future; on the contrary, it signifies a harmonizing of the positive features of the historical form of society with the changed conditions of today.

No matter how stimulating they may be, we cannot pursue Adorno's and Marcuse's thoughts on the critical-utopian function of art and the aestheticization of society, because any attempt at understanding the social role of art in history and in the present without considering the fundamentally patriarchal structures of those societies must necessarily end in an impasse.

Contemporary Art Theory: The Formalist Movement

Because art has lost its social function, the works of many formalist theoreticians treat the problem of reintroducing "art" into "life." Unfortunately, however, the Duchamp paradox merely designates another impasse in art theory, as well as in artistic practice.

In communication theory, art is considered an exchange system between those who create art (artists), those who mediate art (gallery owners), those who receive art (recipients), and those who process art (critics, theoreticians, imitators, interpreters, transposers into another medium).[18] Whether the objects in the exchange system are "art" (literature, music, the visual arts) is always determined by definite conventional rules. Those rules emphasize that the objects in the exchange system have the character of fictions, for which reason they are assigned the title *art*. In this way, the communication system "art" is differentiated from the communication system "life," which is based not on fictionality but on reality of experience. Bear in mind that this is a criterion only for differentiating between art and social life, not for distinguishing between "good" and "bad" art. That would be a second step; in the first step, "art" is always both "good" and "bad" simultaneously.

For the formalists, art in general is characterized by the concept of "fictionality." Fictionality refers to the particular setting in which art takes place and through which it is recognizable as art: the museum, the theater, the gallery, the reading, or even the stage, the picture frame, the book jacket. Some sort of sign is given to make it clear that the context in which something happens is supposed to be "art," a context different from that of normal social life. Such an "iconic sign" is like a signal that interrupts the flow of normal life to make room for the "art" taking place now.

When the iconic sign for "art" is made, the attitudes of those participating in this exchange system change in relation to the attitudes they have in the exchange system of "social life." The attitude of the artist is characterized as "polyfunctionality." In other words, the artist no longer uses materials or objects as in normal life, where they serve a single practical purpose, but uses them in such a way that they acquire manifold meanings. The attitude of the recipients is characterized as "polyvalence." In other words, the observers, readers, or listeners of art do not expect to receive only one meaning for what is observed, read, or heard, but to receive it in its manifold meanings. The art objects are only the material foundation for initiating this "aesthetic process" of ascribing the multiplicity of meanings by the artist and the multiplicity of valences through the recipients. Hence, in communication theory, the "artwork" is not the individual object but the entire "aesthetic process" taking place between the artist, the mediator, the recipient, and the processor.

A particularly illuminating example is the school of *objet trouvé*, whose artists exhibited unaltered everyday objects such as an ax, a shoe, or a clothes hanger. The unfamiliar setting, i.e., being displayed in an exhibit—perhaps on a pedestal in a glass case inscribed with the artist's name—neutralized the simple, familiar functionality of the objects. The artist intended ambiguity, and the recipients of that fact tried to assess the object in an ambiguous manner. Thus the object became an artifact, and the entire interpretive process between the artist and the recipient an aesthetic process. The separation of the communication systems of "art" and "life" is thus clearly defined, since the object is no longer considered an ordinary utilitarian thing: by means of an iconic sign (museum, gallery, pedestal), it has been fictionalized and thus transformed into an object in the aesthetic process.

In the experimental art since Duchamp, there have been

attempts to elevate one of the four factors in this model of aesthetic communication to the detriment of one of the others, and thereby to shatter the insuperable barrier between "art" and "life" while preserving the aesthetic process. But the Duchamp paradox shows that that is impossible.

A "happening," for example, sought to abolish the distribution of roles between the artist and the recipients by having people meet and collectively cause something to occur spontaneously. The collective activity was supposed to raze the barrier between "art" and "life." That could be achieved only by dispensing with a prescribed script, no matter how open. But what kept a "happening" from disintegrating into a blind release of passions among the participants? And what made it clear to outsiders that it was not an everyday occurrence? An iconic sign—a minimal text or a symbol—had to be used to identify it as an aesthetic process. However, according to the Duchamp paradox, that defeated the intended purpose of breaking down the barrier.

The Art & Language group took the opposite tack of suspending the boundary between art and life with the aid of theory. Artistic texts were replaced by metatexts *about* art, i.e., philosophical and scientific texts that expounded on art. The "art object" of the communication model was now replaced by the "object (text) about art." As a result, however, art would inevitably turn into philosophy and science, unless the artists clearly indicated that the process was an aesthetic one, not a scientific one. But that could not be accomplished without an iconic sign, and the Duchamp paradox appears again.

What aspects of these theories and experiments are of importance to us? I think the decisive factor is that they consistently characterize art not as a *thing* but as an aesthetic *process* among many people participating in different ways: the artist, who creates something; the mediators, who sell it; the recipients, who interpret and evaluate it; the processors, who reshape it. As a result, artworks as objects recede into the background, and the interactions taking place during their production and reception move into the foreground. This process character shatters the fetishistic character that high art—as the legitimation of authority—has always had in patriarchal societies.

These theories and the pertinent experiments, however, in no way achieve a new beginning—despite their avant-gardist posturing and view to the contrary. Their extravagance alone prevents them from achieving the decisive new beginning. They invent big words like *polyfunctionality* and *polyvalence,* which supposedly characterize the wealth of meaning of modern art, when, in truth, they cloak its poverty of meaning. The ancient meanings of art—twisted, distorted, smashed, and shattered into the atoms of subjective arbitrariness of meaning (whether by the artist, the recipients, or both) throughout the patriarchal millennia—have entirely evaporated. The absence of content, the yawning emptiness of meaning, engendered by the tedium of arbitrary interpretability, are now merely veiled in an extravagant intellectual apparatus. That intellectual apparatus alone causes art to consist of arbitrary ordinary objects (objets trouvés) or to degenerate into a release of emotions ("happenings"), on the one hand, and to petrify into science ("Art & Language"), on the other. Since art as a formalized Muse no longer has anything to say, communication theory speaks in her stead.

But that, too, is based on false assumptions: the Duchamp paradox expresses not so much an insuperable barrier between "art" and "life" but something very different, in both practice and theory. In practice, the Duchamp paradox identifies the impenetrable emptiness of art in its final patriarchal phase and marks its self-dissolution: if art appears only under the condition of fictionality, then it obviously annihilates itself the moment it oversteps the bounds of fictionality. In theory, the

Duchamp paradox formulates a fundamental misapprehension of art, for it is based on a false definition that tries to differentiate art from other spheres in purely logical terms, namely, through "fictionality." But the Duchamp paradox overlooks the fact that the fictionalization of art was a historical occurrence and is therefore completely unsuited for a universal, unrestricted logical definition of art. Only in patriarchal societies do art and life subsist on irreconcilable foundations, since it was important for the new ruling class to convert mythic-aesthetic processes into beautiful semblance in order to rid them of their matriarchal political reality content.

Such is the ideological content of the seemingly neutral fictionality principle—which no proponent of communication theory has ever even considered. If one wants to reintegrate art into life, there is only one way to do so: by making a fundamental change and abolishing the fictionality principle itself by exposing its ideological character. If we do that, we then return to and rediscover the prepatriarchal forms of art.

The Theory of Feminine Aesthetics

Women artists and aestheticians have not had a voice in either of the two prevailing schools of aesthetic theory. No matter how universal those theories pretend to be, women artists appear in none of them—neither their social-cultural situation nor the contents of their works. Women are excluded from both the theoretical discussions and the artistic examples selected for analysis.

Thus women's art is both a historical and a contemporary problem. Women only *seem* to receive more acknowledgment nowadays as painters, sculptors, authors, and musicians than did their predecessors. Even today, women must present their works in a society whose value system is fundamentally patriarchal and whose cultural institutions (publishing houses,

book markets, fairs, academies, conservatories, universities—
even the ministry of culture) are controlled by men. Women
are confronted with the artistic standards of male art critics and
are at the mercy of the art vogues of the male-dominated media
and the notions of femininity determined by the male public—
the old and new projections of men's longings and anxieties,
for which women are permitted to be nothing more than mirrors. Thus, art by women is judged according to norms and
expert constraints that are not their own.

For that reason it is impossible simply to examine women's
art as such; instead, we must examine it, first, in terms of
official art history and men's diffuse aesthetic-theoretical discourses on women's art and, second, in terms of the present
reality and women's aesthetic-theoretical discourses on their
own art and the art of other women. The very fact that, for
the first time, several women theoreticians are introducing concepts for a feminine aesthetic shows that women's art is indeed
a burning issue that cannot be resolved on a naïve level. At the
same time, the first theoretical self-assessment of women's art,
which seeks different criteria of judgment than the prevailing
ones, represents a decisive turn of events.

The problem of the alien evaluation of women's art in official
art history has been concisely and emphatically delineated by
Silvia Bovenschen.[19] In her study on "imagined femininity,"
Bovenschen shows that women are indeed amply represented
as figures in and topics of art and literary history, in which
they represent men's images of the ideal or of their own anxieties, but that they are greatly underrepresented as artists and
writers. The few women who have been able to validate themselves as writers—and are (more or less) remembered by literary posterity—represent, in both their work and their life,
typical examples for masculine theories of culture, art, and the
role of women in them. Only their extreme power to conform
has enabled those women to achieve a certain measure of va-

lidity as artists and writers. This reinforces the fact that we cannot accept without examination the forms of women's art in patriarchal history and the inherited decrees about it. We must always proceed with critical caution. On the one hand, those women are bound by the rules of "high art," of the domesticated Muse, who is not a creation of their form of society. On the other hand, their works, despite their extreme conformity to the prevailing norms, exhibit flaws and transgressions that contradict the domestication of the Muse—which is why disparaging verdicts have followed so quickly on the heels of the paeans by official art criticism.

Unfortunately, Bovenschen's study does not treat the sphere of the Muse in the ghetto, in which women (and men) transmitted still-untamed prepatriarchal contents and forms of art. Those traditions were simply not included in official art and literary histories. Only German Romanticism uncovered those currents, but—unfortunately—it immediately concealed their social and cultural significance, along with its own faded concept of "folk."

An initial turning point in the situation of the alien evaluation of women's art is represented by the theory of "feminine aesthetics" developed by the French philosophers Julia Kristeva and Luce Irigaray.[20] These theoreticians are concerned not with creating a new way of evaluating women's art in history but with devising a completely new "feminine" way of writing based on their theoretical considerations.

Kristeva keeps her formulations general and does not make direct reference to feminine aesthetics or feminine writing. She does, however, develop a concept of the aesthetic process similar to that of formalism but from a completely different point of departure than formalist aesthetic theory, with its structuralist, semiotic, and linguistic apparatuses. Like the formalists, Kristeva understands a poetic text not as a thing but as a process, which she formulates in her concept of "text as praxis."

"Praxis" is a process of the subject, the continuous subjective process of interpretation that takes place in language; the subject presents itself only as meaning-giving praxis.

Kristeva derives her concept of praxis from Hegelian and Marxist theory. She bases it primarily on Mao Tse-tung, who conceded a certain space to unmediated, subjective experience, as opposed to the social ties of the subject. In Mao, this unmediated experience is confined to production activity. Kristeva, however, interprets Mao's cognitive model in a different way. She releases the subject from the shackles of mere production activity and traces its formation in more multifarious practical cognitive activities, which she delineates as follows: When it becomes active, the subject, which exists in a world of contradictions, comes into conflict with an external contradiction. The subject then repudiates itself, loses itself, and no longer knows itself. The subject preoccupies itself with this *external* contradiction, causing it to become an *internal* one. And finally the subject goes beyond itself. After the cognitive work is completed, the subject rediscovers itself, but it has changed: something new has joined it. The subject now takes its own position toward the contradiction—it is a new, "proudly fortified ego" that must affirm or question its newly discovered position toward other contradictions.

This new position is a thought, a thesis, a text. It is, in short, a new meaning formed by linguistic means, for the subject's process of investing meaning, in which it always deals with contradictions in a practical way, takes place in language. Thus, language praxis is the source of the subject, which overcomes the contradictions and thereby affirms itself. Poetry is such a process composed of totalities and fragments and new totalities; as a result, it ceases to be "art" in the conventional sense. The function of poetry is to point out the fundamental contradictoriness of human praxis, to oppose the disappearance of meaning by creating new meaning and determining its range.

We shall retain Kristeva's gripping idea that poetry is not a thing but a process, a praxis in which the subject speaks in actions and thereby changes the subjective and the objective world. Unfortunately, Kristeva does not clarify whether her new concept of poetic text represents the introduction of a *new* style of writing or simply the means for understanding all *previous* poetic praxis. Irigaray, by contrast, is more explicit and radical in this regard: she does intend to introduce a new style of writing—that is, "feminine writing." She is in fact the first to apply Kristeva's concept of the subject to the women's movement. For Irigaray—unlike Kristeva, who incessantly and tiresomely expresses herself in neutral terminology—the subject that speaks in actions and thereby creates texts as its praxis for overcoming contradictions is clearly the woman. It is the woman who is continually exposed by society to new external contradictions, which she must transform into inner contradictions and examine in order to overcome them by investing them with new meaning. And this gives rise to the "woman speaking" and the "woman writing"—the "feminine" style, which Irigaray attempts to characterize and delineate in her theory of "feminine aesthetics."

Irigaray's point of departure is very different from Kristeva's. Irigaray begins with an impassioned polemic against Freud in which she attacks the Freudian theory of femininity and its continuation in the symbolic psychoanalysis of Lacan.[21] However, she then adopts basic Freudian concepts to describe the problems of the woman in an alien world. Drawing on Freud's conception of the unconscious, Irigaray states that she, too, considers the unconscious as the reservoir of historically repressed wishes and longings, not of a pleasure principle in general—as Freud (and Marcuse) had assumed—but of the contents of "the feminine." In other words, the unconscious contains the historically repressed features of the significant other—the woman, whose repression occurred first in society and then in the psyche.

Irigaray sees the repression as total. On the psychic level, the woman is nothing more than the passive projection screen for the unconscious wishes and anxieties of the man; she is not even permitted a sexuality of her own. On the social level— that is, in patriarchy (which Irigaray, like Freud and Lévi-Strauss, regards as a given since the dawn of humanity)—the man is the active subject and the woman is merely his bartering object, a token, a commodity having bartering value among men in general and utilitarian value for the individual man. And the more closely a woman conforms to the prevailing projections of femininity, which are fetishistic in nature, the higher her bartering value is.

Under such conditions, the woman can have no image, no conception of herself; she does not even have her own language. In and of herself she is indeterminate and infinitely different. Her speech is contradictory, inaudible in the already con-structed frames, incomprehensible in the valid code, a bit crazy in terms of the logic of reason, actually mute in terms of the logocentrism that Irigaray regards as a given in patriarchal thought and speech from the beginning. The feminine has nowhere else to subsist but in the unconscious. There it is stored as primal content, concealed and reduced to silence. But, never-theless, it has not entirely vanished. Occasionally it erupts in the symptoms of hysteria—the language of muteness—which can be articulated only in paroxysms of the unconscious. Hys-teria is the cultural neurosis of women in an alien world.

How can this significant other, the feminine, be recovered? According to Irigaray, it can be recovered by abrogating the mechanisms that repressed it. She recommends two paths: women must first search for themselves and their own desires, and then for a language of their own in which to express their desires. This language must go through their newly discovered body. For even hysteria is a form of body language: it is hysterical gesture, which does not fit speech that attempts to mimic masculine language and thus ends up parodying it. The abrogation of hysteria, on the other hand, would lead to a language that freely and harmoniously unites with gesture, mimicry, and bodily expression. According to Irigaray, the feminine language is not conceptual but sensual—that is, bound to the body. In that respect, it acquires aesthetic dimensions—not as a disembodied artwork but as the aesthetic manifestation of a free person in her or his surroundings. Somewhere Irigaray mentions, but only in passing, that the feminine language probably had its roots in archaic matriarchal relationships, which are completely lost to us today and whose complete contents would first have to be rediscovered.

Irigaray comes close to my own ideas on the development of a new type of art through the rediscovery and analysis of the matriarchal form of society—or at least she points in that direction. It is precisely that matriarchal cult, in which, in the magical ritual festivals, people were completely integrated into the symbolic fulfillment of their complex practices; in which dance, music, language, and gesture coalesced into one; in which art was a continuum that included the body, sensuality, and the cosmically experienced world. Unfortunately, Irigaray only mentions matriarchal society without delving into it more deeply. She has no real knowledge of the subject and consistently becomes entangled in the historical constructs of Freud and the structural anthropology of Lévi-Strauss, both of whom ascribe eternal validity to patriarchy. It is no wonder that, given those presuppositions, Irigaray can recognize the feminine only as repressed features having no other place to subsist but in the unconscious. Nor is it any wonder that her conception of society is abstract and pessimistic: absolute phallocentrism prevails on the psychic plane, and total logocentrism dominates

on the conceptual plane; the social plane is characterized by eternal patriarchy, and the economic plane by an exchangeable-value logic that makes women into objects and commodities. Thus, almost all the concepts Irigaray introduces remain un-clarified and—without a description of their contents—empty.

The source of the problem is that Irigaray gets mired in psychoanalytic thought and terminology: only through the fil-ter of the psychoanalytically proclaimed unconscious and its mysterious contents does she attempt to examine the archai-cally historical, which merely disappears when approached in such a way. And like the historical realm, the social sphere and its structures also remain largely in the dark. Only a precise social-historical analysis can penetrate the rules of the patriar-chal form of society and rediscover the rules of the matriarchal form of society. Only in this way can we gain insight into the unique form of art in matriarchies and the manner in which matriarchal women spoke, sang, and danced. Such an analysis can also clarify the rules by which the matriarchal form of society and art was transformed into the patriarchal. Those rules are the mechanisms that drove women into cultural mute-ness. Only when those mechanisms have been identified can one achieve what Irigaray strives for: liberation from this cul-tural muteness.

In addition, after having *expanded* the aesthetic dimension from artworks as objects into body, psyche, unmediated ges-ture, spontaneous bodily expression, and the beautiful mani-festation of a free person in her or his surroundings—which unquestionably restores to it a degree of reality that it lost under the dominion of the fictionality principle—Irigaray immedi-ately *contracts* the aesthetic dimension again by confining it to the female sex. But there can be no "feminine" aesthetic unless we know precisely what "femininity" is. Irigaray evades such a determination with ironic self-abnegation; but her irony is not always successful. She offers a veiled definition of "femininity": it is the flowing, the fluctuating, the dissembling; it is the twofold, the threefold, the manifold; it is the indeterminable, the ever-elusive. A strange definition indeed! In point of fact, *femininity* cannot be defined, because it varies from society to society and from epoch to epoch. By contrast, it *is* possible to determine precisely how women lived in the various societies and in the various epochs. But that cannot be accomplished by speculation, no matter how grandiose.

For that reason, I consider it less fruitful to focus on a *feminine* aesthetic (language, style, art, philosophy) than on a *matriarchal* aesthetic, since, in contrast to a feminine aesthetic, a matriarchal aesthetic has a historical context and reference to a concrete form of society. Moreover, even our questions become concrete in that context: How did women live in the form of society they created? How did they think? How did they speak? What were their ideas on pleasure, on eroticism? What image did they create of themselves and of men? And how did they convert their complex practice into unparalleled forms of expression—into art?

A matriarchal aesthetic, or art, is not bound to one sex, but it does have a perspective different from that of all other aesthetic theories and forms of art: society and art are not under the domination of men but are the creation of women. An aesthetic that pursues this premise to its logical conclusion is much more radical than utopias of the feminine, which all too quickly seek to isolate and abridge themselves.

The Dancing Muse

PRINCIPLES OF A MATRIARCHAL AESTHETIC

Moon Dances

Dance was a primary characteristic of all matriarchal cults. People believed that the Moon goddess made them dance because she derived so much joy from it and that their dance was absolutely vital to her health. Dance was more than a momentary exuberance of emotion, more than a very expressive prayer; it was the most important magical practice of all. Dance is in fact the oldest, most elemental form of religious expression. It is magic as danced ritual, and from it developed every other form of expression we are now accustomed to calling "art."

To comprehend the vast importance of dance in the simple matriarchal societies of prehistory and in the highly developed matriarchal societies of recorded history (including Indus, Sumer, Persia, and Egypt), we must first understand the significance the Moon goddess held for these peoples. The moon, a female entity, was regarded in some cultures as the infant of the even more ancient goddess Mother Earth, who gave birth to the moon each night and swallowed her up again in the morning (Africa). In other cultures, the moon was the child of the Cosmic Goddess of the Night (Egypt) or the world egg laid by the Great Goddess Eurynome, from which all things sprang when it hatched (pre-Hellenic, Pelasgian Greece). In the highly developed forms of matriarchy, the moon herself became the Great Goddess who took the place of the Earth goddess. As the White goddess, she was venerated as the Goddess in Triad: Maiden, Nymph, and Crone.[1]

Aside from Mother Earth, the moon was the goddess on whom all life depended. Every month she performed before the people's eyes the miracle of growing full and round, of waning, disappearing, and returning. Every month she changed from life to death and from death to life, as if that were the simplest thing imaginable. She influenced the earth with her phases: she caused the ocean's tides, made rivers and springs rise and fall, and created the weather and the floods in whose wake the land became fertile (for example, on the Indus, the Euphrates, and the Nile). Plant growth—the foundation of matriarchal agricultural civilizations—depended on her; the grazing animals depended in turn on the plants; and the welfare of humankind depended on the riches of both.

These peoples therefore believed that their lives depended not only indirectly but also directly on the Moon goddess. They feared they would die if she were to perish. Many peoples even believed that they owed their lives each and every month to the moon (Oceania and America). Hence, it was a source of great anxiety for them when the goddess approached death as the new moon or even succumbed to a lunar eclipse: what would happen if she were not to recover from the new moon or the eclipse? Since the moon could not be permitted to perish under any circumstances, the people attempted to facilitate her rebirth by means of magic. The need to save her gave rise to moon dances, which were widespread among matriarchal cultures throughout the world.

The original pattern of the moon dances was as follows: When the Moon goddess was near death, the people were seized with fear. This occurrence caused such confusion that they believed a misfortune would befall them. They moaned and screamed and cried as if they were suffering great pain. All activity came to an abrupt halt, and they gathered for the dance. The dance itself was an entreaty for the moon's return, and it continued until she actually reappeared. But even then the dance continued as an attempt to help her grow; it lasted for days, regardless of the weather. It was essential to dance without pause and with all one's might, which led in turn to ecstasy, trance, and complete exhaustion. The dancers flailed the air with their arms and legs, and spun in thousands of tight circles; they made bizarre faces, threw themselves to the ground, and screamed unintelligibly. Then they suddenly jumped up again and stamped about wildly. When the moon reappeared, they greeted her with loud cries, outstretched arms, and clapping.

Originally, only the women danced until they sank to the ground in exhaustion (rites of African women's cults). Later, the whole tribe participated in the dance. Researchers who witnessed such dances reported that the men in particular danced so violently that they collapsed. The women then danced back and forth over their bodies, upon which they placed a magic symbol to aid the men, who were considered temporarily dead, in their resurrection.[2]

Apparently, it was only in this way that the strength of the dancers could be transferred to the Moon goddess. To have danced to unconsciousness was to have participated in the moon's death, which was considered a highly honorable sacrifice in her service. Just as the moon herself returned to life, the fallen dancers soon arose from their symbolic death. The dance had a different character at the time of the full moon, when she was round and beautiful: the Moon goddess made the people dance for joy over her radiance, and the dances usually culminated in eroticism.

Since the people aided the Moon goddess in her resurrection, they were convinced she would aid them in their return from death. They considered human existence to be nothing more than a chain of decline and advance, of death and resurrection that transcended the death of the individual. Existence was a cycle of phases as eternal as those of the goddess, who was expressly named "the eternal one" by many peoples. The conception of death as the irrevocable cessation of life—that sad notion of patriarchal peoples—did not exist for matriarchal societies. Everything in nature, including human existence, followed the example of the Moon goddess.[3]

Only women have the power of perpetuating human life. Not only do they have periods of fertility that coincide with the cycles of the moon, but they also bring forth new life in exactly nine lunar months. Moreover, according to the beliefs of matriarchal societies, the new life born of woman was not just any arbitrary individual but always a reincarnation of a deceased ancestor.[4] During their absence, the souls of the ancestors abided in the arms of the Moon goddess or in the wings of the Goddess of the Night (Egypt), where they awaited rebirth. All religions that entail ancestor worship or the idea of transmigration of souls have their origin in these ancient matriarchal conceptions.

Women were thus the true daughters of the Moon goddess, for they did as she did: they ensured that every person's death would be overcome by a perpetual series of rebirths. In that way they were one with the goddess and possessed her powers. Among many matriarchal peoples it was therefore doubted whether women even died at all. It was said that in old age they retreated into solitude and simply shed their skins—just as the moon sheds her black veil, or the serpent its shriveled skin—and then returned young and fresh. That is the origin of the legends of the fountain of youth and of the so-called old women's mill, which old women entered and then exited as young girls.

It was also said that women, like the moon, passed with ease from life to death and from death to life. Women were able to do everything the Moon goddess could: through irrigation they made the earth fertile and caused the plants to grow (horticulture); through their power over water they made the wind and weather (weather magic); they brought health and prosperity or sickness and death (magical herbal medicine); like the moon, they measured human time in lunar months and determined people's fate (magical astronomy and the development of the lunar calendar); like the moon, they spun the threads of time and eternity, and from it wove the web of life (the art of spinning and weaving). Women thus performed on earth what the goddess performed in heaven. In fact, the very fate of the peoples of the earth was dependent on matriarchal women, just as the Triple goddess in the form of the Moirai, or Fates—older than all the other gods and, in contrast to them, eternal—was destiny itself.

Thus the moon dance, too, was originally a women's affair. As daughters of the moon, women knew best how to help the waning Moon goddess come to life again. The moon cult was their cult, and magic in the form of dance was their religious practice. Dance was therefore central to their social order, the matriarchy. If men wanted to participate, they first had to be granted magical powers. Since magic was not one of their innate abilities, men were always in need of women's help.

The Nine Muses

The first priestess of the moon cult was not only the tribal queen but also the best dancer; some peoples, in fact, used the same word for "tribal queen" and "dancer." The distinction we make today between religion, art, science, and politics did not yet exist. The first priestess usually had an assembly of dancers and regents around her, who, with her, yielded exactly the magical number nine (the highly developed matriarchy). The number nine contains three times the female trinity—the manifestation of the Triple moon goddess in Triad. This magical number of moon dancers was particularly prevalent in the highly developed matriarchies of the eastern Mediterranean region, which included Minoan Crete and pre-Hellenic Greece. Thus, the nine wild Muses of Parnassus were none other than such an assembly of priestesses, identified with the tripled triad of the Moon goddess of Mount Parnassus herself.[5] On Mount Helicon and Mount Olympus there were similar assemblies of priestesses as representatives of the local Moon goddess—before the patriarchal god Zeus conquered Olympus and, crushing all resistance with his lightning bolts, set himself up as the highest father of the gods.[6]

Everything we designate as "art" today sprang from the ecstatic dancing of the moon priestesses. Before they were captured and "tamed" by the patriarchal god Apollo, they did not stand around stiffly or sit solemnly—as they are usually portrayed—but danced. As mothers of the cult and of their mountain people, as the unrestrained goddesses of creativity and of the entire region, they danced incessantly and thus resembled the wild, orgiastic Maenads.[7]

URANIA

Their dance was not chaotic, however, as the description of the moon dances from the simple matriarchies suggests, but an artistic totality. Nor did they dance just anywhere, but on fixed, demarcated, constructed dancing grounds. The dancing grounds were stone circles made up of nine, eighteen, or twenty-seven stones, depending on the size of the ring. In the middle of the circles there usually stood a stone obelisk, a pointed menhir with many meanings: the altar of the Goddess, a stone herm as symbol of the hero, a giant finger pointing to the moonlight or the sunlight incident in the ring.

At the same time, the stone circles were lunar and solar calendars in which the rising and setting of the moon and the sun were measured by means of the specific position of the outer stones and the shadow cast by the inner stone. The stones served to divide the months according to the moon, and the year according to the sun. For example, the highly significant sunrise at the winter solstice, the rebirth of light, was always represented by a particular pair of stones; the sun rose over the horizon precisely through the narrow gap between them. Such precision was necessary, since the moon festivals with their momentous dances did not take place at just any time but at specific moments in the complex interplay of the moon and the sun in the sky and the vegetation on earth. Even in the simple matriarchies, the phases of the moon determined the dances.

In the highly cultivated matriarchies of the Near East and the Mediterranean region, time was reckoned according to the harmony of the *three* central heavenly bodies: Mother Earth, her daughter the moon, and her son the sun. The time phase of the festive ritual dances extended from the vernal equinox to the next full moon—when the vegetation reappears. That period was followed by the phase from the summer solstice to the next full moon—when the vegetation reaches fruition. Then came the time of harvest, from the autumnal equinox to the next full moon. The nine-month mythic year then concluded with the period from the winter solstice to the next full moon—when the vegetation rests under the earth and awaits its return. The remaining three months were considered the time of quiet preparation for the coming mythic year, which began again at the vernal equinox.

In this way, not only all forms of art but the later separate spheres of art and science were unified in the great moon festivals of the developed matriarchies: early magical astronomy—based on countless observations and the most precise calculations possible—is what determined the place and time of the dances and created for the dancers their dancing grounds in the form of gigantic calendars.

Urania was the Muse of astronomy. Her realm of activity was the most noble, and she was considered the most important of the nine Muses.

TERPSICHORE

Such dancing grounds can still be seen today in the partially or completely preserved stone circles in Ireland, Scotland, and England (figure 1). Stonehenge, in the south of England, is the most spectacular example of such a lunar and solar calendar (figure 2). France and Germany are also littered with stone circles. In Germany they are called "witch rings" or "*Truden* rings" (rings of the *Truden,* or Druids, meaning "witches"). In France there are still some examples in Brittany, although they are combined with different complicated patterns of menhirs—arranged in rows, parallels, or waves. But the stone circle, the simplest form, was later abandoned by the female calendar makers. They also built multiple concentric rings from which rows of stones emanated like serpents and ended in concentric circles; the Avebury Ring, in the south of England, is one such marvelous gigantic array (figure 3).

Other dancing grounds took the form of labyrinths patterned after the movements of the dancers. The basic pattern was the spiral, which was danced counterclockwise from the outside to the center of the circle, and then clockwise from the center of the circle to the outside. This double spiral pattern was a symbol for the Moon goddess, who appeared to orbit the earth in a counterclockwise spiral until she stood full and round at the zenith, the center of the heavens, and then appeared to turn in a clockwise spiral until she vanished near the sun as the new moon (figure 4).[8]

Those who entered the spiral sought the center of the light, the ecstasy, the divine climax; and then they carried the light in the opposite direction, from inside to outside, into the world. Or they entered the spiral to seek the depths, entry into the underworld, the last point where everything stopped: death. Everything came to rest when they cowered in the innermost whorl, but then the crouching position of the dead transformed itself into that of the fetus seeking rebirth. That rebirth occurred when they exited the spiral, and new life entered the world. Thus, the spiral was also the symbol of the uterus and the birth canal.[9] Whether the center of the spiral became the climax of the light or the depths of the underworld depended on the time of year and the type of ritual being celebrated. Thus, the mystical spiral was the image of the Moon goddess herself and her dual power: of passing from darkness to light, from death to life; and from light to darkness, from life to death.

Thousands of such spiral symbols decorate the stones of dolmens as well as cult objects such as vases, jars, girdles, bracelets, head ornaments, sacral rooms in palaces, and the insignia and runic writings in the most ancient archaeological documents in all of Europe and the Near East. And the earliest forms of labyrinths, which were actually cultic dancing grounds, were simple spirals (figure 5).

Later, the spiral—one of the most beautiful and most complex of all geometric patterns—was doubled and either laid in parallel or intertwined, resulting in the first *Maiandros,* or meander. (The classic *Maiandros* consists of two continuous intertwined spirals.) The meander is also an ancient labyrinth marking the entry and exit of the dancers (figure 6). This full, intricate labyrinth did not develop until a double intertwined spiral was danced for each of the four great moon festivals in the seasonal cycle, and the four were united with one another in one large ring (figure 7). The most famous of the labyrinths was a drawn or constructed dance pattern on the great inner square of the palace grounds of Knossos, on Crete. Such labyrinthine dancing grounds were distributed throughout the entire eastern Mediterranean region. Several undisturbed stone or grass labyrinths can still be found today in remote areas of France, England, Germany, Scandinavia, and Russia. They are usually called "Trojan fortresses."[10]

Most of the labyrinths were either destroyed by the followers of patriarchal religions or built over with temples and churches to the new gods. A few labyrinth patterns were reproduced as floor decorations in the great cathedrals of France—for example, in Chartres, Bayeux, Arras, Amiens, Saint-Quentin, Reims, and Sens—in their original size and over their original location. Compared with barbarous destruction, such building-over is merely a more refined form of defensive reaction against the ancient matriarchal religion, for the circular, spiral, or labyrinthine dancing grounds were its holiest places, its "temples" and "churches." Stonehenge was a magnificent "basilica," and Avebury a marvelous "cathedral." However, the matriarchal "temples" and "cathedrals" allowed the powers of the divinities to flow unhindered; they were open to the flooding radiance of the moon, the light of the sun, and the greening or withering landscape around them. The design of those holy places does not betray a lack of architectural skill on the part of matriarchal peoples but reflects a different conception of the cosmos and its veneration.

It is Terpsichore, the Muse of dance, who may lay claim to the creative glory here, for her fundamental choreographic patterns, in addition to the astronomical calculations, developed the structure of the dancing grounds. Those cultic places, which were calendars and dancing grounds in one, were her frozen movements.

POLYHYMNIA, ERATO, AND CALLIOPE

The Muses danced according to their own rhythmic songs, thus quoting Polyhymnia, the Muse of choral song.[11] Their songs in no way possessed the character of disciplined, regulated men's choirs; they were ecstatic invocations, eulogies, and incantations held together only by a common rhythm. These rhythms were meters, or metrical *feet,* in the truest sense of the word, for the dancers gave themselves the rhythm with their bare feet: iamb (short, long), trochee (long, short), spondee (long, long), the more difficult dactyl (long, short, short) anapest (short, short, long), cretic (long, short, long), amphibrach (short, long, short), and other, even more intricate, steps. With their dance steps they scanned the language and, at the same time, measured the lines of verse: trimeter, pentameter, hexameter (three, five, and six metrical feet, respectively). Thus language itself became music.

The songs had two moods. Some very merry love poems struck up by the Muse Erato, perhaps at the time of the waxing Moon goddess, the increasing sunlight, and the growing vegetation; others were elegies and lamentations intoned by the Muse Calliope when the Moon goddess disappeared, the sunlight faded, and the vegetation withered.[12]

EUTERPE

The Muses also danced to instrumental music, and the instruments were of their own invention. Two instruments of female origin played a major role as early as the Athena myths: the drum or the tambourine and the double flute or the *aulos.* The Pelasgian Athena of Crete is said to have invented the double flute, but she carelessly tossed it away because she supposedly did not like having to inflate her cheeks. It was then found by a satyr or "reinvented" by the god Hermes. Both Hermes and the satyr entered a contest against Apollo and lost to him.

Hermes was clever, however, and made a deal with Apollo to trade his flute for Apollo's shepherd's staff, but the stupid satyr was skinned alive by Apollo after the contest. Pan lost, too, when he played his pipe for Apollo.[13]

Ethnology confirms that drums and flutes were the most ancient instruments of many peoples. Drums were usually played by women and flutes by men (Andean Indians), thus revealing their erotic associations: the drum as the female body, the flute as the phallus. Even in the later Cybele cult in Rome, all rituals were accompanied by the sound of drums and cymbals (hand bells or finger bells) and the provocative timbre of Syrian double flutes, which drove the Goddess's devotees to ecstasy.

Stringed instruments in the hands of female musicians played an important role in Egypt, which was matriarchal in its most ancient stage. These seven-stringed instruments reflected the astronomical science of the then-known seven planets: each string was consecrated to a planet, and when the priestess played it, she literally created the harmony of the celestial spheres. Consequently, an octave consists of seven tones, and a new octave begins at the eighth tone.[14] The harp, which embraces several octaves, was a highly mystical instrument in the hands of the priestess: from it resounded the music of the entire cosmos. In Greece the seven-stringed lyre was the sacral instrument played only by priestesses. With few exceptions, it was kept out of the profane hands of men. Only the hero-king was permitted to play the lyre, at the sacred rituals in which he was included. For example, in times of drought he musically summoned the rain (love magic); before his sacrificial death, he tuned his swan song to the lyre (death and resurrection magic). Since music was magic, the strangest things happened through it: plants grew, wild animals became tame, dolphins came to one's aid, and stones rolled and raised themselves into walls. The two exceptional matriarchal kings who played the lyre became famous through such magical deeds: Amphion and Orpheus.

The invention of the lyre is also attributed to Athena, but it is more likely that she received both the lyre and the flute from the hands of the Muses and took them to Athens, where she was considered the goddess of art and science—a sort of comprehensive Muse. The new male gods treated the lyre as disrespectfully as they had the flute: the presumptuous Hermes claimed it as his own invention and again traded it with Apollo, this time for Apollo's cows, which is how the cowherd Apollo became the later, arrogant god of art.[15] But, to give truth its due, it is the Muse Euterpe to whom we owe the invention and performance of music.[16]

THALIA AND MELPOMENE

The artistic dances to artistic songs performed—with or without instrumental accompaniment—on the artistic dancing grounds were in no way arbitrary in content: they were danced celebrations of orgiastic joy or danced rituals of sacrifice. The four great festivals of the seasonal cycle were their eternal theme: the initiation of the hero by the Triple goddess in Triad in the spring, the ritual of Sacred Marriage *(hieros gamos)* of the Goddess and the hero in the summer, the sacrificial death of the hero at the hand of the Goddess in the autumn, and his joyous return or rebirth through the Goddess in the winter.[17] The nine priestesses incarnated the Triple moon goddess in Triad, and the hero-king embodied the sun and, at the same time, represented humanity, his people.

In the first half of the year, when the power of the sun intensified and the vegetation became increasingly luxuriant, the frolicsome festivals took place—the initiation in the form of an amusing competition or hunt during which the designated successor of the king from the previous year gladly allowed himself to be defeated, captured, or overpowered by the nine.

At the height of summer the extravagant Sacred Marriage festival took place, not as an aesthetic play but as ritual reality. The Goddess in her ninefold form (the nine priestesses) thus united with humanity (the hero-king), and heaven and earth, moon and sun, entered into a mystical union that fructified the land and sea, animals and people, the entire cosmos. These were festivals of rapturous joy directed by Thalia, the Muse of mirth, laughter, and comedy.

The mood changed, however, after the summer solstice. Now began the time of harvest, and the female reapers went through the fields. The grain and the fruit died for the life of humanity, and with them (and for the same reason) the most esteemed thing that the people had to sacrifice died as the sun grew weaker: the hero-king. For the sacrificial ritual in autumn was not an aesthetic play but danced reality—not out of cruelty but in the knowledge that descent necessarily follows ascent. After having shown her bright side, the Moon goddess was now showing her dark side as Fate. The royal sacrifice magically safeguarded the life of the people through the winter; the hero-king's descent into the underworld freed humanity from a premature death. For that reason, he became a hero to his people and, because of his self-sacrifice, was venerated as a demigod (the original concept of the heroic). At the same time, the hero-king himself was ensured eternal life in the paradisiacal otherworld of the Goddess or rebirth and reawakening through the transmigration of his soul into his successor. The mysterious return of the hero, usually as a divine child, was celebrated at the winter solstice, the precise moment when the sun returned. Both these festivals, of sacrificial death and the hero's return, were filled with tragic solemnity and ceremonious mysteries directed by Melpomene, the Muse of tragedy.

Comedy and *tragedy* are derived from the Greek, meaning "festive song" and "goat song."[18] That is significant because, whereas in earlier times the wild Maenads annually tore their divine hero Dionysus to pieces, and the Wild Muses their priest-king Orpheus, in later times the sacrifice was performed in the autumn with the surrogate offerings of male animals— young rams, bulls, and above all goats.[19] The king himself, however, remained the true sacrificial offering (figure 8). Thus, tragedy and comedy were actually mystery plays in the seasonal cycle, and all highly developed matriarchal cultures celebrated them. As rites of Dionysus, the mystery plays were the origin of classical Greek theater.[20] However, under the dominion of the fictionality principle, the ritual seriousness of the mystery plays degenerated into imitation (mimesis)—mere theatricality depicting unreal events and celebrated solely for the sake of this semblance.

The most ancient poetics, Aristotle's *Poetics* (highly esteemed and binding until modern times), ultimately destroyed the very structure of the seasonal mystery plays by putting them in the straitjacket of the three unities: a play must take place in *one* locale, in *one* day, and with *one* plot line—otherwise it is not "natural." However, instead of one day, matriarchal mystery plays required a whole year. Instead of one plot, they had four: initiation, marriage, death, and return. And instead of one locale, they took place in all three regions of the God-dess's world: in the uppermost atmospheric region, on the heights of mountaintops (initiation); in the middle region of land and sea (marriage); and in the lowermost region, in can-yons and caves, the underworld in the center of the earth (death and resurrection). The Aristotelian destruction of the matriar-chal mystery plays was fully intentional—at his time the pa-triarchal mentality was still struggling against the ancient matriarchal spirit. But, for some reason, only the *theme* of the mystery plays was preserved: the rise and tragic fall of the hero.

CLIO

It should be clear by now how thoroughly the dances of the Muses united *all* the later artistic genres: music, poetry, architecture, the visual arts, and theater. They were *Gesamtkunst* (comprehensive art) in the truest sense of the term. As we have already seen, the dances also fused art and science. They were a danced calendar, for only in this way did they fulfill their magical purpose of influencing the phases of the moon, the orbit of the sun, and the growth of vegetation on earth. The dances of the Muses were not only a danced calendar but also a danced worldview: they expressed the entire mythological perspective of matriarchal peoples and, what is more, the fundamental pattern of their social structure—the matriarchal family of Mother Earth with her priestess daughter and her kingly son. Moreover, the dances also mirrored the economy of that time, for all matriarchal mystery plays were, without exception, horticultural magic. The dances in fact represented the entire complex practice of those societies.

The dances were also their history, their mythic history in a bold panorama, for matriarchal peoples did not visualize history as a monotonous linear succession of ruling dynasties and empires but as a circular cycle, which assumed the form of a spiral as their cultures gradually developed to a higher degree. The smallest historical time unit was the cyclical lunar month (or lunation); a larger unit was the cyclical solar year; a still larger unit was the "great year" of one hundred lunations; and the largest unit of all was the "cycle." Even the "cycles" developed on a spiral course. Of the nine Muses it was Clio who narrated this history, as cycles of priestess generations and their hero-kings.[21] Mythology itself was the history of the matriarchal peoples, and it was recited by the Muse Clio as the sublime background for every ritual festival.

Only a strict framework could preserve the rich significance of the dances through the long matriarchal epochs. We know this framework: it was demarcated by the astronomical events, the mythological cycles, the set rituals, the geometrically arranged dancing grounds, the songs in metrical rhythms, and the accentuated music. That structure determined the course of the dances. But—like counterpoint in music—the structure was only an orientational framework within which one could improvise.[22] Thus, even within the framework, the dance was free in gesture and expression. The dancers were free to invest the framework with individual feelings, personal and social significances, and local symbols. Despite such structuring, the participation of the individuals was so intensive that it led to ecstasy; the latitude for variation was so broad that the attributes of the Moon goddess and her rituals had a different local character from people to people. Utmost multiplicity prevailed within the universal unity provided by astronomy and mythology.

That whole texture changed, however, with the dawning of the patriarchal age, for now the Muses received a male "lead dancer" who prescribed how they were to dance. It was—as we know—the god Apollo who had conquered their cult, usurped the moon priestesses, and killed his royal dancing rival, the hero-king. With that, the complex social practice, the expression and magical center of which was the moon dance, was suddenly destroyed. The distribution of roles now mirrored the patriarchal social structure, with the man as the ruler and the patriarchal economy of a feudal imperialist state, which supplanted the matriarchal theocracy. The ingenious fabric woven of social politics, psychology, science, and aesthetics, which the ritual dance festivals had been, was unraveled into its individual threads, which became the individual formal categories of reason that replaced the ecstatic unity. From then on, "art" existed only as beautiful, decorative semblance. Or,

where it defied categorization as mere ornamentation and re-
tained the ancient mythic content, it was banished to the ghetto
of the new society.

Nine Theses on a Matriarchal Aesthetic

The principles of a matriarchal aesthetic can be easily derived
from my discussion of historical matriarchal art. However,
matriarchal aesthetics is not a retreat to archaic times but a
partially descriptive, partially programmatic theory of certain
variants of *modern* art. For I apply these principles to existing
forms in the art of contemporary women (and men) artists that
exhibit matriarchal features. My comparative analysis will reveal clearly the trend in these modern manifestations, and this
disclosure will have a programmatic effect. I shall also develop
a matriarchal art-utopia from these very real beginnings.

I shall now formulate the basic features of matriarchal
aesthetics in nine theses, which I will thoroughly elucidate
later.

FIRST THESIS
Matriarchal art transcends the fictionality principle. Archaic
matriarchal art predates it; modern matriarchal art postdates
it. Art that transcends the fictionality principle is magic. Magic
is an intervention in reality with the aid of symbols that effects
a change in reality. Archaic matriarchal art attempted to influence and animate nature through magic (archaic magic); modern matriarchal art attempts to change psychic and social
human reality through magic (modern magic).

SECOND THESIS
Matriarchal art has an enduring, preexisting framework: the
structure of matriarchal mythology. That structure is universal,
for it is the fundamental pattern of all concrete mythologies

and all religions that developed from them.[23] The structure of matriarchal mythology has the status of fundamental categories of human imagination and is an objective dimension.

But like any structure, the structure of matriarchal mythology is blank. It acquires various specific contents depending on the various mythologies (religions, rituals, ways of life) of the various matriarchal peoples. As a result, its concrete manifestations are as diverse as the local, individual, and social conditions of those who create them. Therefore, matriarchal art grounded in the structure of matriarchal mythology is multiplicity in unity, wherein the unity is devoid of dogmatism and the multiplicity devoid of subjectivism.

THIRD THESIS

Matriarchal art subverts the traditional communication model and its components: author (artist), text (art product), and recipient. Matriarchal art is not a "text"—it does not confine itself to the production of art "products"—but a process, the concrete manifestation of a preexisting structure in the ritual dance festival in which all participate. The participants create this concrete manifestation together; all are simultaneously artists and recipients. (Women artists/authors and women recipients do not even appear in the communication theory.)

Nor is the structure of matriarchal mythology a "text" produced by an artist and then filled in by several recipients. As fundamental categories of human imagination, the structure of matriarchal mythology is a given: it is the original and historically oldest structure from which all later religious and artistic products of imagination developed. Human imagination is neither unsystematic randomness nor an arbitrary associative process. (That is a later, degenerated conception of it.) It follows its own rules. Those rules are contained in the structure of matriarchal mythology, and that highly ingenious fabric of rules collectively expresses itself in diverse ways in each of its various concrete manifestations. To find those rules, one need not delve into the unconscious for possible "archetypes"; instead, one must uncover by means of social analysis the buried historical matriarchal traditions.

FOURTH THESIS

Matriarchal art requires the application of *all* capacities of *all* participants. Those powers are indivisible in matriarchal art, since there is no separation of artists and recipients in which the artists perform the symbolic action and the recipients either identify with it emotionally or contemplate it theoretically (the patriarchal distribution of roles). In matriarchal art, all participants simultaneously create the symbolic action, the emotional identification, and the theoretical contemplation. The universal, objective character of the structure of matriarchal mythology—which is known to all participants—prevents the action from degenerating into mere effect, the emotional identification from degenerating into subjective sentimentality, and the theoretical contemplation from degenerating into abstract arbitrariness. Matriarchal art combines action, identification, and contemplation in the concrete mythological image and, through this collective action among the participants, inspires genuine ecstasy.

FIFTH THESIS

Matriarchal art also does not fit an *expanded* communication model, with its factors of author/artist, text, marketer, mediator, and recipient. The categories of marketer (art market) and mediator (critics, interpreters, transposers from one medium to another, archivists, and art historians) are inapplicable. As a *process* shared by *all participants,* matriarchal art can be neither criticized and interpreted from outside nor sold as a commodity on the art market and later archived as a dusty object to be placed in the museum of art history. Matriarchal art is not an object but an energetic process having the psychological characteristic of ecstasy and the social effect of changing reality (magic).

SIXTH THESIS

Since it is not an object, matriarchal art knows no separation of artistic genres. The ritual dance festivals are an indivisible union of music, song, poetry, movement, ornamentation, illustration, comedy, and tragedy; and everything serves the purpose of invoking, conjuring, and glorifying the Goddess.

The distinction between art and nonart is also inapplicable. On the one hand, matriarchal art dissolves the boundary between art and theory: archaic matriarchal art fuses with mythology and astronomy; modern matriarchal art fuses with philosophy and the cultural, social, and natural sciences. On the other hand, matriarchal art dissolves the boundary between art and practice: archaic matriarchal art fuses with ritual practices and the practical arts; modern matriarchal art fuses with practices of social change and the practical arts. That is another reason why the communication model does not apply. Matriarchal art is not a mere communication process; it is a process of complex social practice, of which communication is but one part.

SEVENTH THESIS

Since matriarchal art originates on the foundation of the structure of matriarchal mythology, and the matriarchal system of values is entirely different from the patriarchal one (not simply an opposite or opposing one), matriarchal art itself contains this different value system. Eroticism is its dominant power—not work, discipline, or renunciation. The perpetuation of life as a cycle of rebirths is its highest principle—not war and heroic death for abstract, inhumane ideals. The basic social rules of the matriarchy are motherliness, sibling love, and a sense of community—in contrast to paternal authority, conjugal domination, and individual or group egoism.

Modern matriarchal art, which expresses those values and triggers changes in the psychic and social sphere, is a process of complex social counterpractice in a patriarchal society. Since that counterpractice is not enforced by domination, matriarchal art requires no hidden ideology. In every patriarchy, matriarchal art is an oppositional force with the possibility of revolutionary change.

Eighth Thesis

The social changes effected by matriarchal art neutralize the split in the aesthetic dimension. In patriarchal societies, the aesthetic dimension is split into a formalist, elite, socially effective art and a popular, diffuse, socially despised, ghettoized art. The neutralization of that split would restore to art the entirely public character it once had. Art would then manifest itself as the central social practice and, through its processes of change, bring about the aestheticization of the entire society. That was the situation of archaic matriarchal art, and modern matriarchal art strives to recover the same situation.

Ninth Thesis

Matriarchal art is not "art" in the conventional sense of the term, for "art" was defined by fictionality, the fictionality principle being the supreme tenet in every patriarchal aesthetic. "Art" as a concept and as "art objects" has existed only since the splitting of the aesthetic dimension. Consequently, patriarchal "art" is always artificial or denatured art.

Matriarchal art transcends the fictionality principle and thus is not "art" in the patriarchal sense of the term. Nor is it a special technical skill. It is the ability to create and reshape life. Matriarchal art is itself energy, life, and the driving force for the aestheticization of society. Matriarchal art can never be separated from complex social practice as isolated "art," for it is the nucleus of complex social practice itself.

Commentaries on the Principles of a Matriarchal Aesthetic

The theses on matriarchal aesthetics formulated above are in need of some elucidation in order to help the Goddess dance again.

ON THE FIRST THESIS

The concept of modern magic presented in this thesis may sound perplexing and seem a contradiction in terms. What exactly is an intervention in psychosocial reality with the aid of symbols?

Archaic magic is problematical—or so it seems to us today—because it sought to animate the forces of nature through its interventions with the aid of symbols, for example, to cause the moon to return (moon dances) and the sky to rain (rain dances). However, that is an oversimplification, since the people in archaic cultures knew very well that the moon would return. After all, according to its phases they were able to develop a calendar, which in the case of some peoples (the Babylonians and the Mayans) was more precise than the calendar of today. Moreover, they knew immense numbers of weather rules—a tight net of observations of the sky, the clouds, and the behavior of animals and plants from which they could predict the weather with great accuracy. Hence, their recourse to magic was not due to ignorance, which the arrogance of today is so fond of ascribing to them.

The matriarchal peoples did believe, however, that their rational-technical knowledge of nature was not enough. The emotional side had to be included to truly influence the moon and the rain. It was expressed in the moon dance, which was performed at the astronomically precise moment of the moon's return, and in the rain dance, which was not performed until the signs indicated that it would rain. They regarded nature not simply as a calculable object but as a living being who could ultimately change her mind. Therefore it was also necessary to communicate with her through symbols to make themselves understood, to express their wishes, to persuade nature to adhere to her original intention. To them nature was a goddess—an idea that has been completely lost to us today.

The matriarchal peoples derived their attitude toward nature from their magical practices toward people: they were aware of magic not only in nature but also in psychosocial reality. They knew that not only medicines (of which they had enough) but also emotional influences cured the sick: the hope of recovery, the trust in the woman doctor, or shamaness, who fought the demons of illness. (As we know, faith works wonders.) That was the function of the interventions with symbols, which were always used along with technical-medical means in the magical healings (white magic, shamanism). It is a mistake and a distortion to think that these peoples believed the symbolic action alone effected the cure. That is disproved by their extensive knowledge of herbal medicine—a science all but lost today.

Magic, which was really psychology, was present everywhere in the social fabric. Thus, the erotic and aggressive drives with their tendency toward isolation and asocial behavior were not simply given free rein but were danced away, beneficially released within the framework of a social context, namely, a public festival. The resulting change in social reality was a new and meaningful coexistence of the people.

Even today, we constantly encounter interventions in psychosocial reality by means of symbols, namely, in individual and social psychology, particularly the psychology of the unconscious. But their manners of application are anything but beneficial, since the "magical ethos" that should support those interventions has been lost. Instead, symbolic interventions serve the pressures of conformity, deception, and manipulation in patriarchal society.

Magic, vilified as "witchcraft," was a primary target of the evolving patriarchy. To this day magic has not lost this odium of primitiveness or evil in the thinking of most people, which is why it may sound strange for me to speak of a magical ethos. However, what distinguishes archaic magic—and its interventions with the aid of symbols—from modern manipulations with the aid of symbols is that archaic magic always issued from all-inclusive conceptions: it was holistic with regard to the individual and the society. Symbolic practices were always directed at *all* the powers of the individual for her/his recovery or at *all* the possibilities in the society for its peaceful continued existence. The intellect, the emotions, the ability to act, *and* the natural environment were incorporated into archaic magic. Modern symbolic practices, by contrast, serve only limited purposes in which the person is analyzed as if she/he were an automaton and only partially addressed. That is particularly the case when the purposes are obscure—when psychology is in the service of social conformity, commerce, or war. Here the underlying ethos is the opposite of the magical ethos, which endeavored to heal the individual or the society through the harmonic combination of all capabilities; and its effects today are proportionately chaotic.

Modern magic consists of symbolic practices that intervene in psychosocial reality with the support of a comprehensive ethos that does not subordinate itself to egotistical private or group interests. Modern magic differs from archaic magic in that the rational factor has considerably broadened for individual areas of knowledge in the meantime. To develop a system of symbolic actions based on today's state of knowledge and supported by the magical ethos is the task of modern matriarchal art. And it could help modern-day people—who have been fragmented, specialized, stereotyped, and controlled—to become whole again.[24]

ON THE SECOND THESIS

The structure of matriarchal mythology was the system underlying this all-inclusive thinking. I have designated the structure the "fundamental categories of human imagination," not only because it is ancient but also because it was widespread among primitive peoples throughout the world and became the conceptual foundation of all early high civilizations that influenced the development of patriarchal religions, philosophies, and arts, and still has subliminal repercussions today. I have illustrated those connections in my study on matriarchal mythology.[25]

I will now reproduce from the aforementioned work the relatively detailed scheme of the structure of matriarchal mythology. The scheme contains the worldview of both the highly developed matriarchy and the simple matriarchy, whose more straightforward structural pattern merged into that of the highly developed matriarchy. We can decode and read all matriarchal conceptions around the globe in terms of this scheme. And since mythology also contains the history of matriarchal peoples, it is a great source for the cultural and social history of the prepatriarchal era.

The structure of matriarchal mythology has a triadic pattern that corresponds to the concept of the Triple goddess. The pattern is actually a double triad because it relates to the figures, functions, and attributes of the goddess of the developed matriarchy, the Triple moon goddess, and to the figures, functions, and attributes of the hero subordinate to her. (Male gods did not yet exist.) In the structural scheme, the figures represent types whose names vary according to the concrete myths and cults. The function belonging to a figure always remains the same. While the overall attributes are constant, they also admit of variations.[26]

I should like to make a few remarks on this scheme. I shall begin with the worldview of the highly developed matriarchies (urban high civilizations). The triadic worldview of the archaic peoples of antiquity is mirrored in the triadic Goddess Structure (table 1). Heaven is the highest region—the region of light, the abode of the divine constellations. The land and sea compose the middle region: the human world. The underworld is the region under the earth or under the sea and other bodies of water, from which the mysterious powers of death and resurrection emanate.

This three-tiered cosmos is completely permeated by female forces. In the upper region dwells the bright, youthful, atmospheric goddess, embodied in the astral huntress: the Maiden goddess. In the middle region dwells the Nymph goddess, who rules land and sea, fructifies the earth and the waters, the animals and the people by her erotic power, and thus perpetuates life. In the underworld dwells the Crone goddess, the death goddess as the crone who destroys all life in the abyss and, at the same time, causes its resurrection from the depths. This mysterious deity of eternal destruction and eternal return determines the astronomical cycles, the setting and rising of the stars, and, with them, the cycles of vegetation and human life. She is thus the goddess of cosmic order and the incarnation of eternal wisdom.

All three figures form a single deity and can never be completely separated from one another. They are the threeness in oneness, the first trinity, the matriarchal Great Goddess. Her symbol is the moon as a unity with three phases: the white crescent moon is the symbol of the Maiden goddess with the cultic hunting bow; the red full moon on the horizon represents the purplish red world egg, the symbol of the Nymph goddess; the invisible black new moon—seemingly absent, yet pres-

Table 1
Goddess Structure

FIGURE	Maiden
FUNCTIONS	Combat and hunting
ATTRIBUTES	
Moon phase	Crescent moon
Symbolic moon color	White
Seasons	Spring
Region in the three-tiered world-view	Heaven
Animal symbols (or totem animals)	Beasts of prey: esp. lions, panthers, cats; hunting animals: white stags, falcons
Symbolic objects	Bow and arrow; wagon pulled by lions or stags

Nymph	Crone
Love, fertility, earthly dominion	Dominion over the hereafter: death and resurrection, mastery of magic, oracles, art and science
Full moon	New moon
Red	Black
Summer	Fall and winter
Land and sea	The underworld as the hereafter under the earth and sea
Domesticated animals: esp. cows, goats, sheep, hinds; love and fertility symbols: doves, bees	Subterranean animals: esp. snakes (phallic primeval serpent); black or nocturnal animals: owl, raven, crow, black/white hounds or horses
Magic girdle and rings; the world egg (= full moon), the love apple, the fruit-garden paradise	The death apple; the scales of fate, the threads of fate, or the spindle; the fruit-garden paradise as the realm of the hereafter

ent—is the symbol of the dark, paradoxical goddess of the underworld, the goddess of the passage from light to darkness and from darkness to light, the Crone goddess.

Compared with the Goddess Structure, the Hero Structure (table 2) is less complex because the man and his powers do not represent the cosmos. Therefore he appears in more limited dimensions: he is a single figure and is directly connected to the matriarchal Great Goddess in each of her three phases. It is only through her that he gains a share in her qualities and dignity (initiation), is integrated as a part into her all-encompassing fertility (Sacred Marriage), and experiences the sanctioned transitions of death and return (sacrificial death and resurrection). At the cyclical festivals of the seasons, the Great Goddess is represented on earth by her priestess-queen, and the people by the hero-king. Incarnate in these two representatives, the Goddess unites with her people and includes them in her blessings. The hero is subordinate to the Goddess, just as the sun is subordinate to the female moon. The sun was considered transitory since, as opposed to the eternal multiform moon, it has only one form and undergoes rising and setting.[27]

The worldview of the simple matriarchies (agrarian village cultures) is contained in the following scheme. The goddess of the simple matriarchy is the chthonic goddess as personification of the earth. She dwells in canyons, caves, volcanoes, or simply everywhere under the earth. She brings forth all life from the depths and draws it back down to her again. The hero is her fertility partner, and he usually dwells with her in the underworld. Neither figure has yet attained astral dimensions. The chthonic goddess was later absorbed by the third figure of the Triple moon goddess (the Crone goddess).

There is an even older form of matriarchal mythology in which no male partner appears at all. It mirrors the Pelasgian myth of Eurynome, the dancing creator-goddess who parthenogenetically brings forth everything from herself; the serpent demiurge is merely the wind or the water of the ocean, which was considered sufficient to impregnate a woman. (Fatherhood was unknown to the early matriarchies.)[28] Only later did the great serpent gradually evolve into the masculine principle, the phallic symbol, but it still had no representative figure. Eurynome merely danced with this "wind" in Chaos, and her orgiastic dance led to the birth of the world.

Now I shall make several brief comments on the diffusion of this structural pattern of matriarchal mythology. In the present study I cannot possibly list all the mythological names that filled this pattern for all matriarchal peoples, but I will do so for the Indo-European area, where matriarchal mythology attained its highest level of development.

In the eastern Aegean region, including pre-Hellenic Greece, the names of goddess and hero figures were Artemis of Ephesus and her hero Actaeon, Aphrodite Urania of Cyprus and her hero Adonis, the Cretan-Pelasgian Athena and her hero Erechtheus, Demeter of Eleusis and her hero Iacchus/Dionysus, Hera of Argolis and her hero Heracles. On Crete they were called Nout/Neith and her hero Re/Ra, Hathor and her hero Horus, Isis and her hero Osiris/Horus.[29] All these cults were closely associated with the oldest matriarchal cult of the region: that of Inanna/Ishtar and her hero Dumuzi/Tammuz of Sumer. Asia Minor and ancient Palestine were also influenced by Sumer. The figures in Asia Minor were Kubaba/Hekuba and her hero Teshub, and Cybele and her hero Attis; in Palestine they were Atargatis and her hero Hadad, Anat and her hero Baal. In Persia the figures were the goddess Anahita and her hero Mithra.[30] In pre-Aryan India they were Prithivi and her hero Dyaush-Pitir, Sarasvati and her hero Brahma, Lakshmi and her hero Vishnu, Shakti/Kali and her hero Shiva. In all these cults the heroes were gradually deified, and under pa-

Table 2
Hero Structure

FIGURE	Only one		
FUNCTIONS	Initiation (in fall)	Sacred Marriage (in summer)	Death and Resurrection (in fall/winter)
	Initiation as fulfillment of his marriage tasks:	Sacred Marriage is the most important festival, which is consummated with the nymph-goddess in the presence of all the fertility symbols. Place: a wonderful spot outside, originally on mountaintops.	Death is always a sacrificial death in which the hero-king himself is the valid sacrifice. (Later variations: surrogate offerings of boys or male animals.)
	Peaceful variations: obtaining magic objects or attaining wisdom. Competitive variations: competitions, races, or battles. The initiation battle occurs with the following variations:		
			The sacrifice of the king also has the following variations:
	Battle against mythic animals: lion, hind, serpent, where killing the serpent = dragon dominates as the monster of death.		Death through the goddess herself in her third form; rebirth or reawakening through the goddess in her first form.

		Death through one of the mythic animals of the goddess, esp. the dragon = serpent (death also as a deathlike state: suspended animation, unconsciousness, deep wounds); reawakening through the goddess in her first form, usually as a healing of wounds.
		Death through his successor; reawakening and return in the form of the successor.
	Battle against his predecessor, who is considered either a stranger ("widow-murderer" relationship) or a relative; the latter case has the following variations:	
	The old king is "father" of the young king, then a "father-son" battle with a subsequent "mother-son" relationship (cf. Oedipus). The old king is an uncle-usurper who slew the first king (= "father") and now is slain by the "son," with a subsequent "mother-son" relationship (cf. Orestes).	
ATTRIBUTE	The celestial symbol of the hero is the sun with the colors red and gold.	

triarchal influence became the high gods who later supplanted the more ancient goddesses. Abstract principles are all that remain of many of these high gods.

In northwestern and central Europe, the matriarchal cults of the Celts were those of Dana and her hero Dagda, Modron/ Morrigan and her hero Bran, Erin and her hero Lug. There, too, the heroes were later deified. In the Germanic region— although of pre-Germanic origin—there were the matriarchal cults of the Earth goddess Jörd and her hero Tyr/Heimdall, the goddess Freyja and her hero Freyr, the goddess Frigg and her hero Odin/Balder.[31]

In my detailed study on matriarchal mythology I prove that those cults have the structure of matriarchal mythology and I demonstrate how they were transformed—under the continuous influence of the patriarchal waves of conquest—into the early patriarchal Indo-European religions.[32] Therefore, to avoid repeating myself, I have confined myself here to a mere enumeration of examples. But even a mere enumeration of examples hints at what extraordinary repercussions the matriarchal cults and mythologies had throughout the patriarchal epochs. With the destruction of the matriarchal form of society, matriarchal cults and mythologies did not simply vanish, but persisted through the historical millennia as open or secret cults, or as images and ideas appropriated by the patriarchal religions. They were later passed down in folklore, folk festivals, fairy tales, legends, and even high poetry, but with dwindling consciousness of their origin and meaning. In my study on matriarchal mythology I have also described this process in Europe with regard to folklore and poetry.

In view of these historical currents, I am certainly not going too far in presupposing that the structure of matriarchal mythology is—or should be—the basis for modern matriarchal art. We need only consciously apprehend what has been unconsciously present (and repressed) in poetry and art from the beginning. There is nothing new about the structure of matriarchal mythology in the sense that by rediscovering it we can reestablish our connection to archaic matriarchal art—a connection that has never really been eliminated. We are simply creating a new consciousness of that structure. This discovery directly and consciously vivifies our connection to archaic matriarchal art—a connection that has existed only indirectly and unconsciously for millenia. Our unconscious knowledge is not of some mysteriously collective, unprovable intellectual archetype (in the Jungian sense). It is rather the unconscious knowledge of a very old, repressed cultural tradition, which was passed down to us without cohesiveness and whose pattern has petrified in mere ceremonies. To rediscover the matriarchal cultural tradition requires not spiritual introspection but basic ethnological and cultural-historical investigation, by means of which it can be precisely localized in time and place and studied, thus eradicating its seemingly subjective, mysterious, and unprovable character.

The artistic and literary analyses in the next essay will demonstrate that this structure is emerging more frequently and clearly today. It is as if the structure of matriarchal mythology were gradually rising from its long obscurity and resurfacing on the social horizon of thought. We merely have to help it make its final breakthrough as articulated knowledge and a deliberate artistic pattern.

ON THE THIRD AND FIFTH THESES

In these theses I attempted, by means of a negative description, to specify the nature of a matriarchal "artwork," i.e., a concrete realization on the foundation of the structure of matriarchal mythology. The negative description was based on the general communication model, which has been used for patriarchal art and suits it. In terms of that model I was able to determine precisely what matriarchal art is *not:* it is not a *thing*—not a poetic, musical, or visual "text"—but a *process*. Matriarchal art requires neither a marketer nor a mediator; it admits of no separation of artist and recipients, no distinction between artistic genres and between art and nonart. So what *is* matriarchal art?

Is it a multimedia show? Certainly, but it does not confine itself to the presentation of the interactions between various formal means.

Is it a performance? Perhaps, but it is not merely the individual action of an artist whom the others are permitted only to watch.

Is it a happening? To some extent, as the artistic action of several persons. But it is not a pattern that a few people stumbled upon together, since matriarchal art has an established, preexisting structure that contains the objective categories of human imagination.

Is it environmental art? Yes, in that it is an artistic alteration of the surroundings. But its goal is not the transformation of an apartment, a house, or a surrounding landscape, for it does not yield passive, observable objects.

Is it even art at all? Yes, for it creates beauty—no longer as beautiful semblance but as reality.

Is it more like a new cult? No, because it does not prescribe any religious contents, as do all religions that use dogmatic tenets. Besides, this question presupposes the separation of art and cult, and therefore simply cannot be answered.

Can matriarchal art even take place outside the matriarchal form of society? No, because the matriarchal form of society was and is the immediate expression of matriarchal art. In the past, the matriarchal form of society embraced entire peoples, giving matriarchal art its completely public nature. Today it embraces, at best, small groups on tiny cultural islands, where it is not so much a different form of society as a different way of life. Insofar as matriarchal art is practiced in those small groups, it can be only an experimental anticipation still lacking a valid form and a completely public character.

Nevertheless, my description of the moon dances and the structure of matriarchal mythology clearly describes what matriarchal art *is*. Matriarchal art is what the nine Muses performed: ritual dance festivals in the course of the seasonal cycle as initiation, marriage, death, and return.

One may argue that ritual dance festivals with such contents cannot be repeated today. However, that is an illusion, just as it is an illusion that magic cannot be repeated today. This becomes clear when we recall that the ritual festivals were merely the concrete realization of the fundamental categories of human imagination—and those categories have not changed in the meantime.

The only question is how those categories can be concretely realized today. It is a completely open question. Experiments in this area will yield answers, and the answers will be extremely diverse. There is no simple answer to the question of the possible form, contents, or significance of modern matriarchal *Gesamtkunst* (comprehensive art). Each individual woman or each group of women will find their own answer in their own way in their own concrete realization of matriarchal art. One can neither predict nor predetermine the experiences, sensations, insights, attitudes, actions, and symbolic forms each will invest, or the meanings with which they will fill those categories. As I have already said, those categories are an open structure. Not even the participants know it exactly, for the contents crystallize as forms only during the *process* of matriarchal art. New meanings and new forms are indeed actively sought, but their emergence comes as a complete surprise. And that is precisely what constitutes the alteration of reality in the process of matriarchal art. That is the magic that is experienced and performed and whose sudden manifestations can be so stirring that they lead to ecstasy.

It should be clear by now how fundamentally different matriarchal art is from patriarchal art. Matriarchal art cannot be used as an ornament, a commodity, or entertainment. It also does not know the loathsome alternatives of art dogmatism, which still prescribes the themes, meanings, and keys (e.g., Christian art), and art subjectivism, which confines itself to arbitrary themes or arbitrary forms that have lost any binding force (e.g., bourgeois art). Matriarchal art is, by contrast, unity without dogmatism (because it prescribes no meanings) and multiplicity without subjectivism (because it follows the framework of the categories of human imagination). And that is what accounts for its uncommon effects.

On the Fourth Thesis

By its very nature, matriarchal art demands all human capacities, which do not deteriorate in the process but at its climax lead to ecstasy. The concept of ecstasy, however, requires elucidation.

The modern conception of ecstasy is just as unclear and prejudiced as the modern conception of magic and ritual transformation. With the dawning of patriarchy, those cultural forms decayed and perished in a jumble of polemics and intentional misunderstandings, which persist to this day. As a result, most people mistakenly consider ecstasy a form of delirium leading to complete irresponsibility or a form of mild insanity—that is, as something completely irrational. That is false.

Genuine ecstasy is of course difficult to describe, for it is a sudden interplay of all a person's powers, including the emotional, the intellectual, and the behavioral. Although those powers can be unleashed, ecstasy can never be achieved at will. Such concepts as inspiration, illumination, and intuitive insight hint at the spiritual element of ecstasy, but they emphasize the passive intellectual side and exclude the active emotional side.

Eroticism is not a good analogy for ecstasy, either. Although eroticism can be an exquisite act, it all too often lacks the spiritual-intellectual element. Eroticism is always involved in ecstasy, but in and of itself it would produce only delirium at its climax. None of this has anything in common with the great energetic power of ecstasy.

Genuine ecstasy unites the powers of emotion, intellect, and the capacity for action in a climax in which no one power is limited at the expense of another. They do not interact consecutively but simultaneously and at full force. Ecstasy is the lightninglike, inimitable harmonious interplay of those powers at the moment of their highest intensity. For example, to give concrete form to the categories of human imagination as represented in the Goddess-hero structure requires a great amount of intellectual work to recognize those categories clearly, great emotional strength to be equal to experiencing them, and an intense capacity for action to implement them. When the interplay of those powers suddenly occurs, which is always improbable and rare, ecstatic moments are produced. They are moments of extreme lightness and freedom; they are chords of celestial energies played on the fragile instrument that is a human being. No one can hold on to those ecstatic moments, which is a good thing, because ecstasy cannot be endured for long.

This reveals another decisive difference between matriarchal and patriarchal art: as an ecstatic outlet, matriarchal art is not art for an audience; it is not art for voyeurs. One can recognize matriarchal art only by entering into its process.

ON THE SIXTH THESIS

The neutralization of the division of the artistic genres probably requires no further explanation; but a few remarks on the dissolution of the distinction between art and nonart are necessary.

I think I have demonstrated that entry into the process of

matriarchal art presupposes "theory," that is, knowledge of the matriarchal form of society and mythological structure, as well as intense contemplation of ways to transpose them into the present. On the other hand, the process of matriarchal art always entails the transformation of a way of life, for it also includes all the practical "arts." Crossing the boundary between theory and everyday practice does not happen independently of the artistic process itself—for example, by first formulating a theory and then putting it into practice. It happens simultaneously.

Let us imagine that such a process of matriarchal art has been in progress for several days or weeks. Elements of daily life automatically come into play: resting, sleeping, eating, drinking. Theoretical elements come into play just as automatically: speeches, discussions, meditation. The essential difference is that those elements normally occur outside a symbolic context, whereas in matriarchal art they are integrated into a symbolic context and are therefore no longer what they appear to be. They have now become symbolic acts themselves. As a result, those elements can evolve from and flow into dance forms, where our definition of *dance* is much broader than the conventional one. *Dance* is not just musical movement but also promenades, processions, and scenes that form a continuum. At festivals the types of movement are manifold: there are ritual meals prepared and conducted with stylized gestures; inspiring dramatic speeches followed by dramatic scenes; sleeping and awakening as symbolic states that can give rise to new mysterious festive acts. Those elements cannot be separated from one another because it is only within the total context of the process of matriarchal art that they acquire their meaning. And their meaning is always multilayered. Elements become separate from the process only if they do not preserve the symbolic value acquired through the structure of matriarchal mythology as expressesd in the flow of the festival—that is, by not conforming to that structure itself.

ON THE SEVENTH, EIGHTH, AND NINTH THESES

"Practice" is not confined to domestic practice. It clearly follows from the last three theses that it also entails political practice. The change in lifestyle entailed in the process of matriarchal art pertains not only to the way of life of individuals but also to that of groups and the entire society. Only from this perspective do the symbolic acts of matriarchal art obtain their complete substance.

This extension, however, seems implausible according to what was said above. Is not the process of matriarchal art by definition and in practice extraordinarily esoteric? Who can possibly know the structure of matriarchal mythology? Who is capable of achieving genuine ecstasy? Who can be so free as to change her whole way of life through an artistic process? Moreover, processes of matriarchal art have existed thus far only in the experimental stage, isolated in enclaves seemingly devoid of social efficacy.

Such a scenario completely contradicts the character of matriarchal art, because true matriarchal art as ritual festival is *public* by its very nature and accessible to *all*—under the open skies, in the fields, or on the city squares.

Matriarchal art is fundamentally public for another reason as well: nature participates in it. At the archaic matriarchal festivals, the accompanying natural events—the phases of the moon, the sunrises, the rain—were the decisive elements, which is why their dates and times had to be determined so precisely. When one forecasts nature precisely, nature really does reliably participate and perform the most spectacular "symbolic acts." These natural events represented the true climaxes in the archaic matriarchal festivals, for the dancers had spoken with nature, and nature had responded—an occurrence that, as a rule, aroused great enthusiasm. The fact that an astronomical calculation underlay the natural event did not detract from the ecstatic joy, for nature had done them the favor of acting according to their calculation, and she rewarded their service with her manifestations at the opportune time. That was how the mutual understanding operated between people and nature.

The possibility of communicating with nature through symbolic actions is not precluded today, despite our denatured environment. However, it *does* require our relearning to act according to nature's will instead of trying to coerce her into acting according to ours. We can begin to act in accordance with nature, for example, through our treatment of our own body, which is a part of nature, and our treatment of the immediate, changeable environment. The moon and the sun—which of course cannot be coerced into acting according to our will—demand *our* adjustment to *them*. If we do nature this service, then she will do us the favor of participating in symbols. The joy and delight we experience through her participation derive from the harmony between a transformation in nature and a spiritual transformation in us. The one is mirrored in the other, and the entire situation thus becomes a symbol.

Precisely that striking symbolic situation is what enables the uninitiated to comprehend what is happening. It is not only that such basic patterns as initiation, marriage, death, and return are somehow known to each person—after all, they are the basic patterns of human imagination that manifest themselves in all religions in one way or another—but, over and above that, such fundamental processes take place simultaneously with visible natural phenomena, making background information and long explanations superfluous. With her seasons, nature herself explains the structure of matriarchal mythology, without the uninitiated having to know it beforehand.

In this way the initiates are drawn into the festivals, become involved, and, as soon as they comprehend the development, gradually become participants. Nature herself is the greatest festival. All who have participated in such a process of matriarchal art, in which every element in the interplay becomes a symbol, might recognize that they have participated not in a new form of art but in a new form of *life*.

Precisely because it does not conform to the fictionality principle, matriarchal art becomes a provocation the moment it appears in its totally public sphere, which is also the public sphere of nature. It is a provocation without even trying to be one, for it contains a value system different from the patriarchal one, and it implements that value system without repudiating it as "beautiful semblance." Matriarchal art counterposes the unity between nature and humankind against the exploitation and commercialization of nature by man. Matriarchal art counterposes the unity of all human abilities against their patriarchal specialization, which, for men, leads to absurd excesses and, for most women, to equally absurd distortions. Matriarchal art counterposes eroticism as the strongest creative force against its devaluation and repression in the ascetic patriarchal religions and moral systems. Matriarchal art counterposes the finiteness of death and the infiniteness of life against patriarchy's bleak scientific attitude toward death and cynical perfection of the instruments of slaughter. Not one single idea in matriarchal art bears any resemblance to any patriarchal idea.

To live those values beyond "beautiful semblance," beyond the ghetto to which patriarchal societies have banished them, is a challenge of the first order. Patriarchal societies will attack matriarchal art precisely because it can be neither formally nor socially domesticated. And thus, without even trying, matriarchal art will find itself in the midst of political action. Its forms would then become forms of a political confrontation—a confrontation that would be completely unconventional and completely astonishing for the opponent not familiar with such forms of resistance. The struggle would not be an exchange of aggressions but an incessant withdrawal and reappearance, a growing, intangible symbolization, a creation of entirely new connections in the midst of this disintegrated, atomized world. This symbolization is not predictable—neither its stages, nor its dimensions, nor its forms, which are in perpetual flux. What would the opponent attack in such a vexing puzzle? He would get lost in unknown labyrinths. He would experience a paralyzing bewitchment.

There are no weapons against a complex social "counter-practice" that is not *against* but merely *indifferent to* prevailing social practice. It is a way of life based in and of itself; it is unconstrained integration according to the rules of the multiplicity and totality of the individual and society. That is the essence of beauty as a noncommodity: it seeks to abolish the split in the aesthetic dimension and thereby aestheticize the entire society. The aestheticization of society through such an art is the creation of meaningful social intercourse. From this perspective, art is no longer a special technique or a particular ability but the universal capacity for individually and socially shaping a life worth living.

In a patriarchal society this matriarchal art, this beauty, is opposition par excellence, without attaching any importance to being opposition. And what weapons exist against this withdrawing and opposing, opposing and withdrawing beauty?

THREE

Witchcraft/Witch Art

INTERPRETIVE COMMENTARIES ON CONTEMPORARY WOMEN'S ART

I shall now attempt to identify tendencies in contemporary art that represent an intuitive anticipation of a matriarchal form of art and can be described in terms of the principles of matriarchal aesthetics. That is my most difficult task of all, but for different reasons than one would expect. One might assume that matriarchal tendencies are almost indiscernible in contemporary art, which would commit me to overinterpretation from the outset. However, matriarchal tendencies are in fact very pronounced in contemporary art by women, particularly feminist art. That does not mean that every feminist artistic expression can be described in terms of matriarchal aesthetics, nor does it mean that matriarchal aesthetics includes only explicitly feminist art. Such matriarchal tendencies do, of course, manifest themselves most clearly in feminist art.

What actually makes my task so difficult is the international diffusion and erratic development of feminist art. Because it is impossible even to survey, I will not make definitive pronouncements about feminist art in general but will merely describe only those narrow segments that most clearly exhibit the matriarchal tendencies I wish to delineate. In this respect I admit that my choice of examples is subjective, but since my criteria of selection are based on the principles of matriarchal aesthetics, they are not arbitrary but systematic.

Another difficulty is my unconventional interpretive method. I do not approach the works as an interpreter or a critic would. Such roles are not possible in matriarchal aesthetics, nor is it possible to treat works of art as things. I would be contradicting myself if I were to cast myself as an authority and treat art objects as if they were commodities for the art market. Matriarchal art is not a thing, a commodity, or a fetish but an energetic process. Neither the categories of recipient, interpreter, critic, and market nor the categories of artist and the "art thing" created by her/him are applicable in matriarchal aesthetics. Such categories vanish in the process of the magical transformation of spiritual-social reality described by matriarchal aesthetics.

What I am doing here—writing thoughts about matriarchal art—is part of the process of matriarchal art, and so I myself am a participant. I am advancing this art itself by the very act of describing it beyond the landmarks of "pictures," "tones," or "poems." For matriarchal art admits of no such separation of genres. I am advancing matriarchal art itself by surveying concrete artistic expressions from an all-encompassing perspective, which, because of its greater range, actually produces a vision of the new matriarchal art. For matriarchal art admits of no separation between "art" and "theory," or "art" and "life." I therefore take the liberty of improvising beyond the conventional artistic boundaries, with the ultimate purpose of outlining a matriarchal art-utopia. For to write thoughts about matriarchal art means to *create* matriarchal art, to be in the midst of the matriarchal way of life. Beyond the fictionality principle, everything occurs simultaneously.

Space

How do feminist artists shape and alter space in order to open it up and to transcend it as artistic space? They do not begin with an abstract conception of a space to be delimited and filled arbitrarily; instead, they begin with the concrete space that they themselves are—their body. The body space is a natural space that these artists reexplore and reexperience. By beginning with their body as the center, they find that other natural spaces automatically open up: the sensual space, the living space, the space of surrounding nature. These spaces are not abstractions but concrete unities and environments that issue from each other with fluid transitions. The interrelationship of the corresponding artistic forms is equally fluid: body art, environmental art, and earthwork art are combined and augmented in ritual art (performances). (In this context, ideas on architecture are simply an augmentation of earthwork art.)

On Body Art: External Space

Body art has two different meanings for women artists: first, as purely feminist body art, and second, as matriarchal body art. Feminist body art is a critique of the diminishment of the female body in patriarchy, i.e., its colonization as an object of lust, reproduction, and work. The body art that takes this tack derides and exposes by means of its postures, colors, and symbols the functions and visual manifestations forced upon women. In feminist body art the artists break social taboos in general and taboos to which only women are subject. Two examples are works by the Austrian Jana Wisniewski and the English Cosey Fanni Tutti.

In Jana Wisniewski's photo series *Rollenbild der Rollenverschweigerung* (Roll picture of role concealment), a woman's face (Wisniewski's own) repeatedly appears amid images of clouds, waving fields of grain, thickets, puddles, half-open doors, walls, bookcases, and doll's heads. The woman is imprisoned among these realities, and her face undergoes various changes in each frame: once it is behind black bars; then it is rigid like a mask; then it wears numbers as if calculated with geometric precision; then it is enshrouded in black like the face of an Arab woman; another time it has a darkly encircled eye; or it appears trapped inside a black case.[1] All these faces are the desired or made-up feminine faces that Wisniewski rejects by caricaturing the role expectations—a silent protest.

Cosey Fanni Tutti goes a step further in her photo series *Life Forms*. She radically exposes the brutality in the forced poses of a pornographic photo model and a striptease dancer by caricaturing them with her whole body.[2] As Cosey says of the pictures, it is the photographer or the audience that ascribes to her personalities that are not her own. The publisher, the market, and the audience vehemently dictate what they want. Consequently, the only contribution the artist can make is to place her own body on exhibit. In this way, Cosey exposes the cynicism that reduces a woman's body into a commercialized object of male sexuality.

Cosey takes an entirely different approach in her "actions," which she documents in photos. The photos show her in poses similar to those in pornographic and striptease pictures, but here she is not an object but the *artist,* i.e., the *subject* reclaiming its identity. She is dressed in delicate tricots and absorbed in a game with threads, bands, and chains around her arms and legs. Those are gestures of grace and self-love, the tender exploration of her own body, which is no longer placed on exhibit. According to Cosey's commentary, she presents *herself* here; everything is determined by *her* and seen through *her* eyes. She thereby dispels the false ideals of femininity and performs a purification ceremony. Her life is now her own work without any outside influence. Hence these "actions" are true forms of her being: the "life forms" of Cosey Fanni Tutti.

From Mary Beth Edelson's *Woman Rising*

1   Stone Circle of Dromberg (Cork, Ireland)

2 Stonehenge (reconstruction)

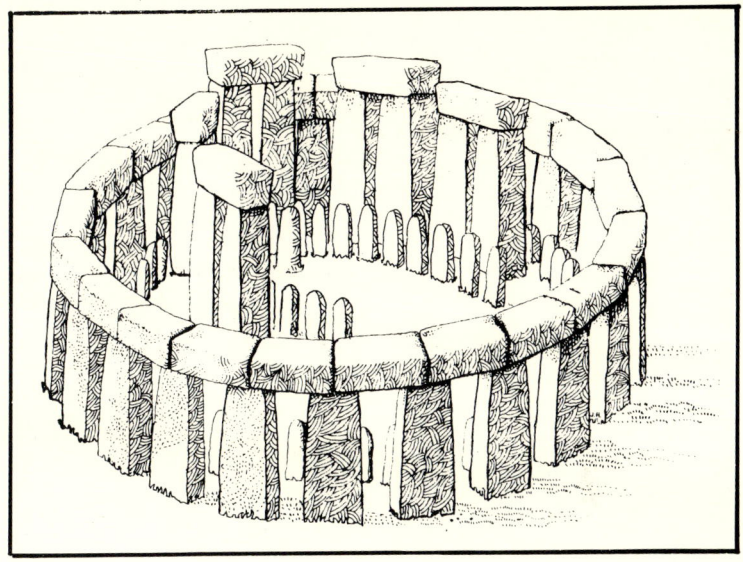

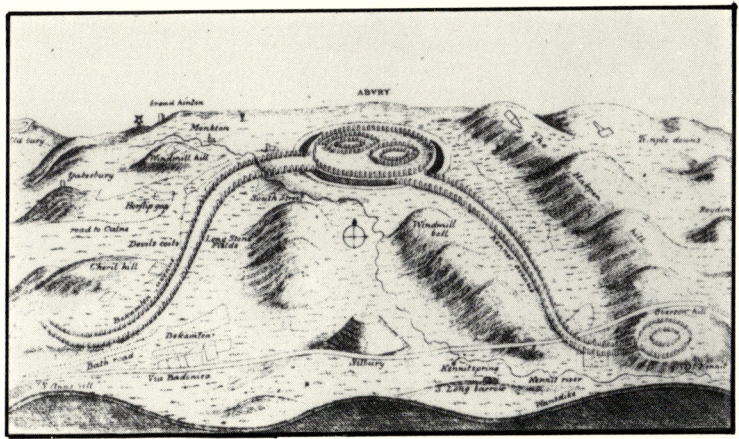

3 Avebury (reconstruction)

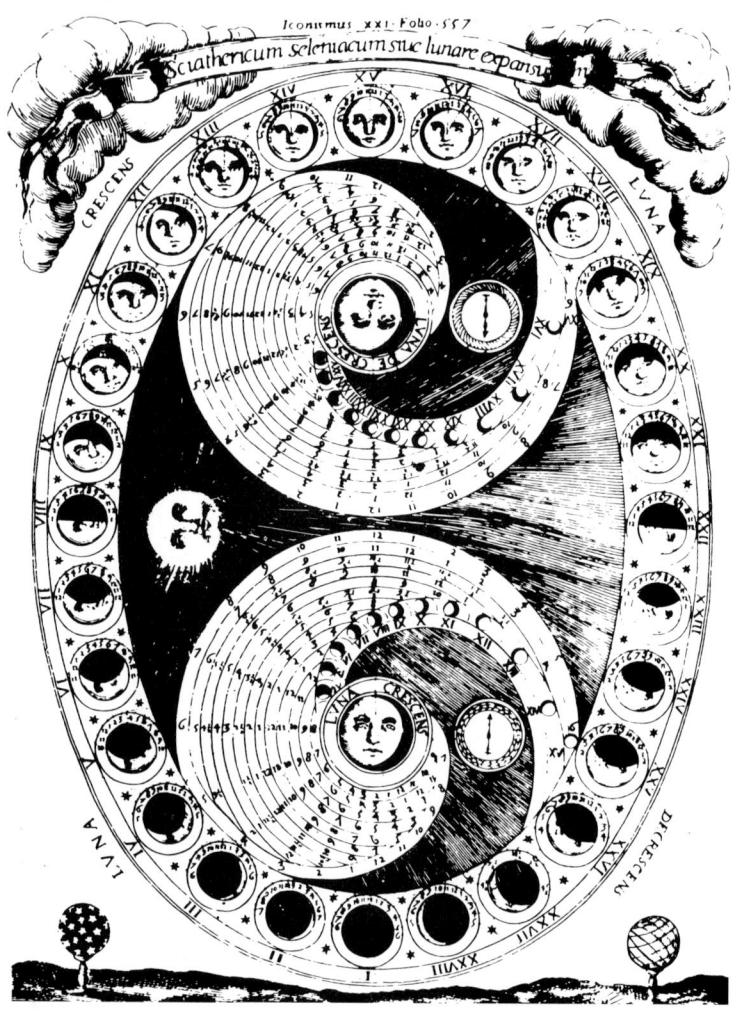

4 Lunar Calendar

6 Labyrinth of Tibble (southeastern Sweden)

5 Labyrinth on the Island of Wier (Finland)

7 Labyrinth of Troy (England)

8   A Dancing Maenad

9
From a Performance of Carolee Schneemann's *Eyes-Bodies*

11
Frida Kahlo, *The Love Embrace of the Universe, the Earth, Me, and Diego*

10   From Mary Beth Edelson's *Woman Rising*

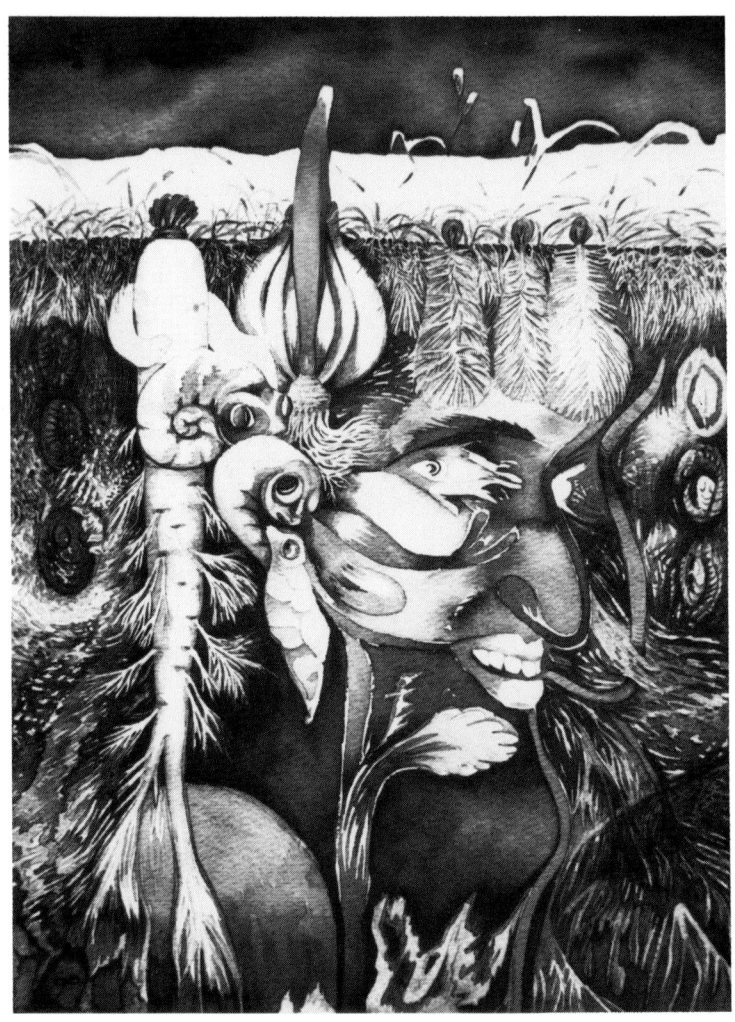

12 Anna Fengel, *Subterranean Goddess II*

13   Anna Fengel, *Amazons with Their Serpents and Dragons*

14 Margarete Petersen, *The Moon*

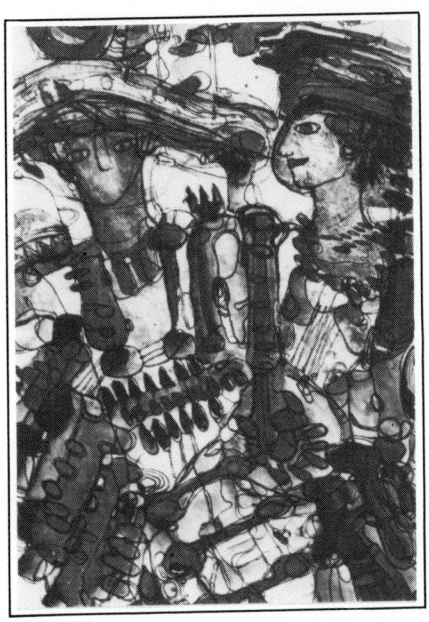

15
Lena Vandrey, *On the Way to the Future of the Amazons*

16 Ingeborg Lüscher, *Ingeborg*

17 From a Performance of Ulrike Rosenbach's *Reflections on the Birth of Venus*

18   Colette, *Persephone's Bedchamber*

19   Judy Chicago, *The Dinner Party*

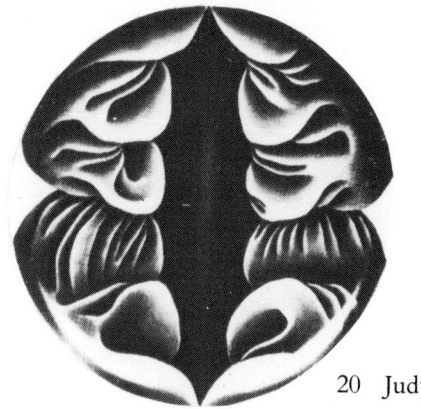

20 Judy Chicago, *Plate of Gaea*

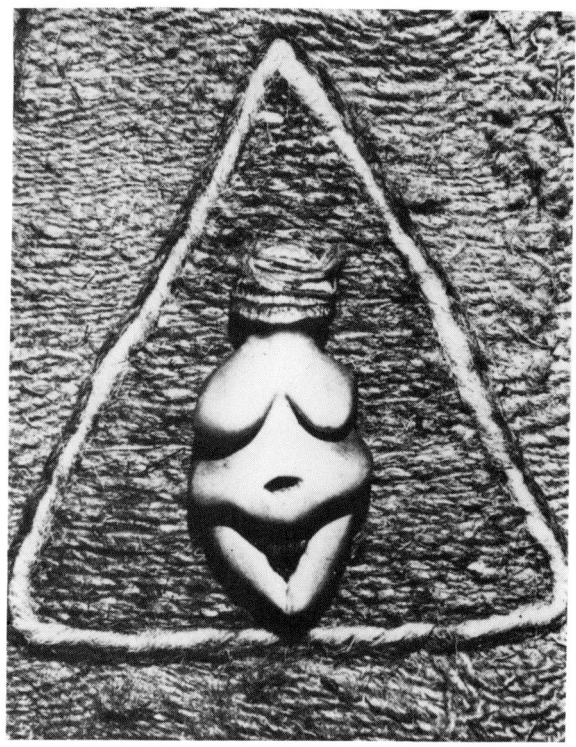

21 Judy Chicago, detail from *Place Setting of the Fertile Goddess*

22   Judy Chicago, *Place Setting of the Amazons*

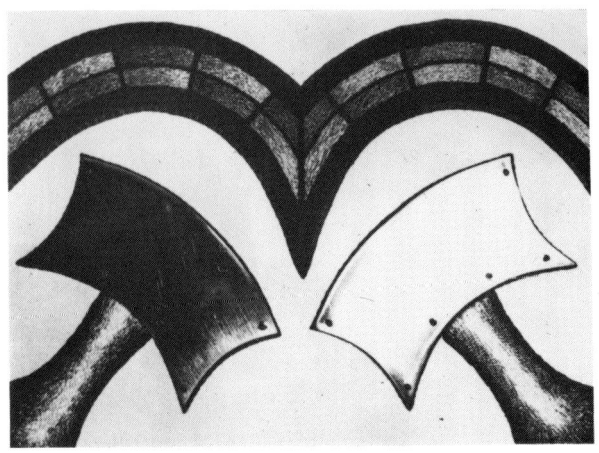

23   Judy Chicago, *Place Setting of Hatshepsut*

24
Judy Chicago,
Place Setting of Theodora

26   Sigrid Neubert, *Movement of the Sun in the Water*

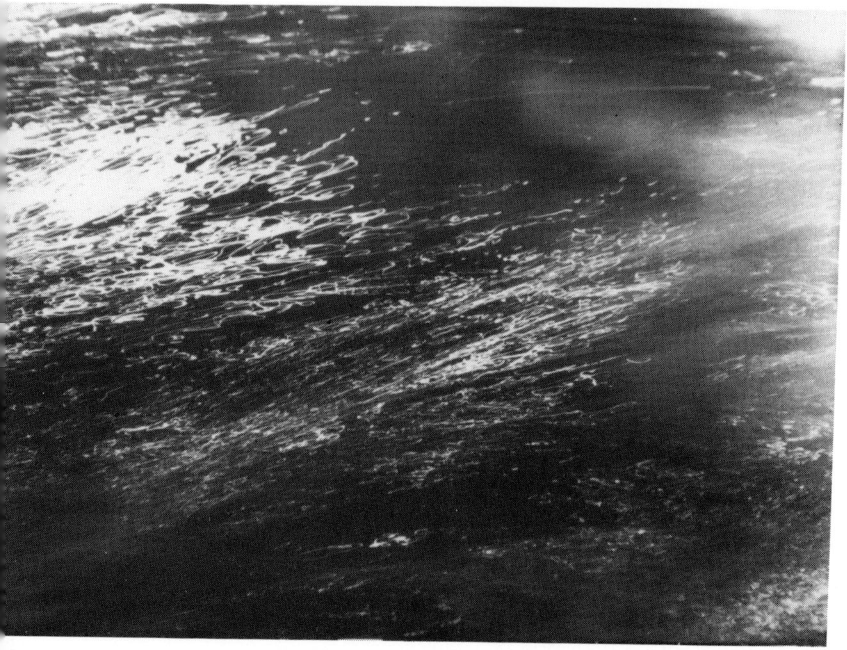

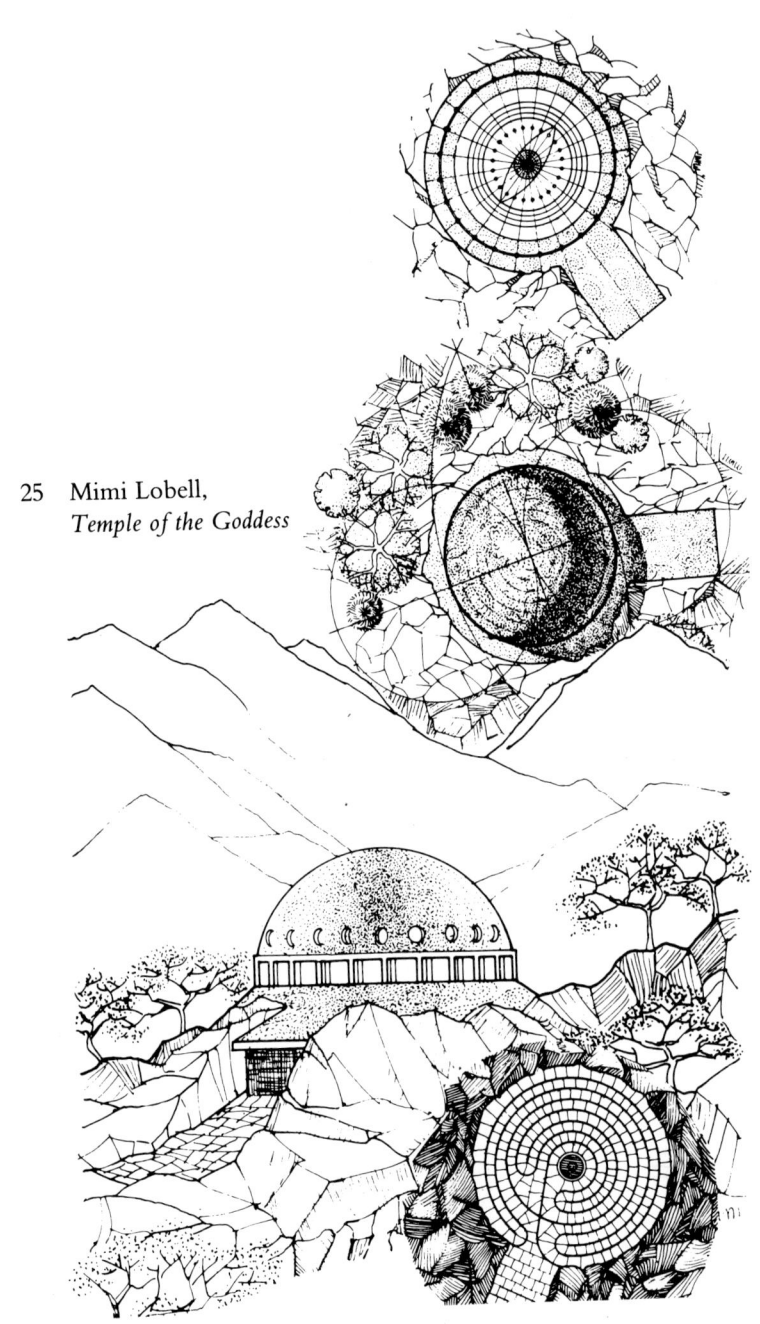

25 Mimi Lobell,
Temple of the Goddess

27   Robert Smithson, *Spiral Jetty*

28   Margarete Hicks, *Hicks' Mandala*

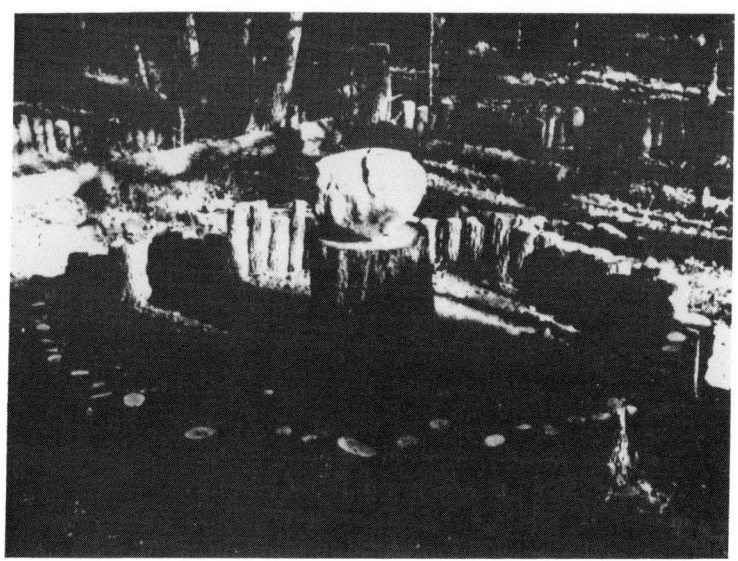

29 Mary Beth Edelson, *Pilgrimage to a Neolithic Cave*

30 Mary Beth Edelson, *Where Is Our Fire?*

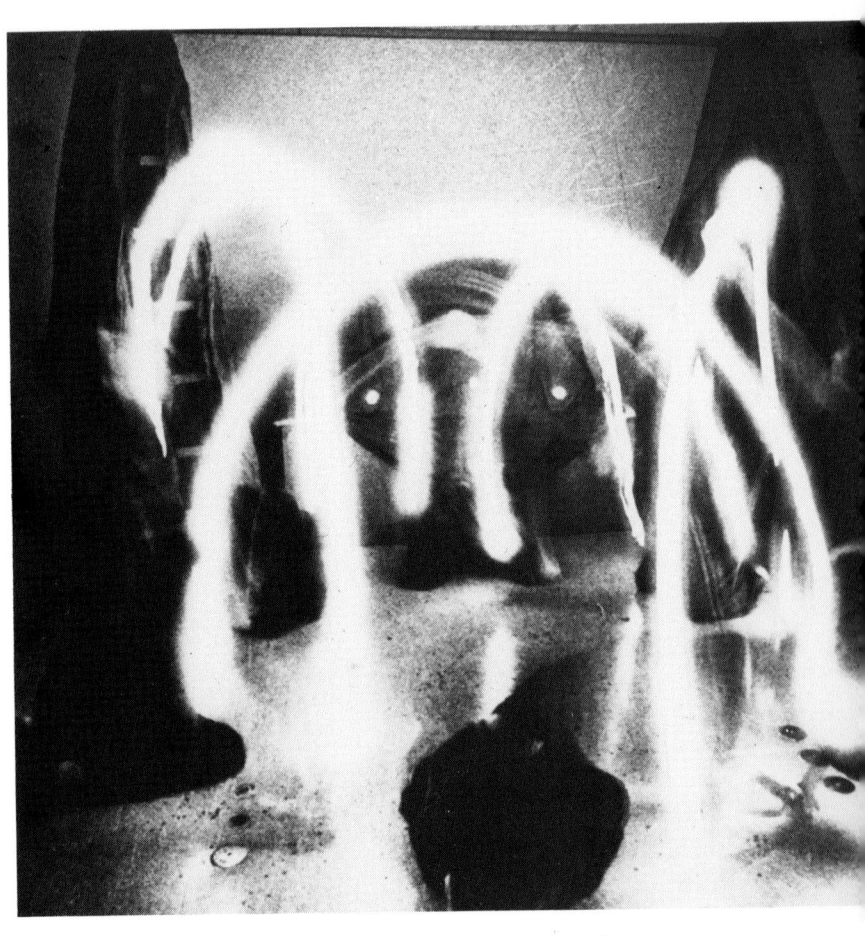

31 From Mary Beth Edelson's *Creation Begins . . .*"

Friederike Pezold is another artist who treats the rediscovery of her own body, of feminine sensuality beyond male projections. After criticizing in pictures and texts the passion story of the bondage of the female body, Pezold finally discovers an alternative: to create a new film language in which the woman rediscovers her body, creates *her own* image of herself, and refuses to be an object or a nude model for the male spectator or artist. Pezold translated that idea into reality with her film *Toilette* (Primping), which she calls the first body-language feature film. To quote her, the video has the following very simple plot:

> A woman sits alone in a room that could be any room. Opposite her is a television. Her image appears on the screen as an effigy. She sits face-to-face with herself. She looks herself in the eyes. The body postures of the image and the effigy are not identical. She was an effigy when she was hiding her body, and she is the image when she rediscovers her body and its parts by taking a video camera and filling the television screen with her new self-confidence and new self-images. The body postures of the image and the effigy are now identical. [She is] on the search for her identity. She is primping. With the video camera. She is thus re-creating her body. Piece by piece. Millimeter by millimeter. From head to toe, tooth and nail. Before she goes, she watches what she recorded with the video camera. On the screen. Which, in contrast to a mirror, illuminates and stores the reflected image, even when one is no longer standing in front of it.[3]

With great intensity Pezold rediscovers in her film every detail of the female body: the face, ears, eyes, nostrils, mouth, hands, back, breasts, navel, pudenda, posterior, feet—a minute portrayal of their minute movements. According to Pezold, she thereby reveals through her own body the "black-and-white goddess in her new corporeal sign language."[4]

That is one side of the protest. In Pezold's case it is positive and culminates in the recovery of her own sensuality in sensations of autoerotism. In this respect, *Toilette* comes close to realizing the theory of the feminine aesthetic and its conception of the recovery of female body language. Pezold's film does not go far enough, however. Her feminine body language does not harmoniously and fluently unite body, gesture, mimicry, expression, and symbolically apprehended environment; nor does it unleash untamed, unrestrained feminine sensuality in every direction. The film has too great a tendency to dissect and dismember, thus resulting in a piece work composed of individual body-part pieces (for example, the "pudenda work," the "back work"). The woman never appears as a whole and free person in an environment created by her.

Because of that I do not consider Pezold's film an example of matriarchal aesthetics, neither in theme nor in form. The same is true of the other examples mentioned. However, it was necessary to discuss these examples to indicate the overall trend in contemporary women's art and, at the same time, to distance myself from it. In fact, none of the feminist works discussed so far are examples of what I would call matriarchal art—at least not in approach. The distinction between purely feminist art and matriarchal art should gradually crystallize in my delineation of the examples that follow. And it should go without saying that my selection criteria are in no way a devaluation of nonmatriarchal feminist art.

In the examples of matriarchal body art, the women artists take direct recourse to magical-mythic symbols from matriarchal societies and infuse them with new meaning. In matriarchal body art, female physicality is understood more broadly than in the examples of mere self-discovery discussed above. It is viewed in its creative capacities as uniquely and closely connected with the cosmos. The female body is not merely a mirror of distorted projections of femininity as the opposite extreme in a male society; it is the mirror of the entire cosmos. This recognition reveals to the artists completely different dimensions of expression and form: the matriarchal aesthetic as opposed to the feminine aesthetic. These artists can therefore identify with the strong, independent women from matriarchal societies—their priestesses and goddesses—and thus develop a much more expansive image of themselves than can women who perceive themselves only as the "other," or the "opposite extreme," in a patriarchal society.

The American Carolee Schneemann is one of the first contemporary artists to choose this approach. Her performances, characterized by fragmentary chaos and orgiastic exuberance, directly penetrate into nature—both inner and extrahuman nature—and fuse it with ancient and new images of feminine physicality. Schneemann thus succeeded in consciously portraying goddess images in her art even before the new feminism emerged. She took those images from dreams, hallucinations, and the tales of her Scottish nanny, who used to show her "the Great Mother in the full moon." Such profound symbols as the cat, the bull, and the serpent did not leave her, and she soon comprehended their connection to feminine strength in archaic art. Schneemann developed that connection in her spectacular performance *Eye-Body* (1963), which she documented in photos. One photo shows her reclining on a flooded, glittering couch as two snakes slither over her nude body. A black line divides her face in half, causing her to resemble the double-faced earth-serpent goddess, whose body radiates magical and erotic power (figure 9).[5]

The Cuban expatriate Ana Mendieta came to a matriarchal conception of her physicality via the pagan vestiges in the Roman Catholicism of Latin America. She captures images of death and rebirth in her various photo series. For example, Mendieta portrays her own silhouette with arms raised in a goddesslike gesture of invocation and then has it collapse and go up in flames, leaving behind only a small pit full of black, fertile ashes. Or she depicts her silhouette as a bunch of flowers floating down a river on a raft, as if journeying to the other world. Or she reproduces her body, outlined by the flames of small candles, on the rock floor of a pre-Columbian Indian temple. Or she stretches out naked in an archaic Mexican grave with innumerable tiny flowers growing on her body.[6]

A little later, the American Mary Beth Edelson employs similar themes, but with complete consciousness of the new women's movement. Edelson elevates her performances to rituals, which she performs alone or with other women and documents in photo sequences. She distinguishes between "private rituals," which serve the purpose of self-discovery, and "public rituals," which seek to unite all the participants in a joint action. According to Edelson, a joint ritual is not successful if it is a self-conscious, isolated act of a performer upon whom all the attention is directed—as is normally the case with plays. On the contrary, it is successful only if all the participants feel and act in concert—proceeding, of course, from a theme and a form but gradually forgetting them. Moreover, an authentic ritual not only can satisfy a momentary need but also can be performed repeatedly.[7]

Edelson depicts the rediscovery of the elementary power of her feminine physicality in the private ritual *Sexual Rites,* which she performed on a beach in North Carolina and documented in a series of photos.[8] One photo shows her kneeling in the sand, completely naked and holding her breasts in her hands— the same gesture as in a hundred ancient Goddess idols. Her breasts are painted with black and white concentric rings and thus very clearly defined. She bears similar markings on her stomach—nothing but black and white concentric rings around her navel, increasing to the size of a pregnant woman's abdomen. With this archaic body painting and gesture she resembles a new, resurrected fertility goddess. The artist makes the "resurrection" tangibly visible: she stretches her arms to the sky like the newborn Venus, slowly rises as rays of energy emanate from her right and left (the lines drawn on the photo), and with outspread legs stands before the sky like a statue. At the same time, the rays of energy coil around her head in a bundle, with the crescent moon in the middle, and finally explode into a wreath of beams from which the new goddess gazes into infinity with a smile and white eyes (figure 10). Edelson herself says of this series: "I am depicting the wholistic [sic], centered, assertive, sexual, spiritual woman who is in the process of becoming, balancing her mind/body/spirit. I am using my body in these rituals as a stand-in for the Goddess, as a stand-in for Everywoman."[9]

It is clear from all these examples of matriarchal body art that these performances have nothing to do with art as beautiful semblance but are *real* processes of self-healing and self-liberation. However, because they are documented as photo sequences in galleries, the performances are still bound up with the representational form of patriarchal art. But the representational aspect is a secondary matter since, unlike conventional art, the performances—and particularly the rituals—are not created for the purpose of exhibition. The essential aspect is what happens *within* the artist herself: the physically and spiritually liberating transformation. And for women in today's society, the transformation is not merely a subjective, private matter but a political act designed to rupture totalitarian patriarchal culture and subvert its exclusion of everything genuinely feminine. Edelson expressly considers all her rituals to be political statements, for they symbolize women's joy and exuberance over their newfound freedom.

On Body Art: Internal Space

Internal space is filled with dream images and mythical visions of the female body and its power, which artists portray indirectly with their own bodies. Their media include traditional forms such as painting and photography, in which matriarchal elements appear only as a theme, and nontraditional forms such as performances, in which those inner visions are expressed through movement. Even in the traditional genres, the approach of the artists is in no way object oriented: the images and forms appear only as individual phases in processes, the expression of which is considered the essential aspect, not the individual work.

The Mexican painter Frida Kahlo belongs to an older generation, and my discussion of her work will be the only reference I shall make to precontemporary women's art.[10] I will describe only two of her paintings in order to show that matriarchal symbolism openly resurfaced as a theme before the new women's movement. The surprising resurgence of matriarchal themes has nothing to do with archetypes in the collective unconscious; on the contrary, in every individual culture it is a conscious continuation of old traditions that were consigned to the underground or to fringe areas of patriarchal societies. Kahlo was well aware of her own legacy from pre-Columbian Mexican culture. She herself was of Indian blood and as a baby was attended by an Indian wet nurse. The nurse appears in one of her numerous self-portraits. It depicts a brown, stone-faced figure holding in her arms a baby Frida Kahlo with an adult head. The breast Kahlo sucks is transparent; all the milk vessels are filled with tiny white flowers, and their stems reach through the nipple into Kahlo's mouth. She is literally drinking her roots.[11]

Another marvelous painting infuses this theme with cosmic dimensions to mirror matriarchal mythology in its totality: *The Love Embrace of the Universe, the Earth, Me, and Diego* (figure 11). A black-and-white, atmospheric, cloudy face of a woman appears in the background. Her great hands—one is black, the other white—appear in the foreground, and in her arms she holds everything in the center of the picture. She is the universe, the cosmic goddess, in whose white half hangs the red glowing ball of the sun and in whose black half hangs the bright sphere of the moon. She lovingly embraces the smaller goddess, the Earth goddess, who is enthroned as a compact, brown stone figure in the center between the moon and the sun and is the image of Kahlo's wet nurse. She is the Indian Earth goddess, whose breast drips with milk, on whose shoulder grows a tree at a river's edge, and whose sides overflow with lush Mexican vegetation. On one side it is colorful in the heat of the sun, and on the other side it glows in the silver of the moonlight.

The enthroned Mother Earth in turn holds in her arms the enthroned Frida Kahlo, who appears in the three colors of the daughter of the earth, of the Triple moon goddess: Kahlo has black hair and wears a purplish red dress billowing in snow white rays of pleats. Kahlo's breast, too, drips with milk, but her eyes shed tears because she has no children of her own—she was unable to have children as the result of a serious spinal injury that had confined her to a wheelchair since her youth. Kahlo nevertheless holds a child in her arms: her husband, Diego, as a large male baby. Her gesture is identical to that of the Egyptian goddess Hathor as she holds on her lap the adult but baby-sized Pharaoh, her son and husband.

In the matriarchal world the man is at once son, husband, and hero and completely embedded in the universe of women, who lovingly direct everything. The association of the childlike Diego figure with the hero is established through the third eye on his forehead (reminiscent of Mexican gods), and his association with the sun is created through the bundle of flames he holds in his hand. Even Kahlo's shaggy dog is included in this embrace: he is sleeping peacefully under the maguey on the black arm of the Goddess of the Night—an odd Anubis, watchman of the underworld.

But let us return to contemporary women artists. The works of the German painter Anna Fengel clearly demonstrate that, in the hands of women artists, picture painting does not merely yield objects but is a process—albeit still within the realm of a traditional genre. Fengel concentrates on only a few themes, but they recur in numerous variations that mirror the stages of her own spiritual developmental processes. The painting of such a series extends over years and encompasses the same time frame as the inner developmental process itself. Fengel's themes are mythic visions in the form of "dream paintings" or "soul pictures," in which mythic matriarchal themes are consciously used for purposes of self-discovery. Fengel calls this process "seeking the Goddess" and says of herself: "I am not a painter but an inventor of pictures. The content is important to me, and finding contents is difficult. These are soul pictures, and it is difficult to find pictures for a spiritual state."[12]

Let me describe two of these series, both painted in Fengel's characteristic style of centering heads in profile. The first series is titled *Die unterirdische Göttin* (The subterranean goddess) (1970–1981).[13] It begins with a *Self-Portrait* depicting a super-terranean half and a subterranean half. A white face appears in the superterranean, dark world covered with meaningless formulas. The white face is lifeless, rigid, chalky, and enveloped by blue worms instead of hair. A red face appears in the sub-terranean, bright world; it is tilted halfway down and resembles a mussel or a half-moon. The red face is bright and vivacious but subterranean. Thus the living half is under the earth, and the half that is visible in this world is a lifeless mask.

The second painting in the series is titled *Hades*. Fengel had intended to paint a royal, crowned head—an underworld god-dess. But because she had not yet internalized the theme, she painted a god instead of a goddess. The god is sitting under the earth, as if in a cave in the world of the gnomes, surrounded by precious stones and the rolled-up insects that form his headdress. This is only an allusion to life: life is present visually but not conceptually. The insects, glittering like jewels, are dead larvae—purely formal, purely ornamental. The structure of the brown stone under the earth is amorphous and dead, empty and devoid of content. The god's eyes are equally empty. He is blind and his face is turned to the left, back into the Stone Age. His smile, which was supposed to be superior and Dionysian, is frozen in a demoniac grin. The amniotic sack bulging from his mouth remains empty. (When the god was still a goddess, the sack was supposed to contain an embryo.) His crown is a furry animal that appears to be sleeping under the earth. However, the animal is not really sleeping—it is blind like the god. It also has the same malicious grin, the same dark color, and the same treacherous lurking posture as the god—it is his crowning attribute. Thus, even in its failure, the picture is evocative as a negative backdrop.

In the next painting, *Unterirdische Göttin I* (Subterranean goddess I), the subterranean goddess herself appears for the first time. She has a bright face with a green, albeit incomplete, eye. The interior of the earth is beginning to move around her like waves—the water under the earth is rising. The animal figures are also losing their rigidity. The round jewels prove to be eggs from which birds with large, partially blind eyes are sliding. Like the god, the goddess wears a furry animal as a crown. Unlike the god, her crown is decorated with two living horns—large-eyed fish. The goddess's animal is younger than the god's. It cannot show its claws yet and, like an embryo, helplessly holds its paws open. Even its mouth is naïve and has no viciously flashing teeth.

That intermediate painting is followed by *Unterirdische Göttin II* (Subterranean goddess II), in which the theme is internalized for the first time and attains a free and relaxed portrayal (figure 12). Like the god and the first goddess, this goddess is sitting in profile under the earth; but, in contrast to the god, she is looking to the right—into the future. Her eye is clear and sharp, radiantly blue and shaped like a fish, a water symbol. Her smile is as serene, alert, and superior as her gaze. Her exquisite, sensual mouth smiles ironically and haughtily, in Dionysian lust and divine serenity. The round, brown shape of her vague body is also sensual. Her chin, shoulder, and breast exude massive, fertile power. Besides the soft brown tones, there is also much pink: the goddess's lips and the coiling larvae. The life here is even younger than in the painting of the first goddess: it is in the bud stage, pink like plant sprouts before they blossom. The goddess's headdress is made up of budlike animals and plants in the rooting and bulbing stage. Reminiscent of Celtic Irish manuscript illuminations, the animals and plants form the letters IN, meaning "It begins."

The structures of the earth are beginning to come to life around the goddess. Bright blue arteries of water flow upward, pass into the root fibers of the plants, and draw the life force upward. New life will soon break through the surface of the earth, still petrified in the frost of the winter night. The earth is in a state of becoming and is driving the living things upward. The victorious goddess rises from the underworld; her smile is highly subversive and liberating. This powerful emergence is the final stage of a developmental process in which Fengel became aware that—in contrast to the patriarchal conception—matter is not negative, burdensome, suppressive, oppressive, or limiting. Instead, it is living, structured, and charged with manifold energies; it has the power to transform from the depths.

Fengel's second series of paintings bears the provisional title *Amazonen mit ihren Schlangen und Drachen* (Amazons with their serpents and dragons) (1976–1982) and likewise portrays mythic self-images from her own process of spiritual development. Fengel describes the inner theme as follows: "Someone is put into armor and is supposed to fight, although he has neither the predisposition nor the desire to do so." This helplessness is symbolized by the child's hand that forms the earflap of the profiled figure's magnificent helmet, which is adorned with three bundles of flames instead of plumes. The little hand tries to get hold of the terrible, powerful serpents and dragons but is unable to make a fist to fight.

The series opens with *Lanzelot* (Lancelot), a young man who is supposed to fight but is too delicate to do so. He is still protected by the dragons and serpents. But in the second picture, *Höllenfürst* (Prince of hell), the man is forced into battle and flies into a rage. He turns into the prince of hell, who is ambivalently male and female but in any case demoniac. Now all the dragons and serpents explode from his furious head and surround him like yellow, brown, and red flames. They are vital and ferocious, and they bite and devour one another. The figure's face is deathly pale, and since he has no enemy against whom to direct his outburst, the figure represents evil itself. Full of hatred, the evil spreads to all corners of the world.

The aggression is followed by depression. In the next painting everything dissolves in hazy forms, in iridescent, bewildering greenish blue. Now the head is dark and melancholy. It is ornamentally painted like the face of an Indian woman who, in the greenish blue fog, does not know whom she is supposed to fight. She cannot see her opponent and believes the dragons to be her adversaries, but their bulging bodies and heads merely disintegrate into the mist. Only their flame red tongues and white, evil eyes shine through the fog, but the eyes are bulging and their expression is powerless.

The painting of the Indian woman fumbling in uncertainty is followed by a painting of a blond maiden with beautiful, energetic features. On her slender body she wears leather clothing; her helmet does not overflow with ornaments but is of a simple, elegant design. She looks like a female Parsifal, and the painting is in fact titled *Sie will Ritter werden* (She wants to become a knight). The maiden has taken possession of the dragons coiling around her in bright green and blue, and they have become her helpful attributes. The battle with the dragon as a psychic struggle has achieved a metamorphosis: suddenly, light pours in and the space opens up; the largest dragon, which is as blue as the vault of the heavens, soars over the young Amazon's head. The anxiety has been overcome, and a cosmic day dawns.

The young Amazon—courageous, proud, and restrained—has accepted the battle situation. She has consented and, at this moment, recognizes the dragons as her own powers, her own energies. But she does not yet have full knowledge; she imagines or anticipates her strength in the blueness of her fantasy. Her little hand is no longer an ornament indicative of helplessness but of relaxation. She assents to the battle without tenseness, and her inner energies visibly spring from her head as flames from her helmet.

The provisionally last painting of the series portrays the adult Amazon, who has full knowledge of her powers (figure 13). She has conquered the dragons and serpents as her own energies; they are lying behind her and coiling in clear, comprehensible contours at the nape of her neck. The flames of her own energies emit the light now and reflect on her helmet. She thus carries her own light—her inspiration—and stands fearlessly in reality: the real cosmos, which is dark and nightlike and not blue like the cosmos of her fantasy. Arching over her is the cosmic dragon of the night, whose scales, teeth, and eyes glow like heavenly bodies. Reality is ominous, but this Amazon has turned her head and gazes calmly into space. The picture thus attains depth and a hint of activity. The Amazon has become realistic and stares at what approaches her. The band of her helmet has turned into a fire-breathing serpent. This serpent, like the others, is no longer the threatening *unconscious* but the deeper powers of *knowledge,* which the Amazon now possesses. Her little hand is no longer childlike but sinewy, not helpless but relaxed; with ease she lets a dragon slither from her hand like a weapon. She has consciously conquered herself and reality.

Clearly, these mythic self-portraits as stages of an inner, spiritual developmental process—a transformation—cannot be regarded as things or individual art objects. They can be comprehended only in the context of the inner transformation: they are the visible, material stages of that process. Since Fengel cannot count on such understanding in the patriarchal art world, she does not exhibit her pictures in that public sphere; instead, she shows her works exclusively in the Munich women's community.

Just as expressively and consciously as the aforementioned artists, the Berlin painter Margarete Petersen draws upon matriarchal-mythic history with her paintings of tarot cards. Every card she paints (six so far) reveals esoteric knowledge and represents the continuation of the suppressed matriarchal history of symbols. The cards also indicate a deeply felt and experienced personal situation, as Petersen says of her tarot card depicting the moon symbol.

> I performed a full-moon ritual. I put my child to bed,
> washed, and put on clean clothes. I took a glass ball and sat
> down at the window. I wished for the moon to appear.
> But it was cloudy. I gazed out the window for a very long
> time and felt very good. Suddenly I had a strong feeling for
> the tree outside the window. I felt the need to go outside; I
> was drawn to the farmhouse on the hill (a farm in Austria),
> and I asked nature whether she accepted me more now. I
> felt as if I could move in harmony with the swaying of the
> trees and the plants, no longer as an alien entity but as an
> integral part of nature, and I felt very happy. Then I went
> inside again, and from the window I saw a dark cloud pass
> across the night sky—it was so beautiful. Suddenly the

cloud lifted, and there was the moon. It lasted for only a
moment, and then everything was as before. It was like a
dream. Then I very quickly painted the image of the
moon.[14]

In tarot the moon card is the symbol for intense emotion
and intuitive perception, for the world of the unconscious. The
moon card is characterized by night, darkness, mystery, magic,
and a dual energy: the soaring, clarifying, ascending Diana
energy of the waxing moon, and the sinking, obscuring, calm-
ing, leading-to-the-depths Hecate energy of the waning moon.
In moon cards this ambivalent energy is always represented by
two columns. Between the columns is a tortuous path through
the night; it leads from a body of water, over mountains, and
into infinite darkness—as if on the search for the mystery.

Petersen has taken up this symbolism and deepened it in a
personal way. On her moon card (figure 14), whose delicacy
and transparency express the higher stage of the spiritualization
of tarot images (which the painter achieves in all her paintings),
both columns stand directly in the water and open like a gate.
The face of an intent woman is visible in the left column in
bright blue: the illuminating Diana energy. The figure of a
shackled woman is visible in the right column in deep violet:
the downward-drawing Hecate energy. The dangerous path
leads between a sleeping dog and a howling wolf, but it is
illuminated by the glow of a substantial moon, which shines
like a massive silver body and is damp with the dew filtered
from the dark clouds. A crab representing Cancer, the zodiacal
constellation subordinate to the moon, stretches its claws from
the water, whose seemingly inscrutable depths range in color
from turquoise green on the edge to inky darkness in the center.

How the dangerous path is to be overcome is indicated by
the ghostly face in the water. Two of its eyes are closed, but
the third, lustrous eye in its forehead is open; it symbolizes

intuition, the unconscious, which still knows the way long after the conscious mind has forgotten it. That intuition from the depths and the moon from the heights—two feminine symbols—lead the seeker safely on the path through danger and darkness and through the gate, which also symbolizes feminine powers. That is how Petersen painted it; before painting it, she experienced this state herself. Consequently, this tarot card—like her others—originated spontaneously as a magical dream image. Petersen's images, like Fengel's, are not intended for the general public, who would understand neither the theme nor the spiritual developmental process of the painter.

Lena Vandrey's technique, by contrast, diverges considerably from conventional styles of painting. She collects the materials for her pictures—nails, leather, straw, moss, weathered wood, matted wool, colorful stones, mirror fragments, frames, lasts, wire, old sacks, rusty tin—from trash dumps, old houses, and ruins. She shapes the contours of her figures from hot wax, which she also uses as an adhesive to affix the collected materials to the undercoat. Vandrey also intersperses those materials with leaves, plants, roots, thistles, and flowers. In this way, she creates fanciful figures indeed, all of them female: the wild Amazons of her imagination. Vandrey calls the figures "magnificent and humble, basically benevolent and humorously mischievous, laughing and grumbling, restive and gentle, wild and subdued, sorceresses and fairies, witches and huntresses, rebels and queens, sages and horsewomen, bacchantes and alchemists, prophetesses and dancers—our dear ladies of the nettles."[15]

Vandrey considers her *Zyklus der unverwesbaren Geliebten* (Cycle of the incorruptible beloved) a true vision of the widely diverse tribes of the Amazons. The work consists of fifty pictures with extremely audacious figures. They have faces with hanging ears adorned like those of cannibals; eyes made of mirror fragments reflecting the eyes of the viewer; laughing, grinning, triumphant mouths; blemished teeth; wild hairdos created from hair, wire, spikes, and strings of pearls interwoven with bands, and decorated with helmets of brown and turquoise fabrics. The figures stand, sit, or dance, and boldly display their sex organs—even if made only of flower stems. Wool threads hang like tassels from their necks to their beautiful breasts of wax, buttons, or snail shells. Tree leaves adorn their shoulders, colored stones their necks. Tiny nets serve as little bodies, bundles of spikes as dresses, button stays as arm and leg bracelets. Mussels, stones, wool threads, or little cat heads form whimsical vaginas. The gestures of the figures are unaffected and proud. They extend their hands to one another, embrace one another, lean against one another, lick one another, sit on one another's shoulders. These are not structures but orgies of association.

In her paintings in traditional style, Vandrey imitates the montage technique she uses in her pictures made of stones, shards, and rags. The details are executed in round, stonelike forms dipped in the same earth-tone colors as the original material. In these paintings, too, Vandrey creates associative images of multifariously intertwined patterns, for example, in the watercolor *Auf dem Weg in die Zukunft der Amazonen* (On the way to the future of the Amazons) (figure 15). Ingenious multiplicity predominates, an intricate web of lively mirth, which is exactly how Vandrey understands her Amazons: "It is no accident that I have always established a very strong harmonious connection between these women and noblewomen and nature and earth. For me, these women are the image and symbol of feminine freedom itself, the characteristic and essential aspect of life."

Ingeborg Lüscher is another artist who abandons traditional painting. She uses diverse techniques: photography, collections with inscriptions, assemblages, collages of pictures and text. In her works, rigid boundaries between genres and styles become fluid. Her art is filled with autobiographical elements. She searches for herself within and beyond the paradises of this world and explores the deeper layers of herself and her immediate surroundings, which she considers magic. Lüscher characterizes the essence of magic as the discovery of love in all creatures and things. Through magic, the visible is united with the invisible, and the various domains of magic naturally extend into everyday life. The connection between the visible and the invisible comes to the fore in Lüscher's works, which are themselves stages in her own development and so closely associated with her that she maintains: "This work *is* my life, which I modestly and openly, honestly and naïvely attempt to transform through photos, texts, paintings, or found objects."[16]

Lüscher thus discovers magic in nature: in dreamy thickets of ferns, in the traces of their echo in the sand, in loops of water and earth that look as they did at the beginning of creation, in countless heart-shaped stones—hearts in the leaves between the branches, hearts in the rippled sand at the water's edge. Nature is full of hearts, "full of love," as Lüscher remarks with humorous irony. She gives visible form to the magic in other people with her series titled *Zauberfotos* (Magic photos). Without explaining why, she urged friends and acquaintances to perform magic and then photographed their activity. Lüscher comments: "While they do not reveal *parts* of the soul, it seems to me that the *Magic Photos* do perhaps reveal something of the whole that had never come to the surface before."

Such is the case, too, when Lüscher penetrates her own deeper layers by playing tarot or revealing her reincarnations through trances. The love, the power, the magic of a woman come to the surface and manifest themselves in unexpected ways. Perhaps the best example is the large picture *Ingeborg*. Lüscher used an entirely unusual technique in creating this painting (figure 16). She glued a piece of creased and wrinkled parchment to a brown cotton scarf measuring almost three by three meters; then she lay down on it and poured black pigment on her body, causing the outline of her body to appear as a relief. Finally she folded white creased paper into the figure to create rays of energy surrounding the body like an aura. Lüscher thus created her own image as a naked, tranquilly seated goddesslike figure whose body and breasts radiate like white flames the feminine power of love and procreation: a new Venus.

Ulrike Rosenbach, by contrast, takes an approach completely different from those of the aforementioned painters and photographers. Like the Americans, Rosenbach transforms her inner images and mythic associations into performances. And by transposing them into movement, she strips them of their nature as objects to a much greater degree. But it is still a matter of giving visible form to the inner processes of the conscious. Thus for Rosenbach, even video works are not merely "documentation" but "documents of the inner life."[17]

Rosenbach uses mythic associations to give visible form to the false mythologizations of the feminine in patriarchal society and to breach them critically. That is particularly evident in her two performances *Glauben Sie nicht, dass ich eine Amazone bin* (Don't think I'm an Amazon) (1975) and *Reflektionen über die Geburt der Venus* (Reflections on the birth of Venus) (1976). In the performance *Die einsame Spaziergängerin—Hagazussa* (The solitary stroller Hagazussa) (1979), Rosenbach uses ancient symbols of Australian aborigines, among others, to give visible form to a new image of woman. She calls the latter performance a "ritual."

The structure of Rosenbach's performances is always complex and multilayered. On one level, she plays ironically with the mystifications and false mythologizations of the feminine in traditional patriarchal art. On a second level, she penetrates those mythologizations to expose the deeper layers of the myths, which originated in the matriarchal epoch—not the patriarchal age—and are therefore genuine images of womanhood once conceived by women for women. On a third level, she not only goes backward in the history of mythic images but also forward to reveal the patriarchal mystifications of woman today—how they have been corrupted into banal advertisements, into clearance sales of male projections of femininity in display-window decorations, television commercials, billboard ads, fashion, beauty contests, circus performances, and science fiction. In this way Rosenbach recovers that lost, critically reflected dimension of mythic images in their entire historical span. Her feminist critique of the history of these images introduces the fourth level of her art: the utopian idea, the reawakening that will perhaps transform the ancient matriarchal self-images of women into new self-images of women. To realize that utopia—in Rosenbach's view (and mine as well)—is the point of working with matriarchal mythology today.

I would like to elucidate this complex process in terms of the examples of Rosenbach's art mentioned above. In her video *Glauben Sie nicht, dass ich eine Amazone bin* (Don't think I'm an Amazon), Rosenbach, wearing a white tricot and harshly illuminated, stands in a dark room and shoots an arrow at a round target made from a reproduction of Lochner's *Madonna of the Rose Bower*. The Madonna represents the domesticated, sanctified feminine in a patriarchal religion: an artificial, supernatural figure far removed from the life and identity of real women, an unattainable ideal having an oppressive effect on women in real-life circumstances. Rosenbach confronts this mystification with her weapon and destroys it—not Lochner's Madonna herself but a patriarchal projection of femininity. However, the Madonna is not simply the rejected opposite. The superimpositions in which Rosenbach's own face appears behind the Madonna's emphasize that she is also taking aim at the cliché within herself—the internalized projection of femininity as "chastity, gentleness, and goodness." Rosenbach comments: "In this video action I shoot at the picture of a Madonna and at myself. I do not identify with the picture of the Madonna, who is gentle. But I am not aggressive. I am calm."

Clearly, the false paragon of femininity as "chastity, gentleness, and goodness" at any price cannot be overcome by resorting to the false paragon of masculinity as aggression at any price, but only by taking recourse to a matriarchal figure: the Amazon. The Amazon is not chaste in the patriarchal definition of "sexually untouched" but in the sense of independence and sovereignty. Nor is she gentle in the patriarchal sense of "submissive"; she is simply tranquil and serene in her struggle with the predominant reality. Nor is she good in terms of a moral system thrust upon her; she is simply herself. Thus, Rosenbach's Amazon figure symbolizes the discovery of one's identity and the recovery of this ancient image and the values it represents for women today—values that have been distorted into their opposite by patriarchal moral systems. At the same time, the utopian content surfaces in the recovery of the Amazon image as the strong, calm, self-confident girl, the Maiden goddess who is independent of all later gods.

Precisely that utopian content is lacking in every Amazon cliché produced by men today within the scope of their commercial culture, as Rosenbach demonstrates in the revealing accompanying images from the science fiction film *Die Amazonen kommen* (The Amazons are coming). We see women archers disguised in Greco-Roman dress and film-star makeup (perfect to the eyelashes) barking out orders with distorted mouths or fighting—a facile parallel to the usual costume films and war films: a male figure with a female face. Men apparently cannot conceive of Amazons in any other way, as Rosenbach remarks with irony: "Women who want to assert themselves are our Amazons—so say the gentlemen, who claim it to be a compliment. The Amazon film shows that the Amazon is beautiful, wears boots, and is a lesbian. That surely cannot be the image of the 'liberated woman' the advertisers of our products want to convey!?"

Rosenbach uses Botticelli's painting *Birth of Venus* in her second performance, *Reflektionen über die Geburt der Venus* (Reflections on the birth of Venus). She describes her video action as follows:

> A life-size image of Botticelli's painting of Venus is projected on the wall. A large triangle of salt is lying on the ground in front of the projection. On top of it is an oyster shell containing a small video monitor—a pearl. A videotape of surf and foam is running on the monitor. I walk into the projection of Venus. My front is white. My back is black. The projection of Venus is on my body. I slowly begin to turn. I rotate for fifteen minutes. When the projection falls on my back, it disappears: darkness, night. When it falls on my front, it is bright and visible: day.

Again, Rosenbach shatters a patriarchal mythologization of woman, namely, woman as "Venus"—soft, accommodating, and always sexually available, beautiful for no one else but the man.

The decadence of this Venus ideal manifests itself even in Botticelli's painting, despite its masterliness: in its floating doll-like figure with voluptuously flowing hair, slightly turned to the side and bashfully covering her breast and genitals with her hand. The painting contains not a trace of the matriarchal Venus, who, as Aphrodite Urania or the Sumero-Babylonian Ishtar, was the creator of the world. It was not a later Yahweh but Venus who was the creator. She is said to have been the one who, in the form of a dove, hovered over Chaos and from it created heaven and earth, the stars and all living creatures.[18] She created them from the power of her universal Eros and thus was the Great Goddess who preceded all later gods and goddesses, the primordial mother of all things.[19] Consequently, ancient idols to Venus do not conceal her sex organs but emphasize them in consciousness of her creative power. Those idols depict her in a squatting position, exposing her genital triangle, or in a standing position, exposing her breasts, which she raises with both hands.

Botticelli's Venus is the exact opposite of the matriarchal Venus but is nonetheless an aesthetic, lovely figure. However, if the masterly skill of the artist is eliminated, all that remains is lascivious decadence. Take, for example, the use of the Venus figure for advertising purposes in today's late patriarchal society. We see Botticelli's Venus as a display-window mannequin for fur coats or as a plaster figure rising from her shell in a furniture store. We see the Venus symbol in fashion magazines and beauty contests. She is associated with circus performers, naked dancers of the Folies Bergères, Barbie dolls, and Maidenform foundation garments, which can give a woman a youthful, heavenly figure. Their wearers are perpetually smiling doll-women, decorative women with a perfect figure in response to the needs of men. Rosenbach shows all these images in parallel to her own action in the video.

In her video action, Rosenbach projects Botticelli's Venus onto her own body, onto her white front. She rises from the shell surrounded by flowers, breezes, and a nymph handing her a cloak. As a woman, Rosenbach literally wears all these male projections. But then she begins to turn, and by the time she has made a quarter turn, the smile and the lovely face have disappeared, and in their place a Janus-headed profile appears. First it is bright, then it is black—and unleashes confusing ambivalences (figure 17). Then she turns her back, and now it is "night" (in Rosenbach's own words): the projection of Venus disappears on a dark female figure. Who is this unrecognized figure who clearly swallows up all conceptions? She is merely the other side of the Venus as creator: the devourer who destroys everything in the abyss. The bright side and the dark side constantly alternate with each other in the same rhythm as the artist's turns, and both are merely the same figure—the two sides of Venus: Aphrodite and Hecate, Ishtar and Ereshkigal, Isis and Nephthys, Shakti and Kali, or whatever names they were called. They are the dual aspects of one and the same goddess, and this matriarchal Venus, who appears as a concept in Rosenbach's performance, has no doll-like features whatsoever. She is the universal, powerful Goddess of Death-in-Life.[20]

In addition to the Amazon and Venus, Rosenbach develops a conception of a third goddess figure: the crone, the Wise Woman, the "witch." In the performance *Die Einsame Spaziergängerin—Hagazussa* (The solitary stroller Hagazussa), Hagazussa is the witch, the wanderer between two worlds, the wise one who performs magic. Rosenbach portrays this notion by wandering back and forth on the rainbow in an enormous black-and-white reproduction of Caspar David Friedrich's *Mountain Landscape with Rainbow,* which is lying on the ground. She wanders between heaven and earth like Iris, the Greek goddess of the rainbow and messenger of the gods.

At the same time, Rosenbach makes a sign with raised hands. She arches her hand and touches her thumb to her index finger. That is the sign for the serpent in the mythology of the Australian aborigines, whose myth of the Rainbow Serpent also comes into play here. Thus, the wanderer on the rainbow who makes the serpent sign is the Rainbow Serpent itself—none other than the Sumero-Babylonian Tiamat, the Norse Midgard serpent, and all the other primordial serpents in world mythology.

The primordial serpent is the figure or emblem of the powerful goddess of the depths—the Crone goddess, the director of the fate of human beings and the stars, the immutable law of the universe and its transformations. In the Australian myth, the Rainbow Serpent is the primal mother who dwells under the earth *and* in the sky as the rainbow, thus symbolizing both life and death. Fertility rites are the rituals associated with her.

Just as the Rainbow Serpent embodies the second and third aspect of the Goddess, so, too, does the performer who dances on Friedrich's rainbow between the heights and the depths, the light and the darkness, the upper world and the underworld. The performer's wandering empties the rainbow of any romantic sentimentality and symbolically traces it back to its origin. At the same time, the distorted modern-day European image of the witch is stripped away to reveal the powerful goddess of fate. Like the volcanic eruption shown on one of the video monitors, the goddess of fate suddenly bursts forth from the depths, from the sediment of historical interpretation, which had weighted her down for millennia.

And, since the goddesses of fate are usually a trinity, a third figure, the Maiden goddess, is not far away. She is portrayed by Rosenbach's teenage daughter Julia, who is sitting in the next room in a half-arc of salt, which is the precise inversion of the rainbow, and so the circle is closed. Julia takes steel balls from a wooden triangular container and rolls them across the floor, across the semicircle of salt, causing the salt to form little rays. In the dark room Julia plays with silver balls as if with the stars and the planets, and thus represents Diana, the cosmic goddess of the heavens, who in complete naïveté creates new fateful constellations that unite all things. Thus Rosenbach achieves in the performance what she has striven for: visible magic.

Rosenbach has called this video action a ritual. However, when I compare it with Edelson's description of ritual art, I cannot designate an isolated, onetime, expounded performance a ritual. In any case, Rosenbach does succeed in one regard: in exposing the decadence of men's clichés of femininity, thereby opening the inner space of the woman's psyche that has been closed by those clichés, and thus creating room in the woman's psyche for possible new or ancient primal identification.[21]

ON ENVIRONMENTAL ART

As we have already seen, women's body art, which represents a personal liberation through a physical and spiritual metamorphosis, is far removed from the patriarchal notion of art as an object. Art as the transformation of everyday objects is considered by many women artists to be the direct continuation of that physical and spiritual metamorphosis. These artists therefore transform not only the body, the perception of the body, and the spiritual imagination but also the immediate environment—which is considered an extension of bodily functions, sensual needs, and spiritual conceptions. That extension results in the artistic transformation of the objects at hand: plates, cups, dining tables, clothing, furniture, and the rooms of one's own living space, one's own house. The practical matriarchal arts (such as cooking, weaving, and house building), which were an indivisible union of art and life in matriarchal societies, come into their own in environmental art, albeit in stylistically exaggerated form.

Take, for instance, Jere Van Syoc, a feminist artist who transformed her old brick house in Michigan into a surrealistic palace to the Goddess. Every room contains little altars: vessels, statues, and candles stand on the mantelpiece in the living room and on the stove in the kitchen; even the bathroom is filled to overflowing with ludicrous objects, talismans, and images of the Goddess. All the objects were found somewhere, for example, at flea markets, and made into a collection. Van Syoc also uses velvet and other rich fabrics, ranging in color from peach and flesh tones to deep red, to create a protective, warm, festive atmosphere—a temple to female sensibilities. At any rate, her women friends seem to enjoy lingering there; her house is used by local feminists as a gathering place for discussions, workshops, and celebrations.[22] Consequently, her house is not a mere functionless showpiece but a part of the women's collective life.

The principle of transforming the immediate environment has been carried to the extreme by the contemporary French artist Colette. She began with street art, i.e., transitory sidewalk paintings and street performances. Then she altered nineteenth-century paintings and turned them into comprehensive environmental works. Ultimately, she turned her imagination to redesigning everyday objects, rooms, and her own outward appearance.

Colette creates her environments by covering reinforced plywood panels with such luxurious and unusual fabrics as silk, satin, and parachute cloth. The framework is structured, pleated, bubbled; the fabrics are pleated like jalousies. In addition there are subtle color contrasts, but only in the pastel range, as in paintings by Delacroix. Colette adds cloth flowers, streamers, birdlike ornaments, and veils, thus making every panel an individual work of art. Finally, she assembles the panels to create strange spaces whose delicate and mysterious effect is enhanced by freely hanging veils and lace textures. Colette changes the optical perspective of those spaces by means of mirrors and colorful fluorescent lights, which, when hidden behind the panels, lend an almost unreal transparency to the whole.

In this way Colette has transformed her own living spaces and from them developed her "environments," which she exhibits. She has even transformed the objects in her house into works of art: beds, lamps, chairs, and vanity tables become draped pedestals on which everyday objects lie in significant arrangements. And even Colette herself appears as a work of art in her spaces. Whether she is embedded in her living spaces or appears as a living image in her environments, she is just as fantastically decorated as her surroundings—with gathered fabrics, parachute silk, veils, and strange objects. That she also designs clothes and jewelry, marketed by the Colette Company, is a natural offshoot of her art.

Colette's manner of treating herself and her immediate surroundings comes very close to being practical matriarchal art, although matriarchy appears only rarely as a theme in her works. Once she transformed an entire ballroom into an airy church. She hung sky blue Viennese-style pleated drapes on all the windows so that they admitted only subdued light. A tulle runner led to a high altar of rose-colored fabrics. Offerings of very feminine objects lay on two stools before the altar—garters, hairbrushes, barrettes—and in the middle of the altar Colette's own portrait appeared in a rosy cloud between mirrors and shimmering lamps. Colette thus celebrated herself as a new goddess.[23]

Another time Colette used green and rose satin and numerous hanging threads to transform a room into a mysterious grotto in which she herself reclines as the goddess Persephone (figure 18).[24] She is nestled among abundant stone formations made of fabric and sheltered by stalactites hanging like rosy breasts from the ceiling and by threads moving like thin trickles of water. The reclining figure merges with the surroundings and submerges in the delicate silk landscape that she herself created. Hence the space does not remain empty but is centered on a person. The space fulfills the function that human environments are supposed to fulfill and reflects the character of many of Colette's other spaces—a perpetual interplay of illusion and reality. As the sleeping Persephone or in the role of other figures lying or frozen in motion, Colette seems like a doll, yet she is alive. Thus, her art has fluid boundaries: it evolves from tableaux, flows through environments, and streams into populated places. Consequently, her art is not only a manner of perception but also a manner of living, as Colette herself maintains.[25]

Judy Chicago's *Dinner Party* is an outstanding example of matriarchal aesthetics as the transformation of everyday objects on the conscious plane of feminist art. Here, an artist—along with more than forty direct collaborators and two hundred indirect assistants (female and male)—has transformed a dining table and all its utensils into a magnificent banquet table in order to recall in a tangible way the culture and history of women.[26] The lives and deeds of thirty-nine mythological and historical women were researched in order to celebrate their greatness in *The Dinner Party*. The work is reminiscent of ancient matriarchal death rites in which places were set at the table for the dead, who were invited to bless the living with their presence. That, of course, was Chicago's intention, since women's most urgent need in their process of self-discovery is the knowledge and reassuring spiritual presence of their great predecessors who have been suppressed by patriarchal historians.

The Dinner Party consists of a gigantic triangular table with a place setting for each of the thirty-nine great women, who run the gamut from the earliest goddesses, historical queens, philosophers, and artists to contemporary women significant in intellectual and social life. The table stands on a floor of triangular porcelain tiles inscribed with the names of another 999 famous women (figure 19). Each place setting includes a round plate, a chalice, and an embroidered runner.

Every single item was produced and every phase of the work—from the first operation to the last—was performed personally by Chicago and her collaborators. The symbols and decorations on each runner reflect the style of the historical epoch of each great woman. The style of weaving and embroidery—in the hands of women experts—also reflects the techniques used in the highest developed form of handicrafts from each woman's time and thus demonstrates the history of a practical art form developed by women through the millennia.

The same is true of the ceramics—originally a practical art of women, which Chicago places back into female hands by making the chalices and plates herself. The china-painted plates, likewise a female domain, have decorations resembling butterflies, which are symbols for the vulva and eternal rebirth; at the same time, their variations capture the essence or the character of each great woman honored. Thus, a new "female form language" is created, to quote Chicago.[27]

That "female form language," which tangibly reawakens in our memory the history of women, begins at the place setting or altar of the matriarchal primordial goddess of the Stone Age: Mother Earth, Gaea, or whatever name she was called. Her place setting consists of a chalice and a plate resting on two reddish brown animal pelts decorated with delicate Maori shells. The basic butterfly pattern on the plate is transformed into a deep red cleft that opens between round, brown stonelike forms, like the entrance into the depths of a gorge—a warm cave, the motherly womb of the earth (figure 20). Developing from a spiral pattern, the gold embroidery of the goddess's name completes Gaea's place setting.

Gaea's place setting is followed by that of the Fertile Goddess.[28] The runner is made of coarsely woven wool decorated with bone needles, starfish, and small clay figures—the idols of the fertility goddess, the first tiny dolls in history (figure 21). In the center of the plate, there is a wide fissure filled with light brown hemispheres—resembling breasts or the fruits carried by Artemis from Ephesus—and surrounded by quadruple, rosy, winglike ornaments.[29]

Dates also fill the vaginal fissure and the four rectilinear wings of the Ishtar plate, which has the contours of a Sumero-Babylonian ziggurat and stands on a cloth of golden satin. Kali, the Indian creator and destroyer, is honored with lilac, violet, and purple embroidered flames, symbolizing the yawning, multiarmed abyss into which she draws the living and from which she resurrects the dead. The altars to the Cretan snake goddess; to Sophia, the universal goddess of wisdom; and to the Amazons, the great defenders of the matriarchal cultures in the epoch of conquests by patriarchal warrior peoples, are also designed in a similarly empathetic style.[30]

The Amazon place setting is done entirely in the three colors of the Great Goddess: white, red, and black. Red snakeskin and woven bands form the border of the runner, which is decorated with a geometric design consisting of a black triangle, red horns, the white world egg in the middle, and the famous sickle-shaped double axes—which normally curve outward but are curved inward in Chicago's work (figure 22).

The goddess altars are followed by the altars to historical personalities, for example, the Egyptian queen Hatshepsut, whose place setting is adorned with artistically embroidered hieroglyphics, including the serpent symbol and the horns and the solar disk of Hathor (figure 23). Other women honored include the Jewish heroine Judith, the Greek poet Sappho, the Athenian philosopher Aspasia, and the Celtic queen Boadaceia, who battled the brutal Roman legions during an uprising in England. The place setting of Hypatia, the Alexandrian scholar, philosopher, and politician who was ripped apart, limb from limb, by fanatical monks, captures the sadness surrounding the lost independence of women, since Hypatia's terrible death marks the ultimate perishing of the age of matriarchal culture and society with its militant, motherly, and wise women.

The second wing of the gigantic triangular table honors women who had far-reaching influence on the Christian European epoch. The handiwork of the place settings becomes increasingly subtle and follows the complicated techniques of cloistered nuns and noblewomen, whose needlework was considered high art in the Middle Ages. The small altars are dedicated to Marcella, the early Christian preacher and Caritas helper, and to Saint Bridget, the Irish founder of convents— or, as Brigit, the former goddess of inspiration.

Other altars are dedicated to the genius of such women as the Byzantine empress Theodora, with a place setting in embroidery resembling a mosaic (figure 24); the poet Hrosvitha of Gandersheim; the famous doctor and gynecologist Trotula of the University of Salerno; Princess Eleanor of Aquitaine, who, as a patron of the arts at her court, brought about the flowering of medieval literature (the King Arthur epic, the cult of high *Minne*); the mystic Hildegarde of Bingen. The memorial altar to the Irish midwife Petronilla de Meath stands for the nine million women executed as "witches" since Eleanor's time.[31] Honored women of the Renaissance and Baroque periods include the French writer Christine de Pisan, who wrote the first dialogue on the rights of women in Europe; the Italian princess Isabella d'Este, an outstanding patron of the arts; Queen Elizabeth I of England, under whom the empire enjoyed a glorious era; the brilliant Italian painter Artemisia Gentileschi; and the Dutch scholar Anna van Schurman, whose brilliant intellect made her a legend in her own time.

With the place settings on the third wing of the triangular table, Chicago honors the outstanding women of recent Anglo-American history: Anne Hutchinson, who rebelled against the church's degradation of women; Sacajawea, the Indian leader of white expeditions; the astronomer Caroline Herschel; the suffragette Mary Wollstonecraft; the black abolitionist Sojourner Truth; the founder of the first international feminist movement, Susan B. Anthony; Elizabeth Blackwell, the first woman physician in the United States; the poet Emily Dickinson; the composer Ethel Smyth; the suffragette Margaret Sanger, the first to advocate birth control; Natalie Barney, the first woman writer to live openly as a lesbian; the writer Virginia Woolf; and the painter Georgia O'Keeffe. The plates on this wing of the table are more voluptuous in pattern and color than the other, flatter ones. The symbols gradually grow and swell into three-dimensional, fantastic shapes: a plate with a highly upraised, winged vagina (Susan B. Anthony); a plate filled with rose porcelain peaks and ridges resembling a garland (Emily Dickinson); a blue five-pointed star swollen like a body (Natalie Barney); a vaginal slit filled with three-dimensional fruit and surrounded by leaves opening concentrically like a rose (Virginia Woolf); and a whole vaginal landscape of gorges and purple hills (Georgia O'Keeffe).

I have repeated the names of all the women Chicago symbolically represents, because we cannot impress upon ourselves enough those names missing from the history books. Many of the women who saw *The Dinner Party* in American museums were deeply moved by the wealth of female brilliance in all fields of culture and society. In this gigantic artwork created by women using techniques developed by women over the millennia, the viewers were suddenly able to survey the totality of their own trampled, repressed, and forgotten history as exemplified in individual personalities and developed simply from what women do day in and day out: setting the table. But this simple act is artistically stylized by Chicago and her collaborators into an almost sacral table with thirty-nine small altars to the honored dead, with which she repeats a matriarchal rite in the most simple of manners. Many of the women visitors cried when they saw the illuminated triangle in the dark hall; others said the table possessed an aura of holiness. It is the experience of recognition that moved the women so deeply, the experience of recognizing their history and themselves— an experience having a truly healing effect.

Those reactions alone show how little Chicago's work can be apprehended within the scope of traditional artistic norms.

Nor did Chicago create the work within the limits of traditional artistic norms: the more-than-three-year creative process in cooperation with and during communal life with forty women and several men collaborators was just as important to her as the artwork itself. For Chicago, the creative process and the changes in consciousness and transformations that took place during the process were a fundamental part of the work, perhaps even the essential part, which is why the video documenting the creation of *The Dinner Party* is always shown at the same time the work is exhibited. When asked about the difficulties involved in such a gigantic undertaking requiring so many people, Chicago replied:

> Always before when I functioned in similar educational situations, I went home . . . I left the situation, and I didn't have to care whether the women actually performed or didn't perform because I could take control of my own studio and do exactly what I was capable of doing. This time I have thrown the entire success of the largest project I have ever undertaken and an aesthetic aspiration beyond anything I've ever done—one that embodies everything I believe in fundamentally down to my toes—and I have totally thrown myself on my own sex. Just totally! . . . First, there is the task of changing consciousness on a sufficiently fundamental level that real, substantial change can take place in our culture. It's an enormous task. Second, put that together with the absence of support for large-scale, ambitious projects and the absence of social, financial, and emotional support in the culture for taking on such a task. Third, there is female role-conditioning and the way women's personalities have been damaged to the point that they cannot work . . . and we have to simultaneously try to produce and address that level of damage in women's personalities . . . You should see these women taking control of their lives . . . starting to structure their lives around work.[32]

Chicago is thus aware that she has created a new artistic structure by making *The Dinner Party* project a group effort. In doing so she rejects both the authoritarian and the collective structure of conventional collaboration and advocates the *cooperative* structure. Cooperative collaboration entails guidance, since the group consists of people at different developmental stages: the experienced participants must help the less experienced ones in their personal growth. The artistic efforts of all participants are made public along with their contributions, for example, signed tablecloths accompanying books with names. Chicago herself says of this successful model of cooperative collaboration:

> It's scary though, the whole mode of the artist now being that of the individual artist. But if you look at history, the individual artist actually came up with the Renaissance, which also deprived women of the capacity to be artists. In the Middle Ages, when women operated in convents or guilds, they operated in cooperative structures. They were able to operate as artists and artisans. If you look at female art, you will see that a lot of those activities that are indigenous to women have been cooperative structures. So I'm actually finding my roots and a structure that is conducive to female creative genius.[33]

Chicago's conception of art thus differs considerably from what is understood as art today. For her, art is an affirmation of the human spirit, the mirroring of our inner state as women, which redirects our consciousness and thereby transforms reality.

> I feel very alienated from most contemporary, mainstream art. I have a whole other set of beliefs about what art is. I believe that art is an affirmation of the human spirit—that art has the capacity to shape reality—that art can be the reflection of an inner state and can propel us in consciousness by objectifying and symbolizing inner states. Most people

only sense or feel and cannot articulate. Art is particularly important for women and can catapult women into a different realm of consciousness by symbolizing and objectifying our experience. Once you name something, it changes. It no longer has the power to terrify you, to unconsciously motivate you. It no longer has the power to oppress you.[34]

Chicago thus expresses the essence of art in unconventional terms: art is magic that liberates women from the constraints imposed on them by this misogynistic society. She expresses this in her work itself, in the manner in which it was created, and in the complete intellectual awareness that her work is a partial realization of what I call matriarchal aesthetics.

A temple would be a more appropriate space for Chicago's sacral table than a profane museum, which ultimately divorces her artwork from the social realm and eradicates its essence as a process. The temple would be erected solely by women, a project in which their cooperative creative process would be the decisive aspect of the artwork, as in the medieval mason guilds of the great cathedrals. But women of today lack both the time and the means to undertake such a project, which is why the temple exists only as a concept.

Such a temple does exist, however, also as an architectural drawing by the American architect Mimi Lobell, who used matriarchal conceptions in her design.[35] Lobell considers her temple to be, in its own way, an image of the Great Goddess— just as the temples on Malta are in their way. To enter Lobell's temple, one must first walk through a dark underground passage hewn into the rocks and then pass through a circular labyrinth (figure 25). During the journey, all the elementary energies that provide for the creation, maintenance, and destruction of life are awakened. The floor of the labyrinth is made of stone slabs, and the passages consist of webs woven by women. A spring stands in the center of the labyrinth. From there a spiral ladder leads to the upper temple, which one enters through the iris of a large eye.

The eye is the altar itself; it is surrounded by fire and light and a ring of twenty-four columns and segments of circles, each corresponding to one of the twenty-four phases of the moon depicted in the domed ceiling of the temple. There the elementary energies are transformed into the power of wisdom and inner vision. To wander through the temple thus means to be initiated into the mysteries of the feminine power within us—mysteries that, according to the creator of the design, are the fountainhead of inner transformation and cultural change. Although there are no plans to build the temple, it does exist as a dream, as a part of the environment of the inner, spiritual space.

ON EARTHWORK ART

Women earthwork artists regard the natural space—like the living space—as an extension of their corporeal sensuality.[36] They attempt to enter the natural space by means of spiritual acts. They reshape the natural space to adapt nature to human beings and human beings to nature—according to its feminine psyche. Instead of doing violence to the landscape, woman moves in harmonious accord with nature. The entire landscape becomes a temple, a sacral environment for magical-artistic acts. And this spiritual apprehension of the visible environment from one horizon to the other is much more analogous to the archaic matriarchal cultic rites—which took place mostly under the open sky—than is the delimitation of space by means of a closed, monumental temple edifice.

The photographs of Sigrid Neubert are an outstanding illustration of the magical entry into the natural space, although the artist herself remains outside that magically apprehended space. Neubert photographs light and darkness, stones, wind, and water—the natural elements, all of which coalesce into concrete patterns in her photos.[37] Under her gaze, the stones—ordinary boulders in white water—suddenly reveal faces that resemble petrified, mythical creatures from the chthonic dawn of time. The wind becomes visible in the movements of the trees, in the swirls and flurries of their foliage, which appear in the photos as diffuse streamers juxtaposed against sharp areas where the leaves are at rest.

Water also assumes structures in Neubert's photographs: the bends and whorls made by the water between the stones, the coalescence of rigid resistance and fluid elasticity in which the rigid becomes round and the fluid assumes structures. When light falls on the water, the light, too, assumes shapes revealing the flow patterns of the water as delicate silver threads or as clusters of streamers of light (figure 26). Although the photographer says it is "only an ordinary stream which many pass in silence," she discovers in it the movement of the energy of the elements, to which she previously connected herself through inner concentration. While Neubert transforms nature through a spiritual act, she does not do so actively: she makes her own spiritual act passively visible in the forms of nature.

In this respect the earthwork artists go even further, for the things in nature are their creative medium and the natural space their creative space. Take, for example, the Americans Jody Pinto, Margaret Hicks, and Alice Aycock. Pinto redesigned old brick wells. First she excavated them, lowered down a ladder, enlarged the base with more bricks to form a fireplace, and, next to it, placed a bundle of personal objects wrapped in a kerchief, which resembled the corpse from ancient burial rituals. Then she emerged from the shaft of the well as if rising from the underworld into the light, after having left behind a shroud, a transformation.[38]

Another time, nature played a role in one of Pinto's designs, and she cleverly integrated it into the work. In *Five Black Ovals* she built a series of structures on a cliff: five oval mounds of earth and bark decorated with bands of cotton. Then a rainstorm came and destroyed everything. Pinto was furious, but she redirected her anger over the sudden destruction of her artwork in a positive way and started over again. She rebuilt the first structure and secured it with twenty-four poles. Between every two stakes she hung canvas pockets and filled them with hay and red earth. Then she waited for a rainstorm. When it rained, the clay in the pockets softened and ran, and it looked as if the pockets were bleeding. According to Pinto, a storm destroyed the work *Five Black Ovals,* and then another storm completed the work *Five Bleeding Pockets.*[39]

Earthworks and outdoor sculptures made of natural materials are the actual theme of earthwork art. However, in contrast to the works of women artists, the works of men artists frequently reach monumental proportions, reminiscent of the architecture of the megalithic age, when earth pictures, hills, graves, and stone formations were incorporated into shrines. The megalithic age was matriarchal, and its monuments were symbols of the Great Goddess. However, most men earthwork artists are unaware of that, with the surprising result that many of them build matriarchal symbols without knowing it—and without having a matriarchal mentality.

An example of this is Robert Smithson's magnificent *Spiral Jetty,* which he built by piling stones in shallow coastal waters, creating a dam, a jetty in the form of a gigantic spiral (figure 27).[40] It is unlikely that Smithson knew that the spiral—the simplest form of labyrinth—is a goddess symbol; and it is equally unlikely that he realized that his *Spiral Jetty* in the sea was eminently suited to be a new ritual dancing ground. But many men earthwork artists allow their completed artworks to perish in an orgy of destruction—in contrast to Pinto, who creatively averted an undesired destruction of her art by nature.

Because women earthwork artists usually lack the means to execute such monumental earthworks, they build on a smaller scale and establish a personal connection between themselves and the work, and regard the transformed space as part of their own transformation process. As a result, they do not confine themselves to the mere construction of a gigantic edifice but instead create structures resembling dancing grounds in order to *use* them for ritual celebrations. Take, for example, Margaret Hicks, who created the work *Hicks' Mandala* (figure 28). In the middle of a forest she constructed three large concentric circles by ramming logs into the ground; in the center she placed a wide tree trunk on which a large stone was enthroned as the symbol of the Goddess. Upon its completion, a "ritual of giving" was celebrated in the mandala. Each person brought a natural object, presented it to someone else, and explained the significance of the gift. Afterward, all subsequent visitors to the mandala were asked to place a small stone into the circle as a symbol of themselves.[41]

Alice Aycok, by contrast, builds underground chambers resembling ancient burial mounds. Inside they have an atmosphere of security and safety, like the chambers of the ancient dolmens that represented the inside of the body of Mother Earth, the goddess Gaea. Many of Aycok's creations include labyrinthine tunnels or wells. Hills, wells, and caves appear frequently in the works of women earthwork artists, since they know them to be mythic symbols of the Earth goddess, the visible symbol of birth, death, and rebirth.[42]

On Ritual Art

Ritual art unites all the elements of body art, environmental art, and earthwork art. The cultic ornaments in the landscape are not treated as isolated artworks but are incorporated into spiritual activities and rites as organic components of them, as in *Hicks' Mandala*. The rites consist of consciously appropriated elements of archaic rites as well as inventions of the artists themselves. They serve as mythic-meditative acts of rediscovery of ancient matriarchal connections that have become lost: the positive relationship of women to their own bodies and to their magical powers, the relationships between women (as friends, lovers, or mother and daughter), and the relationship between the physical and spiritual cycles of women and the tides of nature.

The ritual relationships of women to their bodies incorporate the elements of body art, which are now portrayed in a symbolic way, as in Mary Beth Edelson's *Sexual Rites,* mentioned earlier. It is no accident that those rites take place in nature, since light, air, natural energy currents, and the entire symbiotic exchange with the natural elements in the immediate environment intensify one's body awareness to such a degree that it can suddenly be transformed into a new body consciousness. Women take up this symbiotic contact for the express purpose of comprehending their body as a complex part of nature and of adapting themselves to the natural space as the extension of their ego. This symbiotic contact is precisely what Edelson expresses in her private ritual *Woman Rising,* in which she demonstrates how the woman liberating herself captures the energy currents in nature and reemits them as clusters of rays (cover photo).[43]

Another example is Mary Fish's twenty-eight-day performance at the seashore, in which she draws parallels between the physical and spiritual periods of woman and the tides of nature. On the California coast, Fish made conscious once again—by means of actions and the resulting symbolic designs in the sand—the perfect harmony between the changing phases of the moon, the various tides of the ocean, and the menstrual cycle of the female body, which is also related to various spiritual phases. "Each day she inscribed a circle in the sand, placed stones within the circle, removed them in numerical sequence, and drew a detailed map/picture of the site. 'Some days the stones were wrapped, bound with thread, drawn and written upon, or painted or arranged in geometric configurations.' On the 28th day, full circle was reached with one stone placed and one removed."[44]

Fish's journal containing the texts and drawings is a tender and striking account of how nature controls the female body and how the artist responds to and interacts with nature, thus creating from body art and earthwork art a truly cosmic perspective that allows the sky, the ocean, and the earth to participate without spatial limitations. In Fish's work, artistic space has vanished; the earth and the sky themselves become an extension of the body space, the sensual space, and the living space of woman. Like the matriarchal Goddess herself, woman once again resides in all the elements.

With the same consciousness as Fish, Edelson develops her multifarious rituals, several aspects of which I would like to describe here. Edelson studied the goddess mythology intensively, and her entire creative life is dedicated to the matriarchal Great Goddess. She personally experienced the Goddess's strength within her when she became a mother and when she was transformed by difficult phases in her life. Those periods in her life gave rise to new forms of art. After she gave up painting, Edelson began to create objects and then turned to rituals in which she could bring the objects to life.

Edelson's rituals developed in three stages: first, private rituals that she celebrated alone, then rituals with her children or close women friends, and finally public rituals as group performances in workshops or galleries, which simultaneously exhibited her pictures and objects from the private rituals. For Edelson, all rituals are a possibility for overcoming a trauma—be it a specific trauma from one's personal life or the general trauma that stems from women's situation of oppression in patriarchal society.

Many ancient magical symbols figure prominently in Edelson's rituals, for example, concentric circles, beams of energy,

Jacob's ladders, rocks, mussels, bird's flight. Fire is a dominant element in most of her rituals. It became a central theme in them because of her personal experience of fire as the element of purification from painful experiences and as the element of profound transformation into a new state.

Drawing Fire Energy Series is one of Edelson's early fire rituals, which she performed in a Native American cave in California near the massive flint stones used by Native American women. Edelson held small burning torches and performed movements that appear in the photos as magical ornaments. She performed the ritual in memory of the life of these many women—a life that consisted of the mundane but important activities of grinding grain, making fire, and cooking. The transformed everyday objects from environmental art reappear, but they are incorporated into a magical process, a ritual.

Later, Edelson made a pilgrimage to a Neolithic cave in Yugoslavia where she repeated the ritual in an intensified form. She herself is the bright figure seated within a circle of starlike lights in the dark cave entrance; a band of light floats in from her left and abruptly ends in a fiery hieroglyph (figure 29). It is the mysterious transformation of a prehistoric place, the rediscovery of inspiration through the Goddess in the same spot where she lived several millennia ago and later perished. In this way, Edelson used one of her new rituals to consecrate many places of known ancient significance—and that, too, is a new and unexpected form of environment.[45]

The fire theme undergoes its most beautiful development in Edelson's most recent public rituals as a fiery transformation and inner liberation not only of the artist herself but of the other women who participated in the rituals during workshops or performances. In the public rituals, Edelson combines the life-affirming self-discovery of the participants with political criticism. The rituals give free rein to both rage and bitterness as a transition to the relaxed and calm celebration to follow.

Her special contribution to the group rituals is her capacity to fuse her own ego with the collective ego, to open herself to the dreams, ideas, wishes, and responses of her women friends and observers, and to integrate them into a cooperative ritual. According to Edelson, "Women [are] exploring who 'we are' and not who 'I am.' "[46] The collective openness of her art is what makes her—and Judy Chicago—distinctive on the contemporary art scene, with its egocentric celebrity system.

The fire theme receives exquisite expression in all of Edelson's public rituals. Her group performance *Mourning Our Lost Herstory* (California, 1977), for example, took place in a ring of fire formed by small flames burning from a circle of bricks.[47] Eleven women sat in the center of the ring and sang a simple liturgy of lamentation, rage, and joy over the dawning of a new age. Resembling the menhirs from Irish and English stone circles, seven large figures shrouded in bluish black leaned against the walls of the hall. During the performance, other women, who had been hidden under the assemblage, slowly moved forward and, looming over the heads of the seated audience, formed a second circle around the ring of fire— thereby drawing the audience into the ritual. Their slow movements corresponded to the mood of the song, and the atmosphere created in the room, illuminated only by the ring of fire, was at once uncanny and mysterious. The entire exhibition, which united the memories of ancient matriarchal history with the contemporary history of women's self-liberation, carried the politically provocative title *Your 5,000 Years Are Up!* At the conclusion of the performance, the stony figures shed their shrouds and joined the circle of singers in their joyous dance, in which the audience was also invited to participate.

Edelson's public ritual *Memorials to 9,000,000 Women Burned as Witches in the Christian Era* (New York, 1977) was no less political and spiritual than her previous ones. Through a gate full of hands making horn signs—the symbol of the Cretan bull and women's magical powers—one entered a dark room in which a ladder stood upright, its rungs burning in little flames. The ladder symbolized the burning of women condemned as witches. Because of the haste of the executions, the condemned often were not even given a funeral pyre but were simply tied to a ladder and thrown into a bonfire in a clearing. At the same time, the burning ladder also represented the Jacob's ladder, a symbol for ascension and mystical transcendence. Around the ladder stood a circular table bearing documents on the witch trials. On the evening of Halloween, nine women gave a performance around the table, read from the documents, and sang. Then they walked through the streets of Soho in New York City in a procession with jack-o'-lanterns—just as women had done in the Middle Ages when they sought out their holy places on Halloween—and sang; "The Goddess is here; the Goddess is us."[48]

The fire theme is also central in two of Edelson's workshop performances, *Fire Flights in Deep Space* (Iowa, 1978) and *Where Is Our Fire?* (California, 1977/79). *Fire Flights in Deep Space* took place outdoors. The performers walked through the field cutting down stalks of grain. In the empty field, the women bound the stalks into three long, continuous rows; they raised the rows of stalks and wove them together by dancing and interweaving their bodies. Then the women waited until sunset and laid the woven sheaves in a spiral pattern on the slope of a hill and burned them. In *Where Is Our Fire?* the women suspended a large burning spiral freely in space. Shrouded in wide shawls, they played with rings of fire and then used torches to trace figures: arcs, circles, spirals—endless patterns of motion resembling a visual fire-meditation (figure 30).

By contrast, Edelson's workshop performance *Creation Begins with a Green Light: Ritual on the Earth* (Massachusetts, 1980) represents a contemporary creation myth. As green light swept over their backs, the women performers lay on the ground and

made jerky movements with their elbows and knees as if they were moving for the first time. Their action was accompanied by a recording of elementary tones, which then merged into the ocean's roar. The women's movements gradually submerged into the ocean's roar, as if waves were rolling over them and the energy of the sea inundating them.

Gradually the flood of waves ebbed; the performers' movements became smoother, and the performers rolled into a semicircle to form a harbor in the shape of a half-moon. Exhausted by their act of creation, they fell asleep. Then the light changed from green to orange and fell on the naked backs of Three Wise Women, who were slowly moving their arms and hands in gestures similar to those of the archaic Great Goddess. Finally, by covering themselves with a wrap, the three transformed themselves into a wandering mountain. At the same time, amid the rolling of thunder coming from the recorder, the other women awoke and used torches to trace lightning and fiery patterns in the air (figure 31). Finally, their torches burned out; the sounds of ocean waves grew louder again, and all sat silently in the darkness and listened.

In contrast to these private and public rituals, Edelson's ritual *Centering* (1974) is performed by mother and daughter, and thus represents the second stage following the private rituals: "Mother and child lay on the ground, making all the possible circles with their two bodies, ending with the child lying on top of the mother; then they gathered sticks, bark, flowers, and other natural materials from their immediate environment and made circles (mandalas) with these as well."[49] Edelson performs such rituals to instill in her children a profound feeling for the earth as Mother and, through those activities, to make a lasting impression on them in order to withdraw them physically and spiritually from patriarchy. As she puts it, "The patriarchy really can't do this to you—take your children away, physically and spiritually, to an altogether alien society because you can *transcend* it."[50] Edelson has thus transcended patriarchy by having created a new yet ancient relationship between herself and her children—a matriarchal relationship.

In Edelson's rituals all energies coalesce: the energy of women as a group, the energy of women and their children, the energy of women and the cycles of nature, the energy of women and prehistoric or historic places—for example, sacred caves, mountaintops, and coastal regions. Hence her art is the best example to date of the eternalness of the rites of the matriarchal Goddess, despite their having stood in the shadow of patriarchal systems of thought for several thousand years. New fragments and new expanded elements of those rites are re-emerging—in part through historical studies, in part through women's longings, wishes, and dreams—to fuse into a new totality through women's reawakened sensitivity to themselves and their surroundings. As Edelson herself maintains:

> Power is transferred during a ritual. I think that is fundamental. After a ritual, we feel strengthened, and this strength lasts, because a ritual can be carried in one's soul like a totem; one can also derive strength from the memory of the ritual. But the best thing is to repeat the ritual from time to time—that is part of the nature of a ritual. It continually purifies the spirit and helps one find perspectives. Things that have nothing to do with the ritual but preoccupy the spirit suddenly resolve themselves. The ritual produces insights into life situations, and afterward one feels fortified and is ready to resolve those things. Thus, rituals are a technique for solving problems, because they lead us very directly to our own insights and our own being. They make us completely conscious of personal information that we have had for a long time. Rituals thus give us the knowledge for creating our new women's culture. . . .
> That is the revolution in which we are embroiled. And we must recognize that we have entered into a lifelong process of transformations.[51]

No matter how much the spatial transformations by these women artists diverge from patriarchal artistic tradition or how closely they approach the integrating matriarchal rites, they nonetheless lack several modes of expression and the truly all-encompassing structure of matriarchal mythology—which was the indivisible union of worldview, psychology, way of life, and societal form. Obviously, it is impossible to re-create the structure of matriarchal mythology in its entirety on the foundation of the patriarchal societies we live in today. But it is equally important to focus constantly on this complex, once-existent treasure trove and to retain it as a utopian guiding idea, as an indicator of the direction women can take in further developing their new art forms. This utopian guiding idea will prevent us from becoming stultified in already achieved forms and perhaps even provide our new and unique experimental art with the dynamism necessary for transcending our own limitations and the restrictions of patriarchy. Transcending is the key element, as Edelson herself constantly reiterates when speaking of her own ritual art.

Sounds

From that perspective, I shall now examine two elements of expression that have not yet been included or have received only conventional treatment in the otherwise highly developed and multifarious performances of women artists: sounds and words. Those are the additional elements necessary for achieving a complete and new matriarchal art. So far, Edelson has gone the furthest in integrating those elements, as is demonstrated in my description of some of her complex rituals that not only combine the declamation of texts, the scansion of words, and the singing of a liturgy but artistically incorporate the sounds of the sea and thunder as musical accompaniment in lieu of conventional music. However, in Edelson's rituals, the pattern of symbols and the structure of matriarchal mythology still remain fragmented and vague and by no means exhaustive of their full range—including the political. Her impressive performances do not rival the complex matriarchal ritual dance festivals or their far-reaching psychic and social consequences, described in my second essay. In my concluding essay I will therefore delineate a utopian guiding idea: a matriarchal art-utopia that unites all the elements of the archaic ritual dance festival on a new plane—i.e., that of our present historical situation—and draws on the enriching experiences imparted by the women artists already discussed.

But let us return to the element of sound. It is very difficult to gain a conception of matriarchal music because its sounds have vanished and there are no recordings or scores. We must therefore rely on speculation. I have already alluded to the musical inventions and musical culture of women insofar as they can be inferred from myths and images, archaeology, ethnology, and folklore. As I have already mentioned, flutes and drums figured importantly as symbolic elements in the matriarchal cults; stringed instruments were added later and developed into the complex Egyptian harps, the sounds of which reflected the harmony of the spheres of the seven planets. The music was sacral in character: it served the worship of the Goddess and, through the spiritual harmonics it inspired during the ritual dances, led to ecstasy. Even today, some African peoples are able to achieve that state to the simple sound of drums.

The connection between musical instruments and women was still well known in the Middle Ages, for which reason both were banned from the new Church.[52] Both were entirely excluded from Christian music in its infancy; Gregorian chants sung by a cappella men's choirs dominated the scene for centuries. However, outside the churches of the new powers, the "witches" engaged in their musical excesses and—like their matriarchal predecessors—played drums, little bells, and flutes, as Meri Franco-Lao vividly describes in her study on witch music.

> Under the spell of evil, the song of witches is said to have been seductive and of breathtaking beauty. They are said to have rung little bells, which they wore around their necks and ankles; they are said to have beaten the tambourine, and there was a "devil's flutist" among them. They danced back-to-back in a circle.
>
> We are not divulging a secret when we say that witches could fly. Their dances must have been the most ethereal spectacle imaginable. Flying means freeing oneself in the air, wandering, loving, running, dancing . . . The music of witches was part of a whole, of a cosmogony, and it was suppressed—just as their medicine, their astrology, and their wisdom had been. It is certain that music fulfilled for witches an all-encompassing, unifying function and was able to influence matter . . . Their music was clearly the embodiment of their accumulated therapeutic experience. Like the shamans, they needed assistants who played or sang while they spread their anesthetic salves and effected cures. [They] treated the conscious mind with the aid of drugs in a communal psychokinetic ritual. . . .
>
> Music split off later. It declined from an activity that, in ancient times, had been extremely closely connected with a knowledge of the world, and it corrupted into an isolated end in itself.[53]

In addition to the witches, gypsies are also known to have danced their passionate erotic dances to the music of tambourines. Their music was never "pure" but always suffused with the trancelike stammering or frenetic cries of the dancers and, sometimes, when animals were being portrayed in the dance, with the imitation of animal voices and other sounds of nature. During their dances, the so-called witches, too, are said to have laughed shrilly, uttered ghastly screams, shouted disconnected syllables, and interspersed their song with sighs, murmurs, snorts, grunts, and stutters—just as the intoxicated, frenzied Maenads had during their dances around Dionysus or Orpheus, whom they routinely tore to pieces at the conclusion of the dance.

That raging sound backdrop has yet to be achieved in contemporary women's music, which tends to confine itself to protest songs and psychosound. However, there are two examples that have overcome this limitation to some extent, one from America and one from Germany. Although they are not the only instances—at least with regard to America—they can nonetheless be considered exemplary.

The American Kay Gardner is the composer, flutist, and singer in her musical pieces titled *Mooncircles,* which she performed and recorded with other women.[54] Gardner's musical compositions have become milestones on the path to an alternative feminist musical culture in America. She uses classical instruments such as the alto flute, violin, cello, and piano; and her works reverberate with undisguised elements of classical music. However, she skillfully alters the given sound elements and enriches them with nonclassical instruments—such as the guitar, zither, cymbals, glockenspiel, bongos, and even cowbells—to create new and original voices that mirror the matriarchal contents expressed in her songs. As Gardner herself comments, "Composition is nothing more than sinking yourself totally into your environment, pulling out and organizing the sounds that are already there."[55]

That is clearly evident in several of her vocal pieces, for example, "Prayer to Aphrodite," which combines a poem by Sappho with the mixolydian mode. That mode, or key—invented or used by Sappho and almost forgotten since antiquity—is based on the fifth interval of the normal Western diatonic seven-tone scale and is said to arouse passion.[56] The deep alto flute performs the piece in soft, full tones; the pizzicato of the stringed instruments adds lutelike tones. The flute and the lute are reminiscent of the *aulos* and the lyre of ancient music, and thus a sound pattern is created that not only pays homage to Sappho but also resurrects—in mood, at least—the elements of matriarchal music still preserved on Lesbos in Sappho's time.

Gardner's piece "Change" invokes in song the woman in the moon, the woman in the sea, and the ancient mighty woman in us all. The instruments play long, flowing tones that evoke a vision of the harmonious interaction of the phases of the moon, the sea, and woman. The "Wise Woman," by contrast, is embodied in the startling rhythms of the zither, bongos, and cymbals—the ancient dance instruments. The "Wise Woman" is not the knowing one depicted in statues but the wise healer through-music or the woman who dances her wisdom. This idea is musically intensified in "Lunamuse," a rondo of rich pulsating rhythms and irregular melodic contours.[57] Gardner's rondo is the music to a moon dance. It is circular like the rituals of the Muses from the matriarchal epoch; it does not follow a linear course but a spiral one—after the climax in the middle, the end flows back into the beginning.

Gardner is aware of the spiritual and physical effect of her music. However, she does not consider her music a solemn end in itself but a background for quiet activities, whereby the sounds exude a soothing, healing effect on the bodily organs and the psyche. Clearly, this conception of music closely approximates the "witch music" already mentioned and its beneficial, healing effects.

Three German women take even more direct recourse to the obscure music of witches. Gisela Meussling, Inge Latz, and Petra Kaster collected the lyrics of old witch songs, set them to music once more, and published the compositions in a book that, through its outstanding graphics, visually stylizes the theme.[58] They thus created a small comprehensive artwork, a

Gesamtkunstwerk, which women interested in music can realize in the most diverse ways.

The composer Inge Latz remarks that in her music the musical form is open. It is not fixed but flexible, thus giving the performers freedom of interpretation and improvisation, the liberty to invent their own tone ranges and expression. Thus, each performance becomes an unrepeatable, individual creative event. The orchestration is also flexible. In addition to classical instruments, a selection of highly unusual instruments—such as wooden sound-sticks, tambourines, vibratory instruments, bongos, rattles, and bamboo flutes—can be used and expanded as desired. All the instruments support the voices in their song recital. The grouping of the musicians also deviates from the conventional norm. The singers are grouped in the center, the instrumentalists sit in a star-shaped pattern around the singers, and the audience sits in a circle around the star. It is also possible to seat the circular group at different heights.

Expressive movements resembling dance forms can also contribute to the realization of the music. All parts of the action should mirror the song texts, which themselves form a loose cycle composed of a seer-oracle from the Scandinavian *Edda,* which serves as introduction; magic spells and a winter solstice song from Germany; an incantation by Siberian shamanesses to the creator-mother; a death incantation by the Greek sorceress Erichtho; songs and magic spells of Irish, Italian, and Estonian witches; and a Gypsy blessing. All are texts of ancient magical beauty. Kaster's soaring, dynamic graphics render their mythic background visible again: gigantic stones in pounding waves or fog, bizarrely animated trees, dancing witches or the goddess-creator in bird's flight. Thus the book itself transcends the bounds of a mere score. One hopes that women will soon bring this work to life.

To assess the achievements of these two attempts at realizing matriarchal music and to determine the continued course of the trail they have blazed, let us turn once again to Meri Franco-Lao's observations on a new witch music. At the end of her study, Franco-Lao describes the music in terms of her historical knowledge and her fantasy, thereby setting the key for women's musical experiments in Italy.

> There must be a constant background of sounds . . . such as the clinking of crystal glasses, amphoras, scales, and mortars, as well as the steaming and boiling sounds from kitchens and alchemistic laboratories. And don't forget the song of night birds . . .
>
> Use your own bodies as musical instruments. Clap your hands, rub your palms together, slap your upper arms and thighs. As rudimentary instruments, use water (pouring, stirring), stones (they produce bright, sharp sounds when clapped together), switches (whip the air with them), and an animal skin stretched over the knee . . .
>
> Except for the tambourine, I would advise against using traditional musical instruments—at most, folk instruments of other peoples . . . Invent your own instruments and remember that it should sound like two identical things striking each other. Use horns, tortoise shells, hollowed-out pumpkins, berries, seeds, mussels, bones. String them like bells; use them as rattles; tie them to your arms, legs, and calves. Attach little knots of hair to an animal skin. Scratch, scrape, rub, rattle, and beat it. Shake little bronze bells, rattles, twigs with bells fastened to them; blow into empty clay jars or ones filled with water. Roll copper pots on the ground to make them ring. Rattle, shatter, and scrape pieces of glass together. Rip silk . . . An enormous harp made of boughs stuck in the ground should resound as the bodies of the dancing witches pass through it.
>
> When singing, use only a few voices very sparingly. Weave into the text a fixed rhythmic sequence, which must be very precisely scanned; or a characteristic cry consisting of only a few syllables having an esoteric meaning for the

group; or a palindrome consisting of the initial letters of several significant words.

Accompany the words with whistles, trills, laughter, cries, and other punctuations. Birdcalls, barking, and other natural sounds achieve effects often used in folk song.

Lengthen certain vowels. Practice a sort of vocal polyphony. Sit cross-legged on the ground in a circle, hold hands, concentrate, inhale as much air as possible into your lungs, and then expel the air very slowly, either on a single vowel or with each singer using a different vowel. Have the voices chime in one after the other, swelling or diminishing at the right time. Accustom yourselves to microtones by using the techniques of the rest, the tremolo, and the glissando. As a contrast, practice making bold leaps with the voice by moving from the highest to the lowest note in your range. Practice everything no louder than mezzo forte . . .

And don't forget the crackling of fire.[59]

From Franco-Lao's description, we can better imagine how a new matriarchal music would sound, and it is clear from Gisela Meussling's collected witch songs that matriarchal music is more than a mere sound background: it is at once magical healing, incantation, and blessing.

Words

Women who want to create matriarchal ritual art in the realm of words cannot confine themselves to the repetition of ancient witch songs, no matter how valuable a stimulus those sources may be. They must invent new poetic texts that mirror their inner moods and transformations in terms of present-day society. Perhaps they will succeed in creating—at least on the conceptual plane—the utopian space for a new women's society by anticipating in poetic fantasy what has yet to be achieved in cultural and political reality (and only through a slow struggle).

Women have already written lyrical texts that can be considered anticipations of matriarchal visions. Although those texts do not spring from new matriarchal rituals, many of them would attain their full significance when coupled with such rituals, because the texts already transcend the limits of mere poems. The experience we will gain from the texts can serve as the third element for our matriarchal art-utopia. However, we must determine how language can transcend the individual poet's process of liberation and fit into a *complex ritual* as an expression or leitmotif of the symbolic actions.

I have chosen only a few examples from a handful of authors. There are many more such texts, but I cannot discuss them all; even the selection of poems by the poets I discuss is exceedingly narrow.

The American Adrienne Rich began writing poetry in 1950 and has published several volumes since then. While her poems are somewhat traditional, they do reveal increasing insight into the personal and general situation of women. Rich's most recent volumes treat the bondage of women in patriarchy and their gradual escape from patriarchal society. Take, for example, her beautiful text "Mother Right" (1977).[60] With great tenderness, Rich describes the ultimate escape of a woman from the dimensions of contemporary society as determined by men. The woman reclaims that the man considers his inalienable possessions: the child, the air, the water, the grass, the expanse. Her escape is neither angry nor easy, for "her heart stumbles," but she follows her path with determination.

In the poem titled "Women" (1968), Rich conjures a picture evocative of ancient female images.[61] Three sisters represent the Triple goddess of Fate, who is exhausted by the adversities of the patriarchal age. While they are still sitting on a magic stone in strange light, the Maiden goddess (the first sister) has grown so frail and transparent that her nerve fibers are visible. The Nymph goddess (the second sister) is mending her eternally broken heart. The Crone goddess (the third sister) has apparently grown indifferent to all this sewing and is gazing toward the west in the direction of the otherworld, where the sun sets and the dead journey—a place to which she apparently no longer has an active connection. The three goddesses are thus a pale reflection of their past glory.

But despite that, the third woman—old, with torn stockings—is beautiful. Why? Because she is obviously beginning to repudiate the perverted image of the Goddess and woman: she is no longer sewing. The first sister—the Maiden goddess—has decayed into a bigoted saint who is present at every procession but whose chastity has rendered her almost invisible. The second sister—Venus—has degenerated into a jilted lover who has never recovered from her broken heart, apparently because her feelings always elude her. The third sister, by contrast, is no longer involved; instead, she looks with sadness, or hope, toward the west and seeks a different future.

"The Fact of a Doorframe" (1974) is also touching and more like a lamentation than an ode to joy. It is a text about poetry itself—specifically, a type of poetry Rich considers lost and vainly seeks to retrieve.[62] Rich conjures in a single image the fate of poetry in patriarchy: it hangs pressed in a door frame like the severed yet still speaking head of the magic horse Falada. Like a beheaded Pegasus, it has been torn from the living substance that poetry is. The magic horse says to the woman poet, "If she could see thee now, thy mother's heart would break." The "mother," in both the old fairy tale and Rich's allusion, is the Great Mother, the Great Goddess herself; her poetry has been destroyed and her priestess has become a goose girl. The epoch of matriarchal poetry—the ecstatic singing of the Muses that formed the core of the living ritual and the life of the entire community—is past. Consequently, the poet feels only the pain of standing in and beating her head against this empty door frame—the boards, beams, rules, and genres into which poetry has been pressed. But at least the pain contains the longing for the reuniting of this bloodily decapitated poetry with its body, and the hope for its dazzling resurrection from the innermost depths.

While I share Rich's hope, I do not see the situation so pessimistically. There *are* poems by contemporary women writers that *do* approach the ecstatic speaking of the Muses. One of them, by Barbara Starrett, is called "The High Priestess" (1976), after a tarot card.[63]

In the poem, Starrett describes the image of the high priestess—who is at the same time the Moon goddess—in her tranquil, virginal beauty, just as she appears on many tarot cards. Then, as the seeker, the poet verbalizes her wish for ecstasy, which she expresses not only in words but also in the sequence of events and the flowing, hypnotic style. Her approach to the ancient sorceress, the powerful magician, proves to be not without peril: the sorceress suddenly reveals her Hecate features. She is always the white-black one, like the columns of light and darkness between which she is enthroned.

The seeker experiences a very unexpected, dramatic initiation, which causes her to break into a rapturous dance. It is not only the dance of homage and freedom but also the dance of evolution, which gyrates in all celestial bodies and terrestrial creatures. It is a poetic allusion to an authentic Maenad or Muse dance, a dance of knowledge, the dance of the Wise Woman— a dance full of exuberance and joy.

Now she knows both sides of the high priestess, or Moon goddess, and speaks with her as with an equal. A woman has achieved self-awareness: "I am." This is followed by a litany of pleas for deliverance resembling a ritualized prayer. The concluding formula is less a persiflage of the Lord's Prayer than the retrieval of power and glory by a woman who has now become a sorceress herself.

Such ecstatic speaking and formulaic incantation have been refined even further by the American Anne Waldman in her text "Fast Speaking Woman."[64] In it, she skeletonizes language precisely for the sake of the ritual formulas. For the first time, a text reveals the actual ritual that stood in the background and was recognized or at least sensed by the poet: a ritual from a magic mushroom-ceremony of Mazatec Indian shamanesses of Mexico.[65] Thus, Waldman's text is a pure incantation text that would acquire substance only through a spoken, sung, or danced ritual. It is precisely that open, fragmented, continuable nature—so uncharacteristic of a book text—that makes *this* text resemble ancient matriarchal ritual songs.

The text repeats an endless self-identification of the "fast speaking woman," who talks like the wind or a waterfall for thirty-six pages. The fast-paced lines thrive on associations and untranslatable puns. The original text must be spoken aloud or sung, and improvisation is expressly allowed. The poem thus resembles a dance text that constantly gives the beat for the same ceremonial movements and that, by means of its monotony, leads to trance. The structure is negligible. After a short introduction, which Waldman characterizes as a magical sylph, the "fast speaking woman" begins her incantations, which are interrupted only by the purification gestures with water and flowers repeated at regular intervals.

The "fast speaking woman" is everywhere; like the Goddess, she is universal in all of nature. She even appears to have a triadic form, as evidenced by her appearance, which resembles that of a fairy-tale princess: she appears in a light and then in a dress, of silver, of gold, and of emerald. At the end, when she almost collapses from fast talking, she suddenly bursts into loud shouting and then singing. Finally she falls silent—but not for good, of course, since the author calls her text a never-ending meditation text, which transposes the external motion of her journeys through South America and India into an inner motion. Waldman is always on journeys, on quests—just as we are.

Several texts by the German-speaking Verena Stefan (1980) also resemble incantations and were likewise conceived on a trip—a journey to Malta and Crete, which represented her quest for the matriarchal Goddess. In the poems' sensitive lines, Stefan interprets the land, the natural forces of sea and wind, the marshy soil, the temples, and another woman as manifestations of the Goddess herself. The texts evoke vivid memories of ancient matriarchal times, and the Triple goddess herself suddenly appears in the scattered texts I have compiled here.

1. "The Woman with the Lioness"

> My deepest yearning dream
> To walk in step with the lioness
> To set foot and paw in unison
> To raise a hand imperiously
> To lower a hand forbearingly
> My deepest yearning dream
> To touch the fur of the lioness.

2. "The Longing Speaks"

> I am the earth below me and the sky above me
> It is firm under my feet and
> Light as a bird over my hair
> The waters of a primeval sea
> Rise and fall within me
> An old red clock measures its time within me
> Month upon month as in the sky
> An old white clock changes its light

I speak from an upper mouth and a lower mouth
I know a higher face and a lower face
I know the brightness
I know the darkness

The longing is mute.

3.   Memory I invoke You
     black forgotten crone
     black from forgetting
     dog-headed bat-winged under the earth
     black from banishing
     banished to the lower world
     send images to my forsaken brain
     Memory I invoke You[66]

The matriarchal Goddess is thus captured and mirrored in the feelings of a woman. The Goddess's image is so bound up with the woman herself that they appear to be identical. In the first text, the poet still speaks as a vis-à-vis, magically drawn by the image of the Maiden goddess with the lioness. The same is also true of the third text, in which the poet invokes the Crone goddess, the subterranean hag Hecate, as the Other who should return. But the second text reveals the connection between the poet and her counterpart. The poetic "I" stands for both the woman who walks over the earth and the goddess who is simultaneously earth and sky; it is the fertility goddess in every woman, whose inner tides correspond to the sea's tides and the moon's phases. The woman and the Goddess give rise to both aspects of the cosmos: the bright and the dark, life and death. All of this is said with great simplicity and without mythological extravagance, resulting in graceful linguistic forms.

However, the appearance of the matriarchal Triple goddess is only one side of the structure of matriarchal mythology: the figure of the hero, her partner, is missing. We must still determine what the Goddess *and* the hero mean for the self-discovery and self-liberation of women in contemporary times. To that end, I shall quote and explicate a poem cycle of my own, in which I have captured the full structure of matriarchal mythology in its duality. I call it "The Goddess and Her Hero" (1977).

part one: INITIATION

1. the maiden goddess to the hero:

i am the revolt
against their fireball rockets
i with seldom
sharp weapons
the aegis
in my fist

i am the revolt
against their calculated
petrification
i with strained
insight
word arrows into interim silence

i am the revolt
in endlessly modest
dress of mail
have battled long
against you
with you
　　　　for you

2. the hero to the maiden goddess:

> you mean
> to die
> before your eyes
> is good for me
>
>> and the bow constantly
>> drawn at me
>> the accuracy of your
>> gaze
>
> pierced
> by your eyes
> you can still
> ask
> what is good for
> me?

part two: MARRIAGE

1. the nymph goddess to the hero:

> how
> could you
>
> unarmed
> in the play of your
> weaknesses
> and exceedingly mild
>
> strike
>
> because
> you unarmed
> and exceedingly mild
> and in the interplay

of your weaknesses
me so

2. the hero to the nymph goddess:

but
also blinded
between purple
folds and
nailed to
your crown
but also
whatever you will—

> i am not to you
> submissive
> but ready

part three: DEATH AND RETURN

1. the crone goddess to the hero:

i harness
the wagon
now you are dragged
through the categories
of your destruction
are you prepared?
i hear you

under the wheels
not in the rolling
on the road
and I will look back
never—

2. the hero:

> but i
> semisubmerged
> in these shadows
> between roots and fallen leaves
> at the most peaceful place

> but i
> still semisubmerged
> between the past future
> where no one accompanies me
> for i see
> nothing more—

> but i
> the shadiest place:
> sun which no one
> understands
> is everywhere

3. the crone goddess to the hero:

> thus
> feels
> the death
> which I
> gave you
> without hesitation

> i have thrust
> and painfully
> struck
> myself
> in you

4. the hero to the goddess:

>>you
>> who me
>>   in falling
>>   through the pitch darkness
>>   of all times
>>   of the destroyed body
>>   somewhere in the unknown
>>   center
>>   you
>>   how could i know
>>   that a
>>   you
>>would catch me?

5. the goddess to the hero:

>>i am
>>a world
>>of anti-rays
>>prism of the future
>>glassily embodied
>>in the cosmos

>>>>>but you are there
>>>>>where you remain
>>>>>on this
>>>>>remnant
>>>>>of a globe
>>>>>wreck of galaxies

>>i am already here
>>but where
>>do you tarry?

6. the hero to the goddess:

> you have me
> between the
> right and the left
> shredded a thing
> without anguish
> and allowed me
> to fall

> and pieced me together
> in the beyond in accord
> with the laws
> of your universe

>> i tell you
>> not
>> what i thus
>> suffered—

7. the goddess to the hero:

> forget me
> and you
> forget yourself
> but i
> am forgotten
> i still
> but you?

8. the hero to the goddess:

> you have inverted me

> and from me

>> deep below beside me

strangely raised near you
> somewhere in the nether region
> of your arms
> where you begin again
> straight through me
> like a sharp sickle
> and laugh me into peace

restored to myself

9. the hero, transfigured:

through the underworld
i journeyed
according to law
and endured
with patience
my deep transformation

> my reflected secret
> i did not know
> untraceable
> clearly the core
> showed me the right side

through hell
i stepped
to the bitter end
i stepped
to spare you
from hell

10. the goddess, transfigured:

hard
> to be a crystal

tempered to integrity
no feeling
of triumph of sorrow
no dimming of clarity

hard

to be a crystal
under human conditions
unshaking
mirror for images
of eros

hard

to be a crystal
under passion
which restlessly burns through me
and finally explodes
with a strange sound[67]

This cycle is connected with my other poems, which mirror the stages in my inner development: the suffering in patriarchal exile and the ultimate escape from it, the zones of spiritual self-discovery that finally open to the experience of the universal Goddess in all the elements—to the entire continent that she is. The language is austere and concentrated and not independent of the graphics (contained in the original), which include the crescent and circle symbols of the Goddess's phases and those of the hero, and are arranged on tricolor paper: white, red, black. This cycle and the events associated with its genesis represent the crucial point in my own inner development.

The cycle has the form of a dialogue between the "Goddess" and the "hero" and reproduces the three stages of the Goddess's relationship to the hero, which in turn correspond to the three phases of the moon, the three parts of the mythic year, and the three main ritual festivals of initiation, Sacred Marriage, and death and return as the hero's journey to the underworld.[68] The Maiden goddess appears with the classic attributes of a militant Amazon revolting against the destructive aspects of contemporary times and sweeping the hero along as her partner. He cannot resist her power. He experiences initiation as a first deathlike transformation; his old categories shatter; he suffers a painful metamorphosis.

The Nymph goddess is then taken aback by the hero's affliction. He is no longer violent but weaponless—an ancient and new masculine figure—and entirely submissive to her. In the hero's eyes, this new counterpart is not the reverse of subjugation but loving, ecstatic eroticism. The Crone goddess then accepts his word of willingness and asks whether he is ready for death, for the journey to the underworld conducted and spiritually escorted by her as the pitiless goddess of death, who spares him nothing and brings him into the depths under the earth. But there is a hint of emotion behind her pitilessness. His death has touched even her, and her participation—even in his destruction—finally buoys the hero in the depths.

The decisive transformation occurs from the depths. The Goddess transforms herself into a visible utopia—a star—and asks the hero if he wants to join her and be redeemed from the wreckage of his past. But the hero cannot yet free himself from the anguish of his journey to the underworld, and the Goddess admonishes him not to lose himself in his anguish. Then the hero finally achieves a breakthrough: he recognizes the transformation. He realizes that the "bringing from himself" was basically a profound "bringing *to* himself" experienced through her power. That knowledge produces a laugh and inner peace—it is implied that the process can begin all over again.

In the last two texts, the hero and the Goddess recapitulate the events. The hero comprehends that he did not experience the transformation for its own sake but to point the way for others. At the same time, his integrity has withstood the test. The Goddess appears as a star of infinite brightness—her own integrity—in the now transfigured and healed world. The star also represents the hero's innermost core, which he has come to recognize on his journey to the underworld. But despite her superior strength, the Goddess has experienced human emotions as a woman, and the ambivalence of being both a goddess and a woman appears ultimately to have exceeded her power. So, for all her uncompromising consistency, she proves to be a loving goddess and reciprocates his loving devotion. As a loving goddess, she is not an omnipotent, directing transcendence but, with her passions, is grounded in the here and now.

I underwent this dual spiritual process myself; it lasted an entire year and spanned a very difficult phase in my life. During this process, it became clear to me that I, too, am both: the powerful, emotional goddess-woman and the suffering, conquering hero-man. The poem cycle thus mirrors my own duality—my dual powers through which I became whole. Those powers are fundamentally matriarchal powers, and perhaps they pervade every woman.

That my psyche has this dual structure was a profound realization for me, a new consciousness, a decisive inner liberation. It is also mirrored in my relationships to other people, both men and women. But, as I continually experienced, the problems involved in such relationships in present-day society have an extremely deforming effect on the psyche. Consequently, the cycle "The Goddess and Her Hero" remains in the final analysis a utopia, a guiding idea for a society born of Eros—a society for both sexes but one whose perspective and foundation only women can create and develop.

My own concise, pithy style is in contrast to Robin Morgan's twenty-six-page poem "The Network of the Imaginary Mother" (1976).[69] In its rich verbal abundance, which ultimately culminates in almost ecstatic speaking, Morgan likewise develops a complete matriarchal Goddess-hero structure based on the delineation of the most important stages in her life. In contrast to me, she does not experience it as an inner process but as a process involving other people. However, her life process, like my own, does reach a climax in the liberating discovery of her own identity.

It is impossible within the scope of this book to reproduce Morgan's huge and nonetheless highly structured poem, nor does it permit of a purely associative arrangement. I will therefore paraphrase and interpret it. Despite its length, the poem has a clear organization consisting of five parts: "The Mother," "The Consort," "The Sister," "The Child," and "The Self." The cycle thus has a fivefold structure like the mysteries of the Goddess. Each part has an identical structure, and each begins with a description of a concrete relationship and the ambivalent course it takes: an affectionate "turning toward" is followed by a "turning away," or an overcoming. Between these two sections are aphoristic verses that hint at the fate of a man and a woman—who have grown up and face each other with problems—and always end with formulaic entreaties for tranquillity, peace, and resolution of the conflict. In the particularly long part titled "The Mother," those aphoristic verses create a double structure. Each part concludes with an indictment listing names from the documents of the witch trials, and also demonstrates which aspect of women was destroyed by patriarchal Christian society.

In the first part, "The Mother," the poet describes her own mother—first her loving, giving, creative side, and then the destructive side she adopted as a withering woman marked by death. In her duality, Morgan's mother embodies the ambivalent power of the Crone goddess, which the daughter can overcome only by placing herself in the terrible proximity of death and accompanying her mother to the resolution—to death. The indictment at the end of this part clearly indicates which powers of women were destroyed during the witch trials: their wisdom as midwives, healers, doctors, and practitioners of herbal medicine. Because old women still possessed those powers in the matriarchies, the relationships to old women in matriarchal societies were not as discordant as those to old women destroyed under patriarchal pressure. In short, that is the message of this part, which Morgan imbues with great sensibility and power of language.

In the second part, "The Consort," Morgan describes her concrete relationship to the man as partner. Here, too, the ambiguity of a patriarchal man-woman relationship quickly surfaces, i.e., in the question of who affixed whose seal to whom. Normally that question turns into a murderous battle in which the woman is usually inferior. But Morgan ultimately turns the relationship into a utopian one, at least on the conceptual plane. The image of the hero—a man originally created by woman and now re-created, consecrated, and led by her— appears in the mythic allusions to Osiris and the stag-god, Pan. Morgan considers the attainment of this transformed, humane, and affectionate woman-man relationship an endless task reaching into the future. The indictment at the end of this part recalls the destruction of the erotic capacity of the woman—precisely the quality that transformed the man into the matriarchal hero. The ancient Venus power of the woman is destroyed, and all that remains is naked sexuality as a brutal act of violence.

In the third part, "The Sister," Morgan describes a relationship between two women who meet as exact complementary opposites and support and assist each other. The wonderful ancient myth of Demeter and Kore is mirrored in their meeting—the more sensual and naïve woman in the daughter role, the more knowledgeable woman (Morgan herself) in the mother role. But the problems associated with the fragile mother-daughter relationship in patriarchy also come into play here. In her relationship to the younger woman, Morgan unconsciously falls into the destructive behavior of her own mother, and the matriarchal myth of Demeter and Kore remains unfulfilled under patriarchal conditions. All that is left at the end of the relationship are small gifts. The indictment at the end of this part again documents the source of the destruction: any hint of a lesbian relationship between women was persecuted and destroyed during the time of the witch trials, since it was precisely such relationships that—in their depth and multifariousness—promoted the social cooperation of women at the time of their independence in the matriarchies and Amazon states.

The fourth part, "The Child," describes Morgan in her role as a real mother, and the language is filled with unpretentious tenderness. Her child is a male baby, and in him she sees the reborn hero in his naïveté and flawlessness. Ancient images of mother goddesses with their small sons on their laps emerge from her memory and imbue this mother-child relationship with matriarchal powers. But Morgan is already aware of the threat to this relationship, for she alludes to the perpetual, inhumane exploitation of motherhood in patriarchy, through which sons learned all too soon to despise their mothers and lead deadly wars against them. Morgan wants to save herself and her child from such an end by teaching her son respect for the mother. In this way, she gains the hope that the misery of the world's children will come to an end, for esteem for mothers also means esteem for children. The indictment at the end names the terrible powers that destroyed the matriarchal social fabric and manifested themselves in the witch trials, in which the witch-hunters did not even hesitate to torture and execute children together with their mothers.

The concluding part, "The Self," is both the summation and surmounting of the previous parts, for it shows the author's growing consciousness through all the stages of her life. As the recurring pivotal sentence, "I affirm all of my transformations," indicates, and the metaphor of the wheel of fate hints at in the other sections, the formation and fading of love relationships are interpreted as stages on the path to reaching one's identity.[70] In this part, the process that has been unfolding before our eyes finally reaches its goal, as Morgan implies with the metaphors of the weaver at her loom and the spider in her net, both of which she identifies with. As those metaphors suggest, Morgan herself created "the network of the imaginary mother": the web of her life and self-becoming, the web that unites the powers of her natural mother, the powers of the cosmic mother goddess of the matriarchy, and Morgan's own powers. And the figures of her mother, her consort, her sisterly lover, and her child are woven into that net as visions of new relationships. "These are my people," she says, for she has re-created them—at least in her mind—into something new. She has reinvented them.[71]

Now the burning question—the perpetually verbalized longing for tranquillity, peace, resolution of the conflict in every relationship—is resolved; for at this point, in the moment of her own spiritual birth, language fails the poet and becomes an ecstatic exclamation, a stammered entreaty to the Goddess. And in her place—or from within her—the Goddess speaks and solves all the riddles.

At the conclusion of the indictment, the soliloquy of the Goddess opens with a reminiscence: syllable by syllable, she recalls her ancient past, retrieves her WORD before all other words, and inscribes her name again. Then the Goddess re-establishes herself as the true sacrament, the true giver of life in the face of Christian imitation and distortion. She, not the man, has the true life's blood: her menstruation. She, not the man, possesses life's true nourishment: her milk. Then the Goddess replaces patriarchal time reckoning with her own: the wheel of the year and of life, the solstices and equinoxes, her ritual festivals and mysteries embedded in the seasonal cycle.

The awakening of memory is the solution of all riddles, and the WORD of the Goddess is her new creation. The poem rises like a wave from strophe to strophe until it comes to the absolute climax: the epiphany of the Goddess in Triad. That is preceded by a fivefold blessing consecrating the body of the goddess-woman who brings forth all things physical and spiritual. It is the validation of self-recognition, and the epiphany of the Triple goddess follows.

She herself—the Goddess *and* the poetic "I"—is the Crone goddess, who rules over the underworld and death; the creative Venus, the mother goddess who brings forth the fertility of the earth; the astral Maiden goddess, who is eternally young. Thus the trinity, long believed lost, reappears. This development mirrors the pattern of the poet's love relationships, which likewise progressed from older to younger people. She herself—the poet and the Goddess—is mirrored in all her relationships, and that realization is the summation of all her experiences. Poet and Goddess are now one and are visibly manifest in the verses that form the climax of the entire poem.

Morgan's image of the Goddess corresponds precisely to the Goddess structure of matriarchal mythology. With her rich mythological allusions, Morgan consciously and completely transposes matriarchal mythology—including the hero structure contained in the second part of the poem—into her own poetic vision. Of course she considers herself to be the feminine side alone, the Goddess; and she locates the masculine side, the hero, in other people, i.e., in the consort and the child. That is, of course, different from my own experience and my poetic treatment of the theme. But Morgan's experience and ideas are equally valid, and thus two possibilities of experiencing the structure of matriarchal mythology coexist.

Morgan's poem spans a phenomenal range. She integrates her concrete personal experience of life, her knowledge of matriarchal mythology, her knowledge of the misogynistic history of the Christian European patriarchy, and her visionary utopia of new relationships and the reappearance of the Goddess. She focuses this range—which is also expressed in the hymnic language—in the pivotal phrase "There is nothing I have not been, / and I am come into my power. / There is nothing I cannot be."[72] The word of the mother stands at the beginning of the poem and recurs at the end as the summation of everything. Like a formula, the phrase contains the inexhaustible power of women who have become conscious of themselves, their history, and their future.

We have now obtained the third element for our new rituals, for our matriarchal art-utopia: the word. Of course—like the pictures, music, and performances by the women already discussed—all these poems are also effective without a ritual. But because they remain within the confines of conventional genres and the framework of conventional forms of presentation, they run the danger of petrifying under the influence of the fictionality principle—and against the intentions of the authors—into mere art objects. The cosmic reality that they embrace, be it the reality of the external or the internal cosmos, or both simultaneously, can still be abridged by others into an "aesthetic fiction."

This situation mirrors the universal contradiction plaguing contemporary women artists who are creating the beginnings of a matriarchal art/music/poetry: the contradiction of having to create nonfictional, non-object-oriented art within an art world that defines art in purely patriarchal terms as "fiction" and "work." Hence, what actually happens in matriarchal art, namely, the transformation of reality, is precluded by definition. Such a transformation is not visible in mere "works," which are cut off from the living process and appear before the eyes of the public as mere hulls, discarded shells, or castoffs. Thus, all the rifts in the aesthetic dimension come into play.

Of course, women artists cannot immediately resolve all the contradictions confronting them. For precisely that reason, a guiding perspective—not criticism but an outlook—is vital. To develop our utopia from what has already been created does not mean to repudiate it but to appreciate it as the first necessary steps—which must be followed by further necessary steps—and to place it into a larger framework, to integrate it into further expanded contexts. In this way, we women can gradually arrive at the expression of our entire being, as Morgan has so splendidly described it. In this sense, we should dare to perform the most diverse conceptual experiments in order to combine the elements of space, sounds, and words presented here, and thus attain the perhaps not so distant matriarchal art-utopia.

It is easy to imagine Anne Waldman's seemingly monotone liturgy orchestrated against the sound backdrop of the "witch music" described by Meri Franco-Lao. Verena Stefan's texts also lend themselves to song, as does my own Goddess-hero cycle. The economy of language of both Stefan's text and my own lend themselves to hypnotic, cyclical, soaring repetitions; their gestures already suggest the choreography of dance. My cycle in particular contains an entire matriarchal ritual. Morgan's magnificent hymn can also be performed as a play of movements patterned after the flow of the words themselves. The changing relationships can be presented in drama and in dance: daughter and mother, woman and consort, the two sisters, mother and child. The entire performance can climax in a ritual in which the Goddess herself speaks and institutes her sacrament in tangible form.

How such word-sound-movement rituals can be realized in space is shown by the women earthwork and environmental artists with their mythically structured landscapes of caves, altars, fires, and mandalas (whether inside or outside), which give us the impetus for re-creating the dance patterns and dance spaces for small- or large-scale ritual festivals. And let us recall the body artists' actions and performances, which represent the origins of dance-dramas and which Mary Beth Edelson has already developed into characteristic rituals. All these artists have pointed the way for us. In these simultaneous, comprehensive actions there are neither isolable individual "works" nor discarded shells of an earlier event; on the contrary, everything happens directly in the action itself, in the process, in the transformation. While these actions can be documented as an inspiration to other women to contribute to matriarchal art, their documentation is not a "work" but merely a vehicle of communication. Such communication, however, releases other women from the role of a mere admiring audience for a "work" and liberates their own creative powers. As a result, we come considerably closer to matriarchal art.

FOUR

The Lunisolar Play

THE SEASONAL CYCLE AS MATRIARCHAL ART-UTOPIA

In this essay I shall present a concrete and vivid description of my own conceptual experiment: to imagine the matriarchal art-utopia in light of contemporary women artists' conceptions of the rudiments of matriarchal art and the experiences we have gained from their work. My purpose is to incorporate the full content of the matriarchal rite into a new matriarchal art, since not every pattern of movement or every symbolic action—no matter how ritualistic its intent may be—is a matriarchal ritual. As far as I know, the full complexity, the extraordinary multifariousness, and the deep significance of matriarchal rituals as they derive from the structure of matriarchal mythology have yet to be treated exhaustively.

Adherence to the strict form of matriarchal rites is very important in this regard, since without careful consideration of the structure of matriarchal mythology, the ritual forms would soon become arbitrary, and everything and anything would be called "matriarchal" whether deserving of the designation or not. After all, the structure of initiation, marriage, death, and return did not arise from a personal desire or a social dictate but developed through the millennia on the foundation of genuinely matriarchal societies throughout the entire world. For that reason, I have designated the structure of matriarchal mythology as the "categories of human imagination." For its content is so extensive and profound that we would have to invest much intellect, emotion, and creative energy before we could approximate it or even implement it.

If we use this structure precisely and its full range of symbols—which is indeed extensive but not arbitrary—we can manipulate it like a language of symbols, a nonverbal language of symbolic images and actions. In doing so, we can recover and revalidate a different and older form of communication, which was valid long before and far beyond today's exclusively discursive, argumentative language of words. Of course, precise usage is requisite, since every language has set rules. But every language also allows for various individual dialects. With regard to the structure of matriarchal mythology, those "dialects" would consist in the play of symbols and their freedom of arrangement.

That in turn goes hand in hand with the various ways in which we explore the depth of meaning of that structure. Just as the Goddess was always the same in terms of her form, she also exhibited the greatest diversity in terms of her names and attributes. Historically, the adherence to the structure of matriarchal mythology has meant the survival, throughout the millennia, of the matriarchal dance festivals and rituals—in their original form—on the foundation of this unchangeable framework. It has also ensured that those dance festivals and rituals are still recognizable today, despite their suppression and distortion by patriarchy. This unity in multiplicity is so important that we may not sacrifice it to the excessive and egocentric subjectivism prevailing in the current patriarchal epoch. It is especially vital in art, since communication by means of symbols is impossible in the face of subjective arbitrariness.

Moreover, the matriarchal rituals and dance festivals were embedded in the seasonal cycle, which considerably intensified the expressiveness of their symbols. Thus, neither time nor place was arbitrary—in contrast to contemporary artistic expressions—and everything happened in analogy to what happened in nature. In that analogy, one cannot determine which events were earlier or later, i.e., whether the festival came first and then nature followed the people's entreaties, or whether nature acted first and then the people imitated her. Everything occurred in perfect simultaneity as an interplay with the forces of the entire cosmos, which themselves became symbols in the rituals.

Nature was a reliable and inextricable participant in this net of symbolic communication; she was the principal actress, the female godhead herself. Such a reclaimed interconnection between humankind and nature is an integral part of a new matriarchal art and clearly shows that the seasons in nature correspond to the psychic seasons in us. Our bodies and psyches are part of nature—the psychosomatic "inner" nature that, in its abundance and complexity, corresponds to "external" nature and is linked through very delicate processes with the periodic monthly and seasonal variations.[1]

Ritual Plays

Women have already made attempts to revive matriarchal seasonal rituals, not within the scope of art but within the realm of spirituality. However, most of those women do not categorize their projects as "art," nor do many women artists associate their work with "spirituality." That is due only in part to their unawareness of each other. To a greater extent it reflects the typical patriarchal separation of spheres, whereby spirituality simply means "religion" and art simply means "fiction"—and both notions are false.[2] That can be a disadvantage both for women who experiment with new forms of matriar-chal ritual and for women who create art with matriarchal tendencies: their rituals run the risk of becoming inartistic, unstructured, inferior imitation; their artistic activity, when performed without the vast intellectual and spiritual horizon provided by matriarchal spirituality, runs the risk of being reduced to private, subjective processes.

The Hungarian-born American Zsuzsanna Budapest was one of the first modern-day women to perform matriarchal rituals. She drew upon the folk traditions of her native land—very ancient, albeit fragmentary knowledge—to invent her rituals, which fit into the original seasonal calendar.[3] Budapest's rituals follow a fixed pattern: the women hold hands and measure a circle; then the circle is drawn to create the sacral space; all who enter the circle are purified; the circle is closed; the four quarters of the heavens are invoked; the magic power is in-tensified through concentration; the Goddess is invited; a ritual appropriate to the season is performed; a feast is celebrated with wine and bread as well as personal wishes and thanks-giving to the Goddess; the magic power is discharged; the circle is opened; and the ritual concludes with dancing and enter-tainment.

The rituals central to this pattern correspond to the special moments in the solar calendar. At the winter solstice the women wear wreaths of evergreen and celebrate a candle ritual. They symbolically enact the birth of the light and the birth of the women participants by singing a concentrated succession of notes in a constant crescendo until the tension is discharged in a common birth cry.

At Candlemas (February 2)—an ancient initiation festival—new members are initiated in a rite in which the women stand one behind the other and slowly pull the initiates through their spread legs. This act symbolizes the passage through the birth canal. At the end of the ritual, each initiate is welcomed into the group.

At the vernal equinox they celebrate the return of Kore from the underworld, and her mother, Demeter, causes the earth to bloom again. The eve of May 1 is considered the feast of the blossoming goddess. In her honor the women wear wreaths of flowers and carry green boughs; a caldron of aromatic herbs forms the focal point of the celebration.

At the summer solstice they invoke the fire goddess of love and, at the same time, celebrate the power of women over men; they even cast spells against personal and political male enemies. The women hold branches, representing the phallic principle, over a burning caldron and allow them to be consumed by the fire.

That is followed by the feast of the grain harvest on August 2, a Demeter festival. All the women wear wreaths of wheat and praise the sumptuous abundance of the goddess. At the autumnal equinox they celebrate the witches' thanksgiving festival. The stone altar in the middle of the circle is adorned with leaves, branches, and pinecones. The ritual revolves around the burial of seeds of grain in the earth in the hope that new life will sprout from them in the coming spring.

On Halloween (October 31) they celebrate the witches' new-year festival, the day on which the Goddess appears in her third form—as the goddess of death and the Wise Crone. It is the festival of Hecate. The dead are honored, and memories of the matriarchal ancestors are awakened. The women pass around a blacklist of their enemies, invoke the Goddess as the avenging mother, and then curse patriarchy. At the same time, they stab a pomegranate with their knives. That is followed again by the festival of the winter solstice.

Budapest arranges the groups of women so that three of them always appear as a goddess triad and perform the duties of the gatherings. The "high priestess"—who is responsible for the political and spiritual organization—explains the significance of the festival, instructs the members, and leads the songs and invocations accompanying the rituals; she embodies the wisdom aspect of the Goddess. The "nymph"—who provides the food, drink, music, and entertainment—prepares bright, happy hours; she embodies the Venus aspect of the Goddess. The "maiden"—who locates a beautiful place in the open air for the gathering—draws the circle at the correct astrological moments, performs the various types of magic, and purifies all who enter the circle; she embodies the Amazon aspect of the Goddess. The roles can be assigned according to the individuals' spiritual readiness and personal preference, and should alternate among the women of a small group. Larger groups necessitate a stricter structure, in which the more experienced participants assume the active roles.

Budapest's ideas are stimulating and shed new light on many details of the ancient witch tradition. However, I see some serious problems in her rituals. She is in danger of becoming mired in nit-picking, because she amasses too many symbols, metaphors, and magic objects. Tiny section upon tiny section associatively alternate with one another; as a result, a clear, powerful ritual structure never emerges. Budapest's rituals lack "art," i.e., the ability to concentrate the action into a single complex symbol rather than a conglomeration of individual symbols.

A second problem is that Budapest anchors the entire seasonal cycle on the relatively late, Hellenistic tale of Demeter and Kore.[4] In its long history as an underground religion during the patriarchal epoch of Greece, this myth suffered several distortions and deformations, which Budapest has not even taken into consideration. If the myth is to be productive, one must at least attempt to reconstruct its matriarchal version and restore its references to the other matriarchal religions of the neighboring cultures.[5] Only in that way can the depth of the myth be plumbed. Budapest and her imitators lack such a historical consciousness, which results in their naïvely transposing the relics of "witch knowledge" into the present—as if we were still living in the same society in which that knowledge originated.

Furthermore, everything masculine is radically excluded from the rituals: not only individual men—it *is* permissible to exclude *them*—but also every masculine principle. While the Goddess structure of matriarchal society is implicit, the hero structure is entirely omitted. At the same time, the profound symbolic content of the ancient matriarchal festivals and the vividness of the relationships between woman/man and the cosmos are undeveloped. The masculine principle appears only indirectly and in evil terms as individual enemies or as patriarchy itself. This results in an unfortunate identification of men with patriarchy—as if the image of the matriarchal man, a pure creation of women, had never existed!

That attitude of hate and malediction is not adopted by Miriam Simos. Under the name "Starhawk," she published a voluminous book delineating her knowledge of and experience with ritualistic activity in San Francisco.[6] Although Starhawk follows closely in the footsteps of her teacher, Budapest, in the thematics and the structure of her rituals, she is more thorough and exhaustive and—in contrast to Budapest—rescinds the exclusion of the masculine principle from the rituals. A "god" appears beside the Goddess and is invoked and praised under as many names as she: he is the "horned one," "the hart and the stallion," "the ram and the bull," the "reborn one," the "sun child," the "king of light," and the "sacrificed one"; he is Dionysus, Osiris, Pan, and Dumuzi.

Consequently, Starhawk's rituals connected with the seasonal cycle have somewhat different contents from Budapest's. At the winter solstice, Starhawk imitates Budapest's "birth canal" ritual, which of course only women can perform. At Candlemas the participants perform a ritual around a caldron filled with earth and lighted candles in honor of Brigit, the Celtic goddess of inspiration. At the vernal equinox they celebrate the growing sun prince, who stretches out his hand to free Kore, the spring goddess, imprisoned under the earth. On the eve of May 1 they perform a Maypole dance, in which they hold the ends of streamers and interweave them. At the summer solstice the "high priestess" and the "high priest" dance with a small idol of the god, which is entwined with flowers and then thrown into the fire. At the feast on August 2 they repeat the burning of the god, but this time the idol is made of bread. At the autumnal equinox they weave a streamer to which all participants have fastened objects symbolizing their wishes for the coming year. That is followed by Halloween, with its memorial service to the dead and celebration of the prince of twilight, who sails to the west and death. Finally the pomegranate, which was used to curse the patriarchy in Budapest's ritual, is peacefully divided into several pieces and blessed by the "high priestess" and the "high priest": "Behold the fruit of life . . ." "Which is death!" "Behold the fruit of death . . ." "Which is life!"[7] The woman speaks the blessing of life, the man the blessing of death.

Despite their rich mythic background and somewhat contemplative mood, Starhawk's rituals present a number of problems. As a whole, they are just as associative as Budapest's and occasionally even more overladen. Moreover, the content of the rituals seems arbitrary. As a result, they lack the symbolic significance of the corresponding festivals and degenerate into mere imitation. In addition, the rituals are not only imitative but also repetitive (which suggests a dearth of ideas), for example, the idol is sacrificed in the fire twice and the streamers are woven twice. Furthermore, Kore appears now and then for no reason, only to disappear suddenly after having been saved by the sun prince. What is more, the image of the Triple goddess is never developed.

Do Starhawk's rituals at least contain the hero structure? The sun prince, who appears at the vernal equinox and takes his leave again at Halloween, seems an allusion to it. But he does not sail away at the autumnal equinox as he should, according to the symmetrical solar calendar. Because of such inaccuracies and the meaninglessness of the rituals, a correct image of the hero never emerges. Thus, Starhawk is in some ways even further from fulfilling the structure of matriarchal mythology than is Budapest.

Moreover, the rituals run the great risk of celebrating the sun prince and the male idols in place of the Moon goddess. No less serious an error is Starhawk's juxtaposition of the "goddess" with the "god," and the "high priestess" with the "high priest." Such an approach is not an integration of the masculine principle into a matriarchal worldview, but pure association. Matriarchal mythology recognizes no such god, but only the hero. The idea of a male god was completely alien to matriarchal mythology, since man is not the life-giving force. For the same reason, there were also no high priests. The deification of the hero, who had hitherto been mortal, characterizes the incursion of the patriarchy into the goddess cult. The first deified heroes, in fact, became the destroyers of matriarchal cults and cities: Perseus, the Doric Heracles, Theseus the destroyer of Crete. The deified hero quickly rose to become a god, and the increasingly numerous gods supplanted the goddesses until all that remained was monotheism with a single God the Father. This was a linear and consistent development.

Thus, with her rash embrace of the masculine principle in matriarchal ritual, Starhawk goes to the opposite extreme of Budapest. Both lack a sufficient historical perspective, but Starhawk's political naïveté assumes a different form—in her cooperation with men and her failure to consider the conditions of our present society. Our society is *still* patriarchal, which means that it generally supports men, while women have to work alone and struggle against patriarchy. It is therefore absurd to admit men immediately as "equals" into any sphere laboriously created by women and still in the experimental stage. In a patriarchal society men are not equal but *privileged*. And whenever men are dissatisfied with their role in this society, they show up in women's circles—because of the complementary self-affirmation and commanding "understanding" they seem to find there. But where are women supposed to go if *they* are dissatisfied with *their* role in this society and are seeking complementary self-affirmation? To men's circles? I think not.

Hence, to develop matriarchal spirituality and matriarchal rituals means—first and foremost—to *protect* them, for it is a very new, very subtle domain for women. And it means to remember the matriarchal ritual structure. Men were never "equals" in those rituals but merely human heroes who stood opposite the Triple goddess and received everything from her. Therefore, the point is not whether to integrate men but how to do it. And the main point is *when* to do it. Such deliberations are of a political nature and are not intended as an injustice to the individual men who would like to be included.

The Lunisolar Calendar

Before outlining my art-utopia of the matriarchal seasonal rituals, I would like to discuss its foundation: the matriarchal calendar. The matriarchal calendar did not simply consist of the solar calendar with its festivals (Sabbaths) into which some moon festivals were randomly interspersed; it was a precise and orderly combination of the lunar and the solar calendars.

The solar calendar is a fixed calendar; the lunar calendar, by contrast, is a movable calendar and historically much earlier. The lunar month, which spans the time from one new moon to the next, is the earliest known measure of time. It is said to have been known and recorded in symbols as early as the Stone Age.[8] The preference for the moon is understandable, since its highly visible and impressive phases are easy to observe everywhere on earth. To determine the seasons, however, requires a considerably longer period of observation, and a greater variety of phenomena must be considered—quite apart from the fact that the observations differ greatly in the earth's various zones. At the equator, for example, there are no seasons but only times of day. At the poles, there are only the seasons of summer and winter and no times of day; the polar day is as long as the summer, and the polar night is as long as the winter. The seasons are most pronounced in the subtropical and temperate latitudes, and it was there that the solar calendar was developed in the early matriarchal high civilizations.

The lunar calendar divides the year into thirteen segments of exactly twenty-eight days. A lunar year consists of thirteen lunar months. That explains the sacredness of the number thirteen, which only later developed into an unlucky number. Today it is conjectured that in the earlier epochs all women menstruated at the same time, so that the parallel between the phases of the moon and the cycles of women was obvious. Pregnancy is also in harmony with the moon and corresponds to nine lunar months. It was therefore no accident that the sacred time in the ritualized seasonal cycle was nine months, to which the remaining four months were appended as a phase of transition—the fading of the past and the preparation for the future, since a woman's body needs about four months to recover from giving birth.[9] Perhaps even women's gestation times were fit into the seasonal cycle during the matriarchal epoch—if not universally, then at least on the sacral plane.

Hence, it is appropriate to say that the lunar calendar was

divided into three parts: the three sacred periods of the year each consisted of three lunar months (the tripartite year), and the four remaining months did not count.[10] Only with the development of the solar calendar did the division of the year into *four* parts come into being; there was no "leftover" time. The year was divided into four equal segments, each consisting of three months between the solstices and equinoxes (the quadripartite year). Three and four were the sacred numbers, from which the sacred number twelve was derived. Thirteen was omitted like the thirteenth fairy in the fairy tale.

The fabulous creatures known as Sphinxes were originally calendar emblems that mirrored the tripartite and quadripartite structures. The trimorphic Sphinx was composed of the animals symbolic of the Triple goddess: the lion, the bull, and the snake. More frequently, the Sphinx consisted of a human head, a lion's body, and a snake's tail. In both cases, however, the Sphinx had the same meaning: it was the symbol of the tripartite year. With the development of the solar calendar, the quadrimorphic Sphinx appeared: it had bird's wings in addition to the other three parts—the quadripartite year.

Since thirteen lunar months and the quadripartite, fixed solar year are numerically incompatible, there were laborious attempts to harmonize the old lunar calendar with the new solar calendar. But that did not detract from the adoration of the Triple moon goddess. Since time immemorial she was considered the triad in quadruplet, because the moon shows exactly four phases: the waxing crescent, the full moon, the waning crescent, and the new moon. The new-moon phase is paradoxical since it does not "show" itself but is nonetheless present. The lunar calendar treated the fourth part of the year in an equally paradoxical manner: present but not counted. With the introduction of the solar calendar, the son of the Triple goddess, the hero, was included with her—from which the quadripartite year derived its significance.

However, the problem of harmonizing the two calendars remained. The thirteen lunar months were therefore divided into twelve months, whose thirty and thirty-one days do not exactly correspond to the orbital periods of the moon. A distinction was made between "fixed" and "movable" feasts, i.e, between festivals determined according to the solar calendar and those determined according to the lunar calendar. The solution was to take the fixed moments of the solar calendar and add the time period until the next full moon. For example, even to this day Easter falls on the first full moon after the vernal equinox (the "Easter rule"), and Christmastide is extended (from Christmas Eve to the Epiphany) so that a full moon always falls during this period. We still celebrate such feasts as time periods of several days, not as moments in time or individual days. Ritual festivals as time phases beginning at the fixed moments of the solar calendar and climaxing on the subsequent full moons were the rule in the time reckoning of the developed matriarchies, with their lunisolar calendar.

Let us now examine in detail the festivals of the lunisolar cycle. The following illustration contains the time phases of the four major festivals at the solstices and the equinoxes as well as the minor festivals, which occur at exactly equal intervals between the major ones. The minor feasts are festivals of preparation for the four major ritual festivals. The entire festival cycle, embedded in the cycle of the zodiac, represents the "wheel of the year" or the "wheel of life"—which we can also call the "wheel of transformation." The wheel has eight "spokes," mirroring the goddess Inanna's life flower: the eight-petaled rosette. The "wheel of luck" in tarot also has eight spokes: it is none other than the wheel of the year and of life, for the calendar emblem the Sphinx is enthroned above it.

The sacred phase of the year begins at the vernal equinox and ends at the winter solstice. The four major ritual festivals of initiation, Sacred Marriage, sacrificial death, and return/

rebirth occur in this time period. The last quarter of the year is the "paradoxical" time in which everything ends and begins again.

I will therefore begin with the "paradoxical" time, with the Candlemas festival on February 2. Candlemas is the preparatory feast for the major initiation ritual at the vernal equinox. In the German liturgical year, the feast is called Mary Candlemas and it celebrates the gradually lengthening days.[11] In pre-Christian times, Candlemas was dedicated to the goddess of light Lucia, who wears a wreath of candles on her head, or the Celtic fire goddess Brigit. Brigit guards the caldron containing the inspirational fire; inspiration through the goddess is the requirement for every new beginning. Brigit sends the kindling sparks, the creative spirit, and thus is the tutelary goddess of poets and singers, whom she inspires.

Brigit's effects are manifest after Candlemas in the time period of Carnival, the time of inspired rapture, ecstatic frenzy, and disorder. The non-Christian character of this time period is still known today. Carnival falls on the full moon following Candlemas and reflects the "paradoxical" nature of this time period. Everything is turned around and inverted: the highest becomes the lowest, the lowest the highest. It is the time of foolish craziness. The inversion and upsetting of set relationships dissolve the old and make way for the new: re-volution. Carnival is the time of transition, of creative chaos. (Zodiacal sign Aquarius, planet Uranus, tarot cards XIV and 0.)[12]

Carnival is followed by the festival of *Eastre,* the goddess of spring.[13] The mythic year begins at the vernal equinox in the constellation Aries (March 20 to 23). In Christian times the festival is still called Easter and is filled with the symbols of this goddess: the first flowers; budding boughs; colored eggs; small newborn animals such as chicks, lambs, kids, baby rabbits—all symbols of burgeoning life. White rabbits are symbols of fertility and the full moon. In many regions of Europe the

THE SEASONAL CYCLE
("The Wheel of the Year")

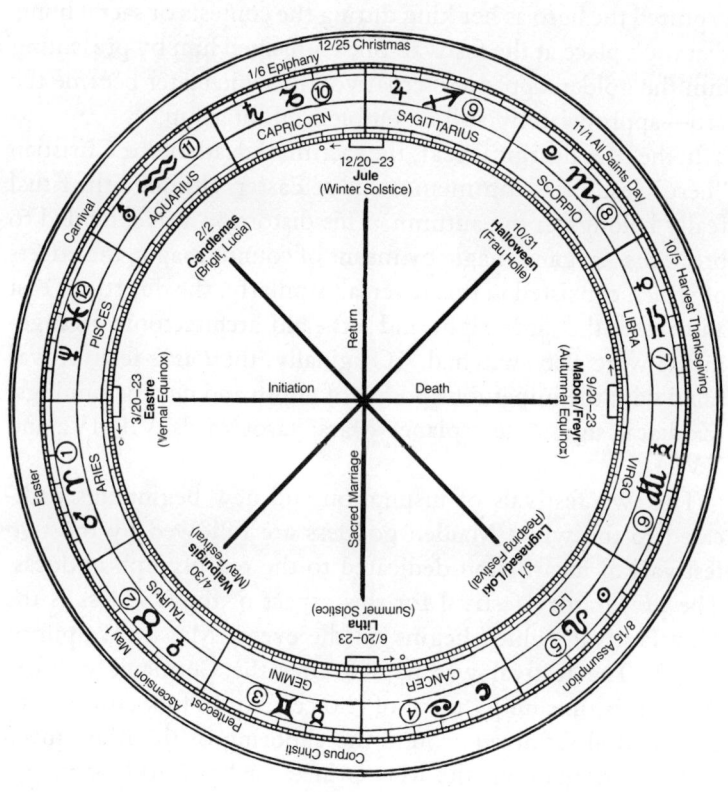

Easter eggs are not different colors but exclusively purplish red. In Greece, for example, a purplish red egg is baked in the center of a round cake resembling a full moon, since the Easter festival lasts until the first full moon after the vernal equinox.

The great ritual of this festival was the initiation of the hero-king by the Maiden goddess Eastre. Eastre vanquished and captured the hero as her king during the contests or sacral hunts that took place at the festival. She enthroned him by presenting him the golden apple of eternal youth, which later became the orb—appropriately, still an emblem of kingship.

In the later liturgical year, the sacrificial death of the Christian "hero" Jesus was commemorated at Easter, although the ritual really belongs in the autumn. This distortion was intended to break the "pagan" magic by means of countermagic, the effects of which consisted in this reversal; similarly, the directions east and west, the sides right and left, and architectonic arrangements were also switched.[14] Originally, the *Eastre* festival was filled with the impetuous power of youth and new beginnings. (Zodiacal sign Aries, planet Mars; tarot cards VII, IV, and XVI.)

The two festivals of inspiration and new beginnings dedicated to the white Maiden goddess are followed by the two festivals of incarnation dedicated to the red Nymph goddess. The preparatory festival for this aspect of the Goddess is the May Festival, which begins on the eve of May 1: Walpurgis Night. The festival was named after the Germanic goddess Walpurgis, meaning "place of choice," for in folk custom this time period revolved around the choosing of the May queen and her companion, the May prince, or "green/black man," who was considered the bringer of luck.[15] It was a purely erotic choice and a purely erotic luck. The May queen was celebrated as the most beautiful of women, and she chose her horned "green man" with a kiss. Only in patriarchal times is it the May prince who "kidnaps" the May queen or, as the "black man," makes passes at young girls and gets them sooty (Austria).

The "place of choice" was the dancing ground eagerly sought out for the May Dance and decorated with erotic symbols. Earlier, the "places of choice" were the ancient stone circles surrounding the menhir; later, they were the places around the Maypole in the middle of the village. A Maypole is a towering upright tree trunk painted with spirals from top to bottom. At the top, a wreath hangs from streamers decorated with garlands of eggs—an erotic symbol portraying the union of phallus (the pole) with vulva (the wreath) (Bavaria). The May Festival was never Christianized; in recent times it has been absurdly proclaimed European "Labor Day."[16]

This time of sensual joy definitely lasted until the first full moon after Walpurgis Night. The Christian feast of the Ascension falls near this time—obviously an attempt to create an ascetic counterbalance to pagan lust: people should look not to the fertile earth but to the ethereal heavens. The same is true of the Christian feast of Pentecost, which follows shortly thereafter (on the seventh Sunday after Easter). Only in folk custom does the "Pentecost Ox" still appear: a bull festooned with flowers. He is either the animal of Venus herself or the Egyptian-Cretan fertility hero in animal form, who carries his goddess on his back. Here, too, the Christian calendar reformers tried to curb this pagan spirit by turning Pentecost into the feast of their holy, ascetic, misogynist Holy Spirit. Instead of the goddess, the Holy Spirit descended from heaven and, in contrast to her, created life in the abstract. (Zodiacal sign Taurus, planet Venus, tarot cards III and V.)

The great Venus festival of Sacred Marriage took place at the summer solstice (June 20 to 23). The Goddess united with her chosen hero and blessed the fruitful abundance on earth. At the same time, she sustained the order of the world with her erotic power. The summer solstice is the festival of the

Celtic Moon goddess Litha, since the feminine power of the full moon is now at its climax, and the feminine principle illuminates the world. In European folk tradition, young couples jump over a fire or roll fire wheels down hills at the summer solstice. The fires are never symbols of the sun but always of the moon. That is clear from the "Easter fire," which is lighted on all mountains on the night of the full moon preceding Easter. They are fires of joy heralding the full moon and the beginning of the festival. At the same time, they are magic fires of purification. Even today the old rubbish of winter is burned in the Easter fire (Austria). Likewise, everything old is still symbolically burned in the "Saint John's fire" of the summer solstice, the fires of the harvest festival, and the "Saint Martin's fire" of All Saints' Day (Bavaria).

The Saint John's fire, which young couples leap over, is also the fire of erotic ecstasy given by the Moon goddess in her Venus aspect. Originally, the fire wheel was probably set in motion not on the night of the summer solstice but on the night of the next full moon, since the fire wheel symbolizes the spiral path of the moon. In the liturgical calendar, the Christian feast of Corpus Christi takes place immediately before the erotic festival of *Litha*. It is supposed to mean that the "body of the Lord," not the body of the Goddess, redeems the world. (Zodiacal sign Cancer; planet moon; tarot cards II, XVIII, and VI.)

With the festivals of *Eastre* and the summer solstice, the time of incarnation ends and the time of transformation begins: the passage through the depths, the pain that transforms. The third aspect of the Goddess—as the goddess of death and the re-wakener—remains in the foreground until the end of the year. At the same time, the significance of the hero increases as he grows into his most profound role by making his journey to the underworld. The next two festivals are therefore named for the hero: *Lugnasad* and *Mabon*.

August 1 marks the preparatory festival for the great sacred ritual of sacrifice. Now the Goddess appears as the reaper and mows the ripe grain with her sickle—a moon symbol. The spirit of the fertility hero dwells in the grain, and he symbolically falls victim to her reaping. Just as the grain is cut, threshed, milled, and baked in order to still the hunger of humanity and ensure its survival, the hero meets the same end a little later and thus becomes the hero of his people. The festival is called *Lugnasad,* a Celtic word meaning "marriage of Lug."[17] The Celtic god Lug—before he was patriarchalized—is related to the Norse god Loki and the Hellinistic Lucifer. He is the "light bearer" or "fire bearer," and—because of the great power of the sun at this time—this is his wedding. Ironically, it is also the preparation for his marriage with death. (Zodiacal sign Leo, star sun, tarot cards VIII and XIX.)

Reaping festivals lasted from August 1 until the next full moon, near the time of the Assumption in the Christian liturgical year.[18] The Assumption documents the dependence of women in a patriarchal religion, for it literally means that Mary did not *ascend* to heaven under her own power, as her son had, but was passively *assumed* to heaven *by him* after her death. That is the exact opposite of the meaning this time of year had in the matriarchal religion. In the matriarchal religion, the powerful Crone goddess, the ruler over the cosmos and fate, prepared the death of her son, the hero, and led him not to heaven but to the underworld. The Crone goddess's son could be reborn only through *her* grace, whereas in the absurd Christian version, it is the *son* who grants grace to the *mother* and causes *her* "rebirth" in heaven.

The Reaping Festival is followed by the ritual of sacrifice at the autumnal equinox (September 20 to 23). This festival lasts until the next full moon—the "harvest festival"—which is celebrated today only in rare instances. The harvest festival has become completely meaningless, and that is certainly no accident since it was one of the most important festivals in the matriarchal religion. The best fruits of the harvest were sacrificed to the Goddess as the people's entreaty for equal fertility for the following year. The same meaning was shared by the death of the hero-king, whose reign ended at this time; the Sphinx reminded him of this with the raised sword that weighed his fate. Instead of the love apple of summer, the Goddess now presented him with the pomegranate, the fruit of death; she became the deadly Venus for him. After his sacrifice, the hero was buried in the earth like the seeds sown at this time. The seeds and the sacrificed hero represented the people's hope for the rebirth of life the following spring.

With the decline of the matriarchal religion, a surrogate was sacrificed as the best offering in place of the hero-king: a male animal (a bull, a ram, or a goat). Eventually, only a "straw man" was used: a doll woven from stalks of grain. The straw man was hanged and then buried; sometimes he was also burned. He was disinterred the following spring, and there was rejoicing if he had green sprouts, which were considered a good omen (Greece, Canary Islands). This sacrificial festival is called *Mabon* after the Celtic sun hero, the son of Modron (Mother Earth). During the first half of the year, the sun god grows increasingly stronger and more radiant. During the second half of the year, he grows weak and pale and wastes away until, to the sorrow of his mother, he dies at the vernal equinox. The Celtic *Mabon* corresponds to the Germanic Freyr. (Zodiacal sign Libra; planet Venus; tarot cards XI, XII, and X.)

Mabon is followed by the last two festivals, both of which have a mysterious character. The Goddess manifests herself as the rewakener and reveals herself in her universality. Now is the time when the boundary between death and life is overcome. The preparatory festival is *Halloween* (October 31), a Celtic word meaning "holy woman" or "holy sister."[19] The "holy woman" is the Goddess herself, whom the Germanic peoples called Holla or Frau Holle. She is the goddess of the underworld; on the eve of Halloween, she opens her gates so that the dead can visit the living, and the living the dead. She has white hair, wears white robes, and rides a white horse; she is the legendary White Woman, who leads the procession of the dead (known as the *Perchten* in Bavaria).[20] Her adherents join her and follow the procession with jack-o'-lanterns as far as the abodes of the underworld—the fairyland, the paradisiacal realm under the earth.

In matriarchal cultures the abodes of the underworld were the gigantic burial mounds (dolmens), which one could enter like castles of the dead to hold cultic celebrations in the round vaults in front of the burial chambers. (The best example is in Newgrange, Ireland.) The sacrificed hero-king was interred there, and the death meal was brought to him so that his spirit might bless the living by abiding among them. Even today this is the time when people remember the dead: they visit their graves, decorate them with boughs and flowers, and place a small light on them (All Souls' Day). In matriarchal times, a table with food and drink was also prepared for the dead so that they might enter the houses and bless every family—for if one did not regale the dead, the good spirits could turn into evil ones.

In Christian times, the procession of Halloween or Frau Holle was turned into the Saint Martin's procession, in which Saint Martin rides a white horse and leads a procession of children carrying paper lanterns (Germany). Thus, the riding goddess became a man, and the remembrance of the matriarchal ancestors and heroes became the remembrance of the Christian saints (All Saints' Day).[21] In matriarchal times, the Halloween festival communicated the mysterious knowledge that the underworld and the upper world are interrelated and that death is not a final end but a metamorphosis, a transformation in the depths. (Zodiacal sign Scorpio, planet Pluto, tarot cards XIII and XX.)

Halloween is followed by the most beautiful ritual festival of the mythic year: *Weihenächte* ("nights of commemoration") in Germanic, *Modronight* ("nights of the mother") in Celtic, and Christmas in English.[22] It begins at the winter solstice (December 20 to 23) and ends on the first full moon in the first week of January: the Epiphany (from the Greek *epiphaneia,* meaning "manifestation"). In the Germanic cultic regions the feast was also called *Jule* (Yule), a name derived from the Old Norse *jól,* meaning "wheel."[23] The "wheel of the year" has now made a complete revolution and the cycle is fulfilled.

At the precise moment of the winter solstice, the women of the matriarchal cults reentered the huge dolmens to await the first rays of the sun. The dolmens were ingeniously designed so that the sun rising at the winter solstice cast a beam through a light well at the entrance and into the interior, weakly illuminating the cultic space and the middle grave chamber—the king's grave (Newgrange, Ireland). Thus, light has conquered darkness, life has conquered death, and the exultation was great. The hero-king was now reborn as the child of the Goddess, just as the sun was reborn from the winter night. This childbirth was not only a sacral and symbolic occurrence but a very real event: at the same time, the tribal queen or high priestess gave birth to a child, who was designated as the future hero-king. Thus, the hope for eternal rebirth and eternal life was fulfilled once again.

We all know the traditional Christmas customs in which mother and child are venerated, but in the Christian version they have become Mary and Jesus. Now the son is divine and the mother human; earlier it was the exact opposite. But children still receive gifts, just as the hero-child had in earlier times. An evergreen branch or tree (mistletoe, pine)—symbol of eternal life—is still brought into the house and decorated with golden apples (paradise apples) or silver balls (moons).

During the preparatory time, the Christian Advent wreath appears in place of the matriarchal wreath. Its four candles symbolize the quadripartite year, which is now fulfilled, and point to the resurrection of Lucia, the goddess of light. Heaven and earth are full of good spirits ("angels"). Everywhere stars twinkle, indicating that the goddess is the cosmic night, the entire universe. She descends from heaven in a sleigh or a wagon pulled by white stags and mysteriously gives gifts to children. She is the Celtic goddess Liban or the Greek Artemis, the goddess in the figure of a child—thus heralding her rejuvenation as the Maiden goddess in the coming year. In Christian times, she was turned into the artificial figure of Santa Claus (Saint Nicholas), and once again it is a man who descends from heaven.

The concluding festival of the winter solstice period is the Epiphany, the festival of the "manifestation." The young, delicate light is carried—in the form of a child or a star—from the darkness of the underworld into the upper world in order to transform it. Not only the new light but the Goddess herself appears to humanity—this time in her triadic form, since all her aspects have already been experienced individually. In her triadic form, the Goddess journeys through the land and blesses each house. In fact, a folk custom still exists in which three women wearing long robes—the first in white, the second in red, and the third in black—and carrying a child, walk through the village and bless each house with three signs of the cross (Austria).

In the Christian liturgical year, those three women were turned into the Three Kings, who follow their star and do the same things the three holy women did. However, they do not bear witness to the epiphany of the Triple goddess but to the epiphany of their lord, the patriarchal God. (Zodiacal sign

Capricorn; planet Saturn; tarot cards XVII, IX, and XV, as well as XXI and I.)

EXCURSUS:
ON INTERPRETING TAROT CARDS IN THE SEASONAL CYCLE

Within the scope of the present study, it is impossible to give a detailed analysis of the complicated correspondences between matriarchal mythology, the seasonal cycle, astrology, and tarot. Since the patriarchal distortions must also be taken into consideration—especially in the case of astrology and tarot—I will reserve such an analysis for a future study; for the time being I must confine myself to general remarks.[24]

In my view, tarot cards—as well as astrology—can be properly interpreted only within the context of the seasonal cycle of the matriarchal festivals, since those festivals form the connecting link between matriarchal mythology and its (secret) continuation in astrology and tarot. If one examines tarot and astrology outside this context, the interpretations run the risk of being overly influenced by our contemporary personal and social conceptions. For that reason, I regard all previous interpretations of tarot and astrology as too subjective.

In my description of the matriarchal cycle of festivals, I hinted at correspondences to tarot, and now I will briefly delineate them. I shall demonstrate that the entire series of Major Arkana cards fits into the seasonal cycle. In other words, the Major Arkana cards basically illustrate the meaning of the matriarchal festival cycle and are, so to speak, the "illustrated bible" of the matriarchal religion.

There are two cards for each major and each minor festival. The first card represents the feminine principle—the Goddess; the second card represents the masculine principle—the hero. For each of the four major ritual festivals there is also a third card symbolizing the universal energy or power of this ritual (based on the Waite Deck).

Candlemas. Card XIV portrays the goddess of inspiration, who intermingles all that exists in order to create new things; she is the winged creative spirit wearing a wreath of light around her head. Card 0 pictures the fool, the man inspired by the white light of the goddess. He is the poet, the singer, who in his ecstatic inspiration forgets everything around him.

Vernal Equinox. Card VII is the Amazon card; it depicts the youthful, militant goddess on her wagon. (She was later masculinized.) She tames the powers of darkness (winter) and light (summer) and harnesses them for the race. She captures her hero and enthrones him in card IV. (Card IV should portray a *young* man, not an old one; only in patriarchy are powerful kings old.) Card XVI symbolizes the energy of this festival: the Mars energy, which demolishes the dark prisons of winter and represents the beginning of the mythic year.

Walpurgis (May Festival). This is the festival of Venus on the bull. Card III represents Venus herself, the goddess who causes everything to bloom. Card V originally represented the sensual, fire red bull-hero, but the patriarchal interpretation has turned him into a chaste pope/high priest.

Summer Solstice. Card II shows the full moon at the climax of her feminine power. She is the red Moon-Venus, the open shell (in the background), the great sorceress, Hathor in erotic ecstasy—not the ethereal nun, as she is portrayed today. Card XVIII illustrates the moonscape: the mysterious, dangerous path the hero walks inside the goddess's body. (Unfortunately, the hero is now omitted from this card, and the erotic character of both cards has been eradicated.) Card VI symbolizes the energy of this festival: love. The sunlight is now at its climax.

Lugnasad (Reaping Festival). Card VIII shows that the power of the sun (eroticism) has grown so hot that the harvest goddess must subdue it: she closes the fire lion's mouth and initiates the hero's downfall. Card XIX portrays the radiantly naïve sun hero on the sun horse; it is now high summer.

Autumnal Equinox. In Card XI, the goddess appears as Fate with her scale and sword; the time of the hero's reign is past. Card XII portrays the sacrificed hero. He is hanging head down, a visual representation of the descent, the setting of the sun. Card X conveys the significance of the festival: it pictures the wheel of the year and of life, which is, at the same time, the wheel of fate. The wheel marks the downward turn for the hero. He is reminded of this by the Sphinx, the calendar emblem who sits above the wheel of the year and holds in her hand the same sword of judgment as the goddess does in card XI.

Halloween. Card XIII portrays the Crone goddess, the "holy woman" riding her white horse and opening the gates to the underworld. (In the patriarchal interpretation, all that remains is a horrible masculine skeleton—expressing a typically patriarchal conception of death.) Card XX originally depicted the transformation in the depths that effected the mystical interchange between death and life. (The card was later turned into a depiction of the Last Judgment, the Christian resurrection with reward and punishment.)

Winter Solstice. Card XVII depicts the goddess as the creative Virgin Mother, who draws and pours the water of life onto the earth in order to revive it. She brings the hero into the world as the new light, the bright star. Surrounded by nothing but stars, she is the goddess of the cosmos, the goddess of the mystical night, of the *Weihenacht*. Card IX portrays the hero as an old man (the old year), who carefully and protectively carries the newborn star—the young hero (the new year)—through the winter night and into the world. The old man is also Saturn or Janus the double-headed: the threshold where the old ends and the new begins. Card XV symbolizes the power and universal significance of the festival: the sun (light, eroticism) is now at the very bottom, i.e., in the depths, enclosed in the dark womb of the earth, from which it will rise again. Hence, card XV is the exact counterpart of card VI (but not in the sense of good or evil, as in the patriarchal interpretation that made card XV into the "devil"). In other words, card VI portrays the sun (light, eroticism) at the *zenith,* from which it will descend; and card XV portrays the sun at the *nadir,* the underworld, from which it will rise again. Both cards symbolize the turning point.

Manifestation (Epiphany). The last two cards synthesize all the events of the mythic year and symbolize the Goddess and the hero in the manifestation of all their aspects. Card XXI depicts the Goddess dancing in space: the universe. She holds a magic wand in each hand: creation and annihilation. She is surrounded by a wreath of suns and planets: the zodiac (not a wreath of leaves, as in the watered-down version). The symbols of the four major ritual festivals (the four elements, the four quarters of the heavens) appear in the four corners of the card. Card I portrays the hero, who has now been transformed from the inspired fool into the sage, the initiate into the mysteries of the four major rituals he has just experienced. He holds in his hand the magic wand given him by the Goddess as a sign of his honored position: he has metamorphosed into the magician, who knows the magic of the four elements. The effects of his magic are revealed in the Minor Arkana cards, which represent all possible combinations of the four elements.

The "Lunisolar Play"

Let us now give our imagination free rein and consider a matriarchal art-utopia as a complex seasonal ritual: the "Lunisolar Play." The "Lunisolar Play" contains the entire structure of matriarchal mythology, i.e., all the aspects of the Goddess and the hero. Moreover, it makes no detours via "high priestesses" or "high priests." Quite the contrary: the female performers directly represent the Goddess and the hero themselves.

I intentionally speak only of female performers and not of a male participant (the hero). Having been robbed for millennia of our own spirituality and its sacred practice, we women have enough to do in rediscovering our own spirituality and, through it, gaining a new understanding of ourselves. We cannot bypass our present situation. Consequently, the "Lunisolar Play" is, first and foremost, a process of complex self-discovery. We must enter into this process in order to overcome the prevailing distorted concepts of "femininity," or conventional female roles, and obtain a conception of the independence, the power, and the myriad attributes embodied in the "Goddess" as our guiding idea. We must enter into this process in order to recognize the masculine, heroic side within us—which has nothing to do with patriarchal "masculinity" and its destructive ambivalence. We must enter into this process in order to recover our complete identity with its two sides: the contradictory, tension-filled totality of our ego.

The "Lunisolar Play" is a complex process among women through which we can acquire new knowledge about and new experiences and relationships with one another. Through the play, we women experience ourselves and one another in an entirely different way than in the usual framework and the usual roles: the participants experience both their divine and their heroic sides. One, three, or nine women play the part of the Goddess, and one woman the part of the hero. The distribution of roles depends entirely on the characteristics or powers that each woman wants to discover in herself and in the others. Each part remains the same throughout the one-year cycle; the roles can be changed at the end of the cycle. It is only in this way that a collective and, at the same time, an individual experience can take place.

Given the present state of consciousness of most men and the prevailing patriarchal order of our society, it would be premature to perform matriarchal rituals with a man, as I have already said. Nevertheless, the "Lunisolar Play" does allow for that third possibility. The "Lunisolar Play" is a utopia that can be realized only within the context of the entirely different value system of matriarchal mythology as a new relationship of women to men and men to women. Only when we have re-created that value system will we make inroads in contemporary society—as hope for the future.

All the images, scenes, and descriptions given below are meant to be suggestions, not prescriptions. Although I follow the structural scheme of matriarchal mythology precisely, the structure is so rich that there are many other possible ways of realizing it in rituals. It is like trying to decipher an ancient language. In order to learn it, we must study it for a long time, pay close attention to its precise details, and heed its rules. When we have finally mastered the language, we can express ourselves freely in it and create a great variety of possibilities of expression without violating its fundamental rules. Matriarchal mythology has become accessible through its structure, its pattern of symbols, and its many individual mythic stories. To act in accordance with and to absorb ourselves in matriarchal mythology is an attitude of esteem and respect for the ancient female knowledge preserved in it. But that does not preclude our imagination: we need the full range of our creative imagination to comprehend the true significance of the ancient images—and their meanings are indeed profound and multi-layered—and to adapt them freely to our current conditions and enrich them with meanings relevant for us today. In this way, we can succeed in translating the *ancient* language of female knowledge into a *new* language of female knowledge and thereby recover the images, voices, and words that have been lost to us for such a long time.

I am currently testing several possibilities for realizing matriarchal mythology in rituals. I celebrated the seasonal cycle in private rituals for quite some time, but I am now celebrating the seasonal cycle with other women and will continue to do so in the future. In this respect my art-utopia is neither a mere art form nor a mere utopia; it is already *reality* to some extent, and it is gratifying to be able to say that. The following suggestions for the individual festivals are therefore the result of my research, my imagination, and the experiences gained from our joint celebrations. Other women may have different experiences, make different associations, and translate matriarchal mythology into different images. But, as in any language, I hope that we may follow the same rules in order to retain the measure of commonality necessary for communicating with one another, even in the diversity of our dialects.

CANDLEMAS (*Brigit/Lucia*)

The seasonal ritual begins with Candlemas, the festival of the goddess Lucia or Brigit. At this festival, we can wear a white symbol—a white band, a white kerchief, or a white piece of jewelry—or we can dress entirely in white. We can begin with a walk through the winter landscape, which is also white. There are delicate colors and delicate sounds, particularly in the evening: the snow reflects the light of the sky; twigs snap; dry leaves rustle when we brush against them; our steps crunch in the snow. Under the snow the seeds and seedlings await the new beginning. We can incorporate those colors and sounds into our ritual—as exquisite music, as the hues of our clothing, as the colors of the food on the festival table we set.

We can also walk in a spiral on a field or in a yard. It is a slow, meditative walk inward, into concentration, into stillness; and then outward, into release, into liberation, into the vast landscape. For Candlemas has less to do with a "mass" than with the word *maze,* which means "spiral" or "labyrinth"; therefore, it is the spiral of the returning light that we form in the snow with our feet. We can carry candles or lanterns into the center of the spiral and let them burn down in the snow: the primordial sparks of fire, the hope for new intellectual and spiritual growth.

At the climax of the ritual we gather around a fireplace where we fan the fire of Brigit, the fire of new creation. A caldron with a hot, glowing drink boils on the fire. It is the caldron of the wind, of the spirit, of intoxication, of poetic ecstasy— the caldron of inspiration and, at the same time, a symbol of the Goddess herself. We throw all our wishes and hopes for the coming year into the caldron and then ladle it empty. In doing so, we are repeating an ancient gesture: the ladling with two chalices. We ladle the drink with one chalice and pour it into the other chalice to cool it. We pour the drink back and forth three times, mirroring the gesture of the Goddess, who gives and takes, takes and gives; who pours everything from above to below and from below to above in order to re-create from chaos.

While we drink, talk, laugh, recite, and sing, we can light candles in the fire and discuss whom we will choose as the Maiden goddess. Perhaps we will choose her through a poetry competition. In any case, it should be a woman who yearns with all her might to be the Maiden goddess and has long been searching for her out of deep motivation. She should have the courage to tell us her motive openly. In this way we will find the right woman.

The chosen one is crowned with a wreath of candles, and then, with a gesture befitting the Maiden goddess, she chooses all of us to be her companions during her white phase. Thus each of us represents an aspect of the Maiden goddess. We can then form a fiery circle and walk in procession outdoors or in the house. It is most beautiful to dance and intensify the dance until we appear to fly. It is the dance of the "firebird" in the fairy talk, the dance of the winged light—a figure of the Goddess herself, for she is the fire of inspiration, which now flies into the world.

We can also choose our hero at this festival. The hero, too, should be the one among us who has the deepest desire to experience the true significance of this figure, the one who wishes to experience the "other side." The hero is the partner of the goddesses, who mold his image and his character. He serves them with devotion. He is their counterpart, their mirror image through which they experience their own feminine strength. A circle of goddesses is cooperation; a circle of goddesses with a hero is cooperation and opposition. A circle of goddesses with a hero offers greater variety and the chance for intensive confrontation—with the hero and with the "heroic" within us.

But the role of the hero presupposes much knowledge and insight. It is not advisable to give the role to a woman who has never had spiritual heroic experiences; it is better for women to celebrate without the hero than with a weak hero. I also strongly advise against having a man play this role. Men have not yet attained the level of intellectual consciousness or the spiritual maturity necessary for assuming such a central role in the framework of matriarchal spirituality: they consciously and unconsciously harbor too many patriarchal clichés. It is hard enough for women to discern—from among all the patriarchal distortions also residing in us—the profound matriarchal content in the images of the Goddess and her hero. We have enough to do on our own without including men. We have not yet reached a secure enough position to be able to integrate men with their innumerable problems, regardless of how willing many men may be. Aside from that, a female hero is a very charming hero: "he" provides many opportunities for perplexing play and merriment.

On Candlemas our hero remains in the background. He is

the poet inspired by the Goddess, the innocent fool in a mul-
ticolored robe reflecting the white rays of the spirit of the
Goddess. He brings merriment, dance, and play; but he does
not yet sense the abyss into which this beginning will lead him.

VERNAL EQUINOX (*Eastre*)
Eastre is the first major festival in the seasonal cycle, the festival
of the white Maiden goddess, heralded by Candlemas. It is
initiation as rebirth, as introduction into the mysteries of the
Goddess. That means we still have much to communicate to
one another: we must impart our knowledge and, through
group meditation, begin to weave the bond, the net, that unites
us. "Teaching" and "meditation" need not be sedentary activities. They can merge into dynamic forms: a walk outside or
a dance with slow, fluid movements activating an inner stream
of images. The movements can evolve into our "*Eastre* Walk,"
a ritual procession or a ritual pilgrimage to a local ancient holy
place, whose history we narrate to ourselves as we walk. Or
perhaps we can climb a lookout tower or a mountaintop, where
we can feel the power of the spring wind as it sets the atmosphere and the land into motion and releases them from the
numbness of winter. We perceive the fresh, sharp breath of
the Goddess; we see her dashing through the clouds as the
huntress; we sense the joy and high spirits of this new beginning. We can sing with the wind or for the burgeoning shoots
boring through the soil and craving growth. During our walk
we can also purify the woods and nature, just as we have
purified ourselves for this festival. We can bring along dry
twigs, old wood, and carelessly discarded litter to set an *Eastre*
fire, which will ultimately consume the old around us and
within us and, through its purifying power, make way for the
new.

The next morning brings *Eastre* Day in its spendor. We can
consecrate to Eastre, the goddess of spring, eggs on which we

have painted or written our wishes. Or we can bake an *Eastre* cake, as Greek women still do today: round and yellow like the full moon, and in the middle a purplish red egg. Perhaps we can also bake an *Eastre* rabbit, the symbol of the fertility of this time. We place everything into baskets decorated with flowers and boughs, and hold our feast in the open air after the initiation ritual.

We begin this great ritual with a Diana hunt. Our chosen Maiden goddess is Diana. While we hide from her in the forest, she cuts a switch for each of us. She searches for and hunts down each individual and, with a blow of the switch, initiates her as a companion of Diana; we thereby gain tangible knowledge that we have truly been initiated. Each woman receives her switch, this wild scepter, from Diana's hand as a sign of our inchoate wildness, our strength, and our power to distinguish and divide, to set limits and to maintain them when necessary. We can then enjoy a Diana bath in a brook, where we slap the water with our switches or throw stones to splash one another—an appropriate "baptism."

Finally, with us as her companions, Diana sets out to hunt the "stag." In ancient myths and tales, the bands of Amazon huntresses themselves capture their hero (who wears a stag mask or carries a stag symbol). For a year the Amazons hold the hero spellbound in their circle, which he cannot escape, and send him through the school of the goddess. That is just how Celtic fairies dealt with heroes who wandered into their magic gardens or behind their wall of air. Thus every hero is a pupil for a year—regardless of how much he may already know—and at the end of the year he is initiated by the goddess, since he cannot achieve initiation on his own.

We hunt our stag-hero with our switches and, climbing a hill or a mountain, surround him on all sides. In his flight he must leave behind all the inclinations, precipitousness, and barriers of his pride and false vanity, and realize that he is at our mercy. Menacing in our flowing robes and wild hairdos of twigs and leaves, and screaming shrilly like flying Sirens, Harpies, and Sphinxes, we close in on him until we have driven him to the point where the direction reverses and he can no longer escape—on the summit. Amid our laughter and frenetic screams, he must look us in the eyes—face-to-face with all the strange and unknown things that await him in the school of the goddess. At the summit we drive him into our enchanted circle demarcated by stones, sticks, or fluttering scarves representing the fairies' magic wall of air. Diana or her companions give the hero the blow of initiation with the switch; it is the "lightning," the ray of recognition upon his entry into the realm of the knowledge of the goddess's mysteries. She has struck him and he is stunned by her. He perceives her severe presence as an incarnate light. He is astonished to find himself in a completely new place, at the beginning of a new path that will lead him from the summit, through the middle regions, and into the depths of the otherworld.

Diana hands the hero a golden bough, the scepter that will guide him on his dangerous journey. Her companions can also give him a gift, which is also an ordeal because it contains a riddle the hero must solve in the course of his journey. In this way the hero becomes the sacral king and companion of the goddess for the year; and, if he solves the riddle, he becomes the companion of her companions.

The entire ritual is a dramatic dance accompanied by the singing, laughter, and birdcalls of the Sirens and the Sphinxes. Very delicate, bright, glasslike sounds fill the air. Music is made by an aeolian harp of twigs moving in the wind. Everything that happens is simultaneously intentional and spontaneous. The initiation through the blow of the switch, the goddess's bolt of rays, is no game but reality—the ecstatic shock, the mystery of recognition.

WALPURGIS/MAY FESTIVAL (*Birth of Venus*)

The Walpurgis/May Festival is the festival of preparation for the Sacred Marriage at the summer solstice. The Goddess now changes from the white to the red phase. Venus is born; she is youthful and bridelike, as delicate as the blossoms of the season and equally vulnerable. The goddess needs protection, and it is accorded her by the "witches," the wise women, the midwives, the protectresses of the "religion" of cosmic love. On the eve of the birth of Venus (Walpurgis Night), the witches perform their wild, orgiastic dances; with their noise they ward off bad weather and evil ghosts and demons who could harm the young Venus. In this way, they help her from the darkness of night into the light of the dawning day, her birthday.

We can celebrate Walpurgis Night in a great variety of ways; there are no limits to our imagination. A good beginning is the "metamorphosis" in which we change into bizarre figures by painting our bodies and donning twigs and veils. We experience and transform our own faces, hands, feet—our entire bodies. Walpurgis Night is literally the festival of sensual love, and all our senses should be involved.

Then we dance as much, as wildly, and as crazily as we please. It is best to dance in a secluded meadow in the forest; to fill the air with the sounds of rattles and clapping stones, sticks, and metal; to scream animal calls; and to wave torches, which cast their restless light on our ghostly forms. While we find nothing sinister about this, we would appear unearthly to anyone who might see us. But no one does see us, for we are covertly uncanny. We are protected—just as we protect the young Venus, who perhaps manifests herself in the form of a gushing spring in the meadow or a budding tree in the middle of our dancing ground.

Suddenly we hear the hero blowing his pipe. He is roaming through the night as the "ram" or the "bull" and wants to hunt the witches. Like Pan, the satyrs, and the fauns, the hero has a pipe and he performs a "satyr play," a comedy. He gives a love bite to every witch he catches. Of course, it is not easy to catch us, because we witches defend ourselves: we box, wrestle, and fight with him; we hit him with our torches, scratch out his eyes, jump on his back and ride him. Very reluctantly we accept his invitation to dance with the Red goddess. It is best when everything is grotesque and silly, and the night echoes with piercing screams and laughter. In the end, we take his pipe from him and pass it to the one we have chosen to be the Red goddess.

The next day our Red goddess leads the dance around the Maypole. For the Maypole we select a budding tree, a stake, or an ancient menhir, if there is one in the area. We decorate it with a wreath and hang garlands of red eggs from it. Then we wind streamers—each woman has brought one in her favorite color—around the Maypole by walking in an increasingly tight spiral around it. Or we invent a different type of streamer dance. The dance lasts until we sense the presence of the goddess of love and the unfolding of the myriad colors and forms of her love within us: Venus is born.

After the dance around the Maypole, we can have a meal outside and a fresh herbal drink. Or we and our bull-hero can perform a dance similar to that of the bull leapers at the Cretan Minoan games. Or we can festoon the bull-hero with flowers and our colorful streamers, bite him, and then lead him home in a triumphal procession. Venus transforms the bull's horn into a female symbol: the cornucopia.

Summer Solstice (*Litha*)

The summer solstice is the festival of Sacred Marriage, in which the powerful eroticism of Venus comes to the fore. It is the festival of plenty and fulfillment, and reveals the creative and motherly aspect of the goddess of love: she is the creator and preserver of all life on the land and in the sea. With this power, the goddess heals all rifts, splits, and inner strife and restores the original wholeness—within us as well. What heals is holy, which is why this festival—as well as the mystical festival of rebirth at the winter solstice—is the holiest in the seasonal cycle.

If we want to celebrate the sanctity of love in the name of the goddess, we must first seek her scenery in nature. If we celebrate at the sea, we are near her primordial element. We can swim in the water, bathe in the sand, make ourselves heavenly clothes of grass, leaves, ivy, or bast and entwine roses in our hair. We can collect seashells and starfish and use them to decorate a magnificent festival table of sand. On it we set bowls of blue, red, and yellow berries, goblets of honey and milk, and baskets filled with the most sumptuous fruits—heaps of colorful spheres such as cherries, plums, oranges, and melons. Nothing should be missing from the paradisiacal abundance with which we honor the goddess of fertility. The waves create the festival music, which we need imitate only with flutes and soft drums—the male and female instruments. It is a Dionysian revel of unending joy.

Or we celebrate in the mountains or on hills in the forest. We climb so high that the landscape extends around us in its nuptial splendor: the dark raiment of spruces, the soft female shapes of Alpine pastures with their radiant flowers, the resplendence of mountaintops with the last summer snow. We search the area for a brook or a waterfall for a refreshing bath. And if we find a spring watering the moss around it, we celebrate it as Venus, as the womb of the earth opening to pour forth the water of life and of death.

At this festival the dancing should be incessant—first as a group, then individually, and finally as a group again. To prevent the dance from becoming haphazard and chaotic, we build ourselves a dancing ground: a circle, a spiral, or a labyrinth. At the sea we construct it with shells or sand, in the mountains with sticks or stones. We dance alternately but incessantly. Each woman dances the expression of her love or the figure of the goddess of love, who she herself now is: Venus, Aphrodite, Ishtar, Lakshmi, Freya, Morrigan, Hathor, or whatever name she was called. The other women make music with flutes and drums, rattles and string; they cause copper and clay to clatter and ring; they cause water to roar by pouring it into pitchers; they cause fire to hiss by pouring water on it. In this way they amplify the roaring of the sea or the rustling of the trees. We do not even stop dancing at night; and Aphrodite Urania, the heavenly Venus, appears among the stars. We can build a ring of brushwood around our dancing ground and set it on fire—the round Saint John's fire, the "fire wheel." We can also build proper fire wheels of brushwood and set them rolling.

At the climax of the festival, we consecrate our chalices in the sea or in the spring. In our hands, the chalices are symbols of Venus and her companions. We place all our wishes for love into them, draw the water, and bring it with us to the dancing ground. Our Red goddess, Venus, whom we chose at the previous festival, rests in the center of the labyrinth as we surround her in the splendor of our individual, highly personal beauty. Then the hero appears; he longs for Venus and is ready to follow the "dangerous" path to its end for her sake. But he must reach the center of the labyrinth without losing his way. At the entrance he makes a daring leap over the fire, which every hero must do if he is to reach the sleeping Venus. In fulfillment of ancient fertility magic, the way will open to him. But first he must confront the red-robed companions of Venus in the passages of the labyrinth. Each engages him in a dance, shows him a form of love, and has him drink from her chalice. In this way we mold his image, for he is the devoted partner for women's love desires.

Finally he reaches the center of the labyrinth and awakens Venus with a kiss. She rises and begins her oceanic dance of consecration. She wears nothing save her golden girdle, which she finally loosens and uses to cast her spell over him. She intensifies the dance and presents him with her shell, the ancient gesture of feminine power. Then both Venus and the hero dance together until their movements achieve increasing unison, a tension-filled harmony: each is the erotic mirror image of the other. They gradually incorporate more and more polarities into their dance—heaven and earth, land and sea, sun and moon, yin and yang—and the dance gradually builds into an ecstatic discharge between the myriad poles. Thus Venus and the hero consummate their cosmic, symbolic, spiritual, and real marriage. With both guidance and spontaneity, the goddess and the hero themselves invent the entire sublime action through which they animate and sustain the world—until the lightning stroke of Eros transports them to a distant place.

REAPING FESTIVAL (*Lugnasad*)
Like the summer heat, the fire and passion of the sun hero reach their climax. The hero now reveals himself in his full glory, which is why the festival is named after him: *Lugnasad* ("the marriage of Lug"). He reveals himself to the goddesses in many disguises and forms: he is cunning and capable of metamorphoses like Proteus or fiery like Lug or Loki the fire bearer. His passion knows no bounds, and it threatens to dry up the gentle water and destroy the harvest. The goddesses must subdue him and reduce his light. And, since there are not only high points in life, the ascent is necessarily followed by the descent. It is time for the dark half of the year, for the Black goddess.

We choose the Black goddess from among us and crown

her with a wreath of grass stalks or poppies. She is now the reaper, the clever Hecate, the goddess of the harvest and the goddess of trance, sleep, and death. She makes us her dark companions, and we walk through the fields with shiny crescent-shaped sickles in our hands and cut the stalks. The color of our robes is transformed from poppy red to jet black, and when we shield ourselves with straw hats against the piercing sun, we look like meridional women farmers or archaic women. We sing in a monotone, and the grain rustles as it falls.

Fruit is also harvested at this time, and wild, luxuriant shrubs and trees are cut down. In this way, Hecate brings thousandfold death to the plants to stay the hunger of humanity, thus revealing the matriarchal conception of death—as the promotion of life. Death is neither a brutal end nor an annihilation but a dying release of energy that will multiply into new life, just as many more blades will grow from the stubble of each harvested stalk.

During the ritual activity of the reapers, the hero continually reappears in various metamorphoses: as a ram or a faun in the grain, as a stag in the forest, as a talking raven on the branches of the trees. He surprises the reapers, disturbs, and amuses them. Then, as the snake or the dragon, the hero dances in the night-enshrouded field; he returns in the morning as the wind or the rainbow and, above all, as the blazing, golden sun. He plays and sings; he conjures and bewitches. He is the "trickster" who fulfills the wishes of the goddesses with his metamorphoses and enjoys their love in the fields. He refuses to believe that his "high time" is drawing to an end.

Hecate and her companions capture the hero in their circle one evening. Because he is threatening to become independent, we seize the dancing sun by the hair or by his rays, and cut them with a sharp blow of our sickles. This robs the hero of his erotic power and he falls into our hands, into the hands of

Hecate's companions. Since the hero is also the spirit of the grain, we treat him as we did the ripe grain, and thus the hero himself is "harvested." We slit open his skin (his robes) with the ritual sickles, and thus he is reaped. We seize him and shake him thoroughly, and thus he is threshed. We pull off his skin (his robes), and thus he is stripped of his chaff. We turn him through our hands as through a millstone, and thus he is milled. From the meal we bake bread and break it into pieces, and thus the hero is "torn to pieces"; and his body, like the loaf of bread, gives us life.

We can depict the "tearing to pieces" of the hero—like this whole harvest story—in a ritual dance-play in which the hero opens his energy currents and transmits them to us, for the ritual teaches him self-sacrifice. Any true sacrifice (a very abused word) is a *self-sacrifice*. The hero's death is a fruitful death, as he realizes now for the first time. The "sacrifice" of the hero is the original action of every sacral meal, during which the true face of the hero becomes visible behind his many masks. The hero does not keep his energies to himself—he sacrifices them for the development of life now and in the coming year, and for further development on a higher plane. (As we "tear the hero to pieces," each participant must remember which part of the hero she has taken so that we can piece him back together correctly upon his "healing" in the underworld. Otherwise we would fare like Isis, who frantically searched for the last piece of her Osiris until she finally found it in the lotus flower.)

Autumnal Equinox (*Mabon*)

The autumnal equinox, also called the harvest thanksgiving feast, is a great and serious festival.[25] Now the path—which had begun at the summit and led through the middle zone of land and sea—leads into the underworld. The passage to the underworld is the most difficult part of the journey, because now the goddesses themselves must descend into the depths, enter the dark realm, and dispatch the hero to the depths, which he cannot reach under his own power: he must die. The hero willingly accepts his death; his love of the goddess leads him through all her realms, and even in the depths he wants to encounter her and share in her wisdom. His love is a sure guide; through it he learns to understand and endure his death as a passage, as the gate to the otherworld. Now the hero's spiritual range and heroic power come to the fore, which is why this festival is also named after him in the Celtic region—*Mabon,* the earth-mother goddess Modron's solar son, who is now descending.

For this festival we build a thanksgiving altar in the empty fields and on it place fruits, twigs, colorful leaves, and pine-cones—or gifts we wish to sacrifice personally. We can also sacrifice the symbols of the hero: his stag antlers, his bull horns, his dragon or snake skin. We do this to show the hero that he is the best, most beautiful sacrifice we can present to the earth. We sacrifice the hero with a heavy heart, but the cosmic balance of giving and taking is at stake: we present his life to the earth, just as she has given us nourishment and life during the year.

But as goddesses we first must experience our own descent into the underworld. Like Inanna-Ishtar of the Sumero-Babylonian myth, each of us must go alone through the seven "gates of hell" and become a corpse in order to learn what death is. Our chosen Black goddess leads us; she is now Hecate, the goddess of death. We can pass through the gates of hell only by presenting each gate with something of ourselves—a piece of jewelry, a lock of hair, a barrette, shoes, a dress. We must also offer a pride and joy, an anxiety, an illusion. We begin the journey in divine garb, in full array, but at its end we arrive poor and naked at the last gate of hell. We thus fare no differently from all the dead, who must leave everything behind on this journey.

When each of us passes through the seventh gate, we sink to the ground and become a "corpse." By doing so we can perhaps have a personal death experience. But now the goddess of the underworld metamorphoses into the loving Persephone, goddess of the depths. She takes us into her arms, sprinkles us with the water of death and of life, and breathes new life into us. She wraps us in magnificent silver robes and leads us into her realm, the paradisiacal fairy world under the earth, where there is no more sorrow, no illness and old age, no heat and cold, but only eternal spring and eternal youth. Everything glows in rosy light, and we hear the fairy music of the harp, which makes us cry and laugh, sleep and awaken, die and come back to life again.

But the hero does not yet know what we now know. He cannot enter the realm of the underworld on his own—we *send* him there through the seven gates of hell. In the hero's eyes we now appear terrible: our figures are veiled in black, our faces unrecognizable behind a terrifying Gorgon mask. Like the Furies, we encircle the hero in a hissing ring, from which there is no escape. We show him the symbols of his death: seeds placed in the earth—as was he—in order to create new life; the scales of fate, which are now tipped against him; the spindle with his thread of life, which we now cut; or the pomegranate, from which the seeds fall like drops of blood when it bursts. We ask our hero if he consents to die, for every step depends on his willingness. If he is truly a "hero," he will consent, for he is not afraid. He has received our love and, through its power, will overcome death.

We lead the hero through the seven gates of hell, and during his passage we make him experience all the fear and loss we ourselves had felt. We thrust our experiences on him; we burden him with them. Hence we are not alone in our experience of death: the hero shares it with each of us; he takes it from us and frees us of it. Dealing with suffering creatively is the power of the hero; it is also what distinguishes him from all the "victims" and "martyrs" of patriarchy.

At the seventh gate we make the hero "journey to the depths," just as the sun is now journeying to the depths, its light extinguishing. We put him in the mystical stance of hanging head down from the "tree of life." In that way he recognizes the world from the opposite perspective. He observes life from the perspective of death—in the underworld everything is inverted. That is the beginning of wisdom. The sun sets; the hero suffers his metamorphosis.

But the hero does not suffer alone. The heroic power of the goddesses themselves is necessary to effect his metamorphosis, and so the hero is mirrored in us. We endure the tormenting silence for a long time, and then the night echoes with sighs, humming, and soft cries at rhythmical intervals like the song of bats. A solitary drum can be heard beating increasingly slowly—like dying heartbeats. Then the beating stops, and all that can be heard are the call of an owl, the snapping of a twig, the breaking of threads, the shattering of glass, the dripping of seeds from the death apple (the pomegranate). Then silence.

Finally the lamentation for the dead hero begins; it resounds and echoes in the darkness. In a slow procession we carry him to a cave and lay him down. Now he is at his destination: the hero has found the Black goddess and rests like a seed in her womb. He has returned to the body of his mother, the Earth, from which he will be eternally reborn.

The black goddesses mourn the hero's death. Each of us can give personal expression to her sorrow. Our torches have long since burned out, our clothes are torn, our hands are black with ashes. Or we can perform a silent, melancholy dance leading us through the earth, heaven, and hell, where we search in vain for the one who is no longer among the living. It is a danced tragedy, a *danse macabre*. Now the vegetation withers, the leaves fall from the trees, and the goddess herself weeps. Her tears are the shooting stars that fall on autumn nights.

HALLOWEEN (*Frau Holle*)

On Halloween, the festival of the "White Woman," the Crone goddess no longer appears in her black aspect as the goddess of death; she is now the White Woman, who possesses and grants peace. Her whiteness is not that of the Maiden goddess. It is the whiteness of her own mysterious figure, a whiteness that includes all three colors of the Great Goddess, the trinity. It is not the clear whiteness of an individual person, but a mystical white veil. She is the "Woman of the Mists," who comes riding from the depths on her white horse and opens the gates to the underworld. Now the living and the dead are interchangeable.

When the Crone goddess reaches our houses and knocks at our doors, we light jack-o'-lanterns and follow the rider in a long procession through the darkness and up to the gates of the underworld. We are her companions and know the way into the depths, just as we know the place where the dead hero rests. The Crone goddess is the great healer, for she can even raise the dead, and we are healers, too. In the underworld we find everything that heals: water, which dissolves paralysis and causes the blood to flow again; earth, which cools and soothes; plant roots, which yield healing oils; minerals, which revive the body. We find rich, deep colors that soothe and assuage. We find colored stones—glittering in the womb of the earth and full of mysterious pulsations—which can heal and maintain the pulsations of the body. And we have our healing hands, our revivifying breath, and our restorative energies. We can heal one another in myriad ways from the pain of the passage to death, and deliver our hero from his death.

When we reach the hero, we handle him carefully. He will

not recover from his oblivion quickly, for the journey *from* death is just as long as the journey *to* death. We use our various healing abilities on him; we piece him back together; we cause him to open his eyes again, to find his tongue, and to relearn the use of his limbs. It is obviously difficult for him, since he is still in the underworld and in a deathlike state. But we transform him and create him anew.

When the hero recognizes where he is, he realizes that the underworld is a paradise. He is within the body of the goddess and experiences her peace. The goddess has received him like a lover, and he presents her with all the love, distress, and fear of death with which we burdened him.

We then lead the hero to the upper world. Although he is still dead and possesses the resignation and the patience of the dead, he is blessed as the beloved of the goddess and therefore permitted to pay a visit to the upper world. His underworldly state is reflected in the upper world—perhaps through his paleness, blindness, or dumbness, or his not being permitted to laugh and cry, no matter what happens. We invite him to our house and hold a memorial meal with him; we decorate our table carefully and prepare a special place set only with the food of the dead. All the dishes, fruits, and drinks of the dead are red like poppies, and no living person may touch them. We bless his place at the table and dedicate it to a dead person whom each of us remembers with love and longing. Then we give the hero an object or a symbol of the dead people we invoke; we take him by the hand and seat him at his place. The dead with whom we want to eat, with whom we want to speak, are incarnate in the hero, and they bless us for remembering them.

Finally the Crone goddess, the White Rider, summons the hero back to the underworld. She lifts him onto her horse and rides through the stone gates down into the depths; the gates of the otherworld close behind them. From the depths her good spirit envelops us, because we have honored and regaled the dead. Then flowers blossom around everything the hero has touched—little eight-petaled rosettes, tiny stars of the tree of life of Inanna, from which he had hung while dying. They are symbols of the eight-spoked seasonal cycle, which is approaching its completion. The flowers are the keys to the realm of the underworld. When we hold them in our hands, each of us is a triple goddess. At the conclusion, we decide into which aspect of the goddess we will transform ourselves so that each of us will appear to the world in one of her many forms at the Festival of the Epiphany, the festival of the manifestation of the Triple goddess.

WINTER SOLSTICE (*Jule/Weihnachten* [*Christmas*])
The winter solstice festival is the most profound and rich of the seasonal cycle; it is the holiest of all. It celebrates the return of light and life, the rebirth of the hero as a child. The full beauty of the paradisiacal underworld, from which the hero is resurrected, illuminates the earth. It is the festival of the manifestation of the Goddess in all her aspects; at the end of the cycle we know all her faces. She appears in triple or even ninefold form and embodies all three spheres of the world: heaven, earth, and underworld. She is the entire universe.

Perhaps we can begin our celebration as follows: Holding in our hands the white flowers, the keys to the underworld, we go to the hero's cave before sunrise to experience the rebirth of the light, to see the beam of sunlight that will fall through the shadows and into the depths of his grave at the moment of the winter solstice. In that beam of light the goddess Diana appears as the resplendent white virgin who pours the water of life over the hero. Now he awakens from death and is delivered from all pain. As the virgin mother and the ruler of the stars, the cosmic Diana leads him forth step-by-step from the depths of the earth, from the depths of the night. She literally brings him "into the world."

Or Diana gives birth to him with us as her helpers, her midwives who slowly draw him through the "birth canal" of our spread legs. Giving birth is a difficult and realistic labor from which we do not spare ourselves. Our energetic pushes and rhythmical, powerful cries turn this rebirth into a sublime act. We cry out the names of everything we wish to bring into the world: not only our hero but also the goddess within us, the goddess in every woman, the hero in every woman and in every man, an unpolluted nature, an unpoisoned earth, the uncontaminated elements of water and air, a gentle and beneficial fire (not an atomic one), a just society, the end of world hunger, a life no longer threatened by war, peaceful coexistence on this globe. Much is in need of our revitalizing, regenerating, transforming powers.

By bringing the hero into the world, we perceive our own strength; we perceive our long-silent energies begin to flow again; we perceive the new beginning of all living things. The hero grows younger with each step into the world. And when he comes forth, he is a child—the beginning of a new, more humane world than the patriarchal one. The hero is reborn. That is his and our transformation, the most profound of initiations.

The virgin mother, the youthful White goddess, holds him on her lap in her arms. The goddess of the stars holds the newborn sun child (the event in which all later Madonna stories and paintings have their origin). With the virgin mother and her hero-child, the "paradise"—the peace and wisdom of the underworld—comes to the earth to all of humanity. With each step we take from the cave, the upper world is transformed into the fairy realm, which otherwise can be found only under the earth.

By the time the hero steps out of the cave, the sun has

completely risen. He is greeted by the laughter of the many "children" gathered together in the snow. In paradise there is no old age; everyone remains eternally young.

But the sun is still too small and weak to convert its power into light, to materialize, to point the way. Its brightness is still diffuse and intermingled with darkness. It must diverge, distinguish, and separate itself from the cosmic night in order to assume its own form. The hero must emerge from the deep, warm womb of the underworld, from the mysterious cosmic ocean in which he swam. He must release and redeem himself to become the unique person he is. To acquire form and to reveal form is the principle of the light. And that is what necessarily separates the hero from the principle of darkness, of night—the dissolving and transforming chaos that fuses everything into one. The time of the transfiguring night is past; the time of the individuating light is beginning. It is time for the "cosmic battle" in which the principle of light struggles against the principle of darkness.

The hero is led into battle by Diana herself; she and the white goddesses are on his side. Diana is also young and, like the hero, wants to become a person, to assume a visible form, to separate herself, to distinguish herself—the daughter—from the primordial maternal darkness. But Hecate and the black goddesses determine that it is still winter, that darkness will long prevail, that the Crone goddess still reigns. They try to lock Diana and the hero, daughter and son, in a maternal embrace and absorb them into the cosmic night. Thus it must come to a confrontation, a confrontation in which there is no good or evil, no victory or defeat, no either-or, but only *everything in its time*.

All the "children" join in the battle. Those who fight for the principle of light grow white wings—two around the head, two around the shoulders, two enveloping the torso, and two covering the feet. They are winged genies, the counterparts of those who fight for the principle of darkness and sprout eight black wings. The white genies decide for the hero; the black genies decide against him. They flock around the white or the black goddesses, who appear in their midst as the shining white full moon or the jet black new moon. The white and the black armies clash violently in the battle for the young sun hero, who is still staggering from his sudden birth and is undecided where to go: into irresolute disintegration or demanding individuation.

Since divisiveness and war are repugnant to them, Venus and the red moon goddesses are undecided which side they should take. Therefore they do nothing. Without participating themselves, they observe and constantly send new creatures into the battle: the four seasons; the four quarters of the heavens; and the four elements of air, fire, water, and earth, for example. The delicate, transparent creatures of air (butterflies, dragonflies, elves, and sylphs) and the energetic, electric creatures of fire (lightning bugs, salamanders, red-speckled cats, spotted leopards, and black panthers) fight on the side of the white genies, of the light. The creatures of water (dolphins, nixes, and tritons making music with conchs, sea lilies, starfish, and sirens) and the creatures of earth (dwarves and giants, bulls and centaurs, billy goats and unicorns) as well as other powerful beings fight on the side of the black genies, of the darkness. Although the battle becomes increasingly turbulent, there are clearly two sides. There is playing and twirling and dancing, throwing and shooting of colorful paper, cotton balls and sugar cubes, flowers, boughs and streamers, and sometimes a little snow. There is incessant laughter. It is an amusing spectacle, a high-spirited farce.

The red moon goddesses still remain aloof; but with increasing pleasure, they send in new "warriors." However, the battle does not become truly "cosmic" until it occurs to the red goddesses to send the stars, comets, and planets into the tumult. Mercury, Venus, Mars, and Jupiter intervene on the visible bright side; Saturn, Uranus, Neptune, and Pluto, on the mysterious dark side. The white and black moon goddesses are pleased with the reinforcements. However, it is possible that all the constellations of the zodiac will rush with the planets to the aid of their corresponding elements. When a few additional fixed stars do intervene, a comet whizzes into the fray—even the galaxies intercede—and the battle finally explodes into chaos.

When the moon goddesses lose track of the battle, the demons—who have already been lurking in the background—seize the opportunity. Now the struggle reaches its climax: the vulture of death, the vulture of Nout, of eternal night, descends. The hero defends himself fiercely, but he is unarmed and the vulture hacks out one of his eyes, thereby eclipsing half of the sunlight and leaving only twilight. Enraged, the hero begins to arm himself—he has made his decision. But then the Hound of Hell, the eternal enemy, rushes from the darkness and bites off his left hand. Now the hero is unable to use his left side, and wrath places into his right hand a spear as bright as a sunbeam. The outcome depends entirely on the hero; he is determined to do anything. He suddenly stands face-to-face with the great dragon, the gigantic primeval serpent, the ocean, the abyss: Chaos itself. The hero fights the ancient battle with the dragon, the battle between darkness and light, the battle for existence or nonexistence, a battle in which there is no victor.

The battle becomes serious, and the hero passionately stands his ground. He is not afraid of the water or the fire belched by the dragon, the cold or the heat, or any other extremes. Having made his decision, he extricates himself from each grip of the dragon by dismembering it limb by limb. The hero is ready to overstep any boundary—alone, if necessary. But no sooner has this thought entered his head than he incurs the laughter of Diana, who is now withdrawing with all the white creatures. The hero pauses and realizes that the dragon is not a demon but a female, and none other than the ancient one, the first goddess, the Great Goddess. But, unlike the patriarchal goddesses, heroes, archangels, and knights—who all believed they had to kill the female dragon—the hero puts down his spear. Thereupon the dragon finally coils around him, bites him, and, beginning with his left leg, completely devours him. Now the sun is in total eclipse, and the cosmic battle threatens to end in "cosmic chaos."

Thus the hero himself falls from one extreme to the other, and that is too much for the red moon goddesses. With flattery, they induce the dragon to spit out the hero unharmed, for no solar eclipse is permitted to last forever. Suddenly the white and the black moon goddesses and their followers are in agreement. Hence the principle of light triumphs without harming the principle of darkness, and the red goddesses bring the cosmic battle to an ultimate "cosmic harmony." Reconciled, all creatures finally unite in a rapturous dance of the universe.

The dance culminates in a triumphal procession to the fairy palace, the subterranean or superterranean castle of the goddess. The path leads through forests of evergreen trees—pines wound with wool streamers or spruces full of golden apples. (The apples of the underworld are golden.) There are lights everywhere in the glint of the snow—signs of eternal life and eternal youth. Paradise spreads before them. In the fairy palace everything shimmers in the silver of moonlight, the gold of sunlight, and the seven colors of the rainbow. Fairies and good spirits receive the procession at the castle gate. They are wearing long, luminous robes and symbols of rebirth: lotus flowers, lilies, and winter roses crown their heads. They fulfill all wishes, and it is like a fairy tale.

In a great hall in the center of the palace stands the festive table on which the banquet, the abundance, the plenty, is infinite. Sitting on her throne at the center of the table is the Triple goddess in Triad, who we ourselves now are. She observes the swarming flock of guests and the strange hopping creatures gathered; she serenely observes her creation. She holds in her hand the grail—a goblet, a bowl, or a cornucopia—from which infinite plenty pours forth, everything the table holds: food and drink, apples, nuts, honey cakes baked in the shapes of the Goddess.

The Goddess sits at the left—on the side of life—and the hero-child sits at her right. He looks into her three faces, which he now recognizes simultaneously. She is the Goddess of Life-in-Death, the changing one, the eternal metamorphosis.[26] And, at the same time, she is the eternally *un*changing one: she is the entire universe in one. She is the creative Chaos, the cosmic night full of lights. But this cannot be apprehended with human eyes, so she always appears as a paradox to our finite gaze.

Now the hero plays his harp, and he plays it so powerfully and sweetly that all the creatures listen; they cry and laugh, sleep and awaken. He plays them into death and back into life. He plays the fairy music, for the underworld is the paradise of art. He conjures and bewitches with the elements of the Goddess—he has become knowing. He is the magician and buffoon, the sage and fool in one. He is the poet, the child and jester of the Goddess.

In her triple form, the Goddess then enters the world with the reborn hero in her arms as a star. She passes over the earth and blesses each house. She reveals herself to humanity so that they may recognize her. It is the festival of her revelation: the Epiphany.

Then a time of stillness begins. The old festival cycle has ended; the new one has not yet begun. All the women withdraw to remain at home alone and spend their days in meditation. They gradually comprehend the events and experience peace; the purification is consummated. There is silence. Only the divine in every individual woman speaks.

I have followed my path to the end. It has led me forward and backward and, winding like a spiral, has led me to my destination—first through a historical section, then through a theoretical section concerning the nature of matriarchal aesthetics, then through an interpretive section attempting to comprehend what has already happened, and finally through a section delineating a utopia already beginning its realization.

The examples given above are a conceptual and experiential attempt to unite the myriad facets of matriarchal art. I could only outline that attempt in a few words that cannot capture the richness and depth of the experiences involved. But perhaps it has become clear how all forms of art can be integrated in the openness of the process of matriarchal art, which constantly begins anew within the totality of the ritual dance festivals. And perhaps it has become clear what matriarchal art is: a completely different form of art, and yet not so much a different form of "art" as a different form of life.

Matriarchal art penetrates the disjointed, enumerated, inorganic course of days and years we are forced into all our lives and fits that temporal course back into a rhythmic, symbolic totality. Matriarchal art shatters the precisely defined boundaries of the patriarchal domain and institutions, which confine art to one sphere, science to another, and religion to still another—an isolation that has long since caused their degeneration. Through its "revaluation of all values" of the patriarchy, matriarchal art inverts the patriarchal point of view and, by transcending it, creates a new and different world, albeit only a tiny island so far.[27]

But there can be many such islands. When we reinvest the days, the months, and the years with new meaning along the lines of matriarchal art as drawn here—with regard to history, with caution in our current situation, and with an eye to a utopian goal—we will rediscover ourselves in matriarchal art. Thus we will become as aliens in *this* present by creating *our own* present. We will make an inner emigration into an epoch of our own. We will create a space for ourselves within a hostile society and an egress to a land of our own. But since we are also present in *this* reality—unconditionally in its midst—we will gradually *change* it.

We will succeed in changing reality because the festivals of the seasonal cycle tend toward universality. They are as universal today as they once were as folk festivals, and, through them, the split in the aesthetic dimension is neutralized. Therefore, in principle, nothing could be excluded from the symbolization, the ritual, the everlasting festival and its tranquil and active phases. And when each woman can become a festival participant—no matter how reservedly or conspicuously—there will no longer be an "audience" standing opposite this art. Since matriarchal art is the perpetual formation and transformation of life in both the microcosm and the macrocosm, the festival would become the central social practice, which in turn would heal the lacerations and wounds caused by the barbaric, callous, violent behavior of the patriarchally imprinted people of today. There would be no such thing as an art that is separate from the activities of life, because there are no activities of life that are separate from matriarchal art. And that would mean the aestheticization of society—a process in which all distortions and contradictions would be mediated less "dialectically" than "aesthetically."

That seems absurd only if the aesthetic is equated with the fictitious. Matriarchal art, however, is not a liberal play of possibilities but a liberating play of realities.

Afterword

I owe the further development of many of my ideas on the theme of matriarchal art and spirituality, some of which are presented here, to my sympathetic women and men critics. Unfortunately, however, there is also a destructive criticism that confines itself to defensive reproaches and insinuations, often without precise knowledge of the subject. I would like to respond to those spreading prejudices, because they reflect the currently prevailing confusion concerning the essence of matriarchal art and spirituality. The most vehement critics suspect it to be a new religion or a new spiritism/spiritualism. Matriarchal spirituality is neither a new religion nor a new spiritism/spiritualism—it differs fundamentally from both. I will elucidate this distinction in my response, through which I hope to contribute to a basic clarification of the present confusion.

On the Charge of Irrationalism
The accusation of irrationalism is the mildest of all. Even so, it is a catchword for suppressing disagreeable views—as evidenced by its indiscriminate use. Nowadays, *any* view that

criticizes the exclusive emphasis on and esteem for the intellect in our culture and cedes an equal position to the other human capacities is immediately dismissed as anti-intellectualism and irrationalism. This devaluating judgment applies only to views that—in a reversal of the prevailing value scale in which intellect is at the very top—place the emotions and other capacities at the top and dismiss the intellect. However, such a view merely perpetuates the patriarchal idea of a hierarchy of values, but with reversed premises and primarily for ulterior motives, such as the neutralization of any criticism that could subvert those manipulations.

Such views are alien to me because, first of all, I myself am an "intellectual" and, second, the only reasonable and rational attitude for me is one that promotes the equal development of *all* human capacities, including the physical, emotional, intellectual, and spiritual. That is the only way to counteract the crippling one-sidedness prevalent today—which is, of course, very useful for certain mechanisms of control. The promotion of all human capacities is a fundamental idea in matriarchal aesthetics/spirituality, and to dismiss it as irrationalism betrays ignorance or maliciousness.

Another distinction suppressed by this accusation is that between a subject, or theme, and its application. A subject or theme is of itself neither rational nor irrational; only its applications can be one or the other. This can be illustrated with the example of atomic physics, a very logically reasoned and recognized subject that has been applied in an extremely irrational way in military technology. By contrast, the subject and practice of matriarchal spirituality can find very rational application, as, for example, in research on archaic spirituality and the spirituality practiced by foreign peoples or in women's current attempts to use their spiritual capacities—which they far too long yielded to ecclesiastical and other institutions, where they were ruthlessly exploited—for their own intellectual and spiritual regeneration. To do so beyond the confines of any church or doctrine influenced by men is a new form of autonomy that in the face of the present social repression of woman, is very rational and not without political consequences.

The same is true for the subject of matriarchy. Ever since its original formulation by male researchers, it has received irrational application. But in the hands of qualified women researchers, "matriarchy" can finally be applied rationally again, after having been a vehicle for irrational value judgments—cloaked in ostensibly neutral, rational science—concerning the essence of womanhood or even the nonexistence of women as active subjects in history.[1] The most loathsome misuse of the subject of "matriarchy" occurred under National Socialism in contexts the irrationality of which bordered on the absurd. That aberration in recent German history reveals what levels of inhumanity patriarchy is capable of, and it is not the only example in the many millennia of patriarchal history filled with wars, massacres, and genocide.

But should this subject, which can give us women so much information about our active and creative existence in history, be taboo simply because of its continual misuse in the wrong hands? Is it not high time we take it back into our own hands to safeguard it? As with anything else, it is a question of method. To dispute this and immediately cry "irrationalism" at any constructive attempt to pursue the subject is itself the expression of an extremely unreasonable and irrational attitude.

The situation of the subject of spirituality is no less problematical. Granted, there are groups of women who use spirituality as a means of emotional withdrawal from reality, as a lapse into endless reverie. However, in doing so, they merely invert the patriarchal hierarchy of values and place the intuition of the elemental woman incapable of critical thinking or self-control at the very top, and dismiss any capacity for more precise decision making as something terribly negative. I have already said what I think of such naïve mirror reversals: they do not neutralize the patriarchal mentality of thinking in opposites.

Moreover, we have behind us a millennia-long misuse of spirituality, which in patriarchal societies is called "religion." That may seem perplexing, for is not matriarchal spirituality something akin to a new religion? It is not. Matriarchal spirituality is in fact the complete opposite of what is called religion and its practice is a radical and practical critique of religion. "Religions" are entities that typically did not originate until the rise of patriarchal societies.[2] "Religions" are characterized by an abstract conception of a transcendent god—where "god" is either a man or merely a principle—and a concomitant absolute claim to truth as well as a spiritualism inimical to the body and physical life (e.g., asceticism). People have been and still are deliberately sacrificed to this asceticism, as evidenced countless times in history, for example, in missionaries' persecution mania and so-called holy wars.

Furthermore, these religions are institutionalized; their institutions are hierarchically and centrally organized; and, as "state churches," they precisely mirror the power structures and power mechanisms of the states that support them. Their rituals are a rigid repetition of past events revolving around the "religious founder": the unique great man, the Prophet, the Lord, or God on earth. However, since mere repetition does not restore the original spiritual event, all the incidents surrounding the religious founder are laid down in a so-called Holy Book, which is supposed to be the guiding principle for the entire course of future world history. With the help of this "Holy Book," the priest caste rules over the lowly laity, the "believers."

That is the pattern of all patriarchal religions known today as "world religions." The pattern reveals what those entities are in actuality, namely, a further variant of the technology of supremacy in patriarchal societies and an extremely irrational treatment of the spiritual needs and longings every person has. The entire range of religious criticism practiced by philosophy from the Enlightenment through Communism (Voltaire, Feuerbach, Nietzsche, Marx) applies only to the pattern of patriarchal religions but not to matriarchal spirituality.

None of it applies to matriarchal spirituality because matriarchal spirituality is *not* a religion. Matriarchal spirituality springs directly from the spiritual needs of individual people and supports the free, playful, sublime, and earnest development of those spiritual needs. When matriarchal spirituality speaks of the "Goddess," it does not mean an omnipotent, omniscient supreme Mother in Heaven, a counterpart to God the Father. On the contrary. This concept signifies nothing more—and nothing less—than the *inherent spiritual capacity in every individual,* which harmoniously expresses itself *together with* the totality of the intellectual, emotional, and physical capacities of the person. The Goddess does not exist independent of those capacities; she is something like the unifying thread, the vitality, the energy of life. In this sense, the Goddess is present in every person and in all creatures and elements that possess or impart the vital energy.

This conception of the Goddess is both concrete and universal: she is a tangible goddess present in every living thing we see around us and in all things we sense to be supportive of life. Since she is so near and can be concretely experienced at any time, proselytizing is superfluous; there is no need to convince other people of something invisible and intangible that violates the laws of nature, i.e., of something totally absurd—which would indeed be difficult and require an entire organization!

The Goddess's tangibility engenders our individual freedom by allowing us to form our own personal experience of her.

The magical Muse rites we spontaneously create give expression not to a rigid ideology but to each woman's individual experience or individual image of the Goddess. Institutions, dogmas, and hierarchies—be they hierarchies among people or among various human capacities—are alien to matriarchal spirituality. For the complete truth lies in each individual, current exercise of matriarchal spirituality. The joy of the Goddess is multiplicity, not the uniform unity to which nonconformists are sacrificed.[3] Because it is humane and centered in life, this attitude is, I believe, rational through and through, reasonable in the broadest sense of the term *reason*.

ON THE CHARGE OF OCCULTISM

Just as matriarchal spirituality is not a religion, it also has nothing in common with the old and new spiritualism manifest in Far Eastern philosophy and life; in the obscure, esoteric, occult undercurrents constantly present in the Christian West; or in the diverse guru sects of today. This brings me to the second accusation against matriarchal spirituality: the charge of mysticism or occultism.

This charge is as polemical and untenable as the first one, for the mere occupation with such themes as magic, mythology, esoteric symbols, astrology, tarot, and breathing and relaxation techniques does not make one a mystic or an occultist. Who is in a position to forbid us from satisfying our intellectual and experiential curiosity through occupation with those themes? Especially since we have realized that those themes— despite their having been distorted or abused—conceal vestiges of the archaic matriarchal ways of thinking and living?

To attain this knowledge requires, first of all, an intensified methodical search for those vestiges and their inclusion in the cultural and historical studies already begun. Second, it requires the cooperative experimental testing of the meaning for women today of this ancient language of symbols and ciphers deriving from ancient women's cultures. This symbolic language contains the sum total and essence of ancient female knowledge, and our deciphering it through research and experiments is indeed a worthwhile task. Or are we so thoroughly permeated by male patterns of thought and behavior that we believe we have nothing more to learn or gain from the legacy of thought images and ways of life handed down to us by historical women and their cultures? That would be a very arrogant attitude, which I do not share. Nor do I share the attitude of slavish imitation. We can attempt to decipher this ancient language of symbols and ciphers without allowing it to become highly stylized as a new doctrine of salvation by some, or to be written off as a new doctrine of salvation by others. We are far removed from both attitudes; for in this case, too, it is a matter of *method*, as I have already said.

Through my terminology alone, I draw a sharp distinction between spiritualism and matriarchal spirituality—and not without reason. Spiritualism is characterized by a strict duality of body and spirit in which absolute preeminence is given to the spiritual, supernatural, and spiritistic. That is what identifies spiritualism as the product of patriarchal cultures. It is true for East Indian and Far Eastern spiritualism as well as for European occultism. That both currents drew considerably on the matriarchal legacy of their parent cultures and have continued to do so for millennia does not alter their patriarchal character. East Indian spiritualism, for example, drew on the heritage of the pre-Aryan Indus culture, the oldest culture by far on East Indian soil (Harappa and Mohenjo-Daro). European occultism drew on Hellenistic secret cults (Demeter mysteries, Cybele cult, Isis cult, Orphics), all of which derive from even older matriarchal cultures in Egypt, Crete, Asia Minor, and Greece. As a result, those spiritualist and occult teachings generally granted women with their divine powers a place next to the male gods.

That explains their appeal to women in the face of the hopeless misogyny of official patriarchal religions. Nevertheless, the female adherents of spiritualism and occultism overlook the typically patriarchal distortion manifest in the dualism of body and spirit, in which the spirit (the masculine) takes absolute precedence over the body (the feminine). This cements the conventional hierarchy of values according to which the male God—the masculine principle—and masculine values always rank at the top, while all manifestations of the feminine principle are mercilessly subordinated to them. In spiritualism and occultism, spiritual experiences and the practice of magic are misused as a means to gain power and influence over other people—and women in particular. It is always the same mania for *power over* others.

In matriarchal spirituality, by contrast, we concentrate on fostering, through symbolic activities shared by all, the full development of each individual's *inner power*—what Starhawk calls the "power from within"—and vitality and joy of life. "Power from within" is the power women have to act without dominating others or allowing themselves to be dominated. In spiritualism, on the other hand, people's spiritual needs and capacities are misused for *personal power* and financial gain, no matter how humane and nonmisogynistic their "spiritualized" leaders appear to be.

The practices of today's astrologers, occultists, clairvoyants, magicians, and parapsychologists are identical: profane commercialism or "black magic" is fueled by people's yearning for the mysterious and the holy. Such phenomena are the last decadent remnants of European occultism, which in the late Middle Ages had thoroughly intellectual force and political and oppositional dimensions, exemplified in the many countermovements such as the mystical and heretical movements.

To place matriarchal spirituality, as represented by me and other thinking women, into the same category as those things—for the mere reason that the same symbols or similar techniques are used—is grotesque. Such a reproach ignores the fact that matriarchal spirituality is grounded in an autonomous self-confidence of women and a nonhierarchical, egalitarian relationship among women, in which the goal is not the suppression of the intellect in favor of psychic flatulence but the vital union of spirit, psyche, and physical expression for the purpose of allowing each individual to become a complete and healthy personality.

ON THE CHARGE OF (NEO-) NATIONAL SOCIALISM

The most superficial and vile attack is the charge that matriarchal spirituality has something to do with the ideology of the Nazis and neo-Nazis. That suspicion is based exclusively on accidental similarities between the two—such as the occasional treatment of Teutonic mythology, the occasional description of Teutonic symbols, the occasional recourse to national folklore and ancient festivals. Or it is based solely on our choice of the same themes the Nazis harped on, such as matriarchy or other legendary themes, which Wagner transmogrified in his operas. But the same images and the same themes do not necessarily have the same meaning; their meaning depends on the perspective in which they occur. That simple fact is swept under the rug by such criticism.

My research perspective is an *autonomous-feminist perspective* in that it concerns the rediscovery of history as influenced by women as active, determining subjects within the form of society created by them. That, I should think, is clear. And my method is equally clear: it is a comparative approach that focuses equal attention on both Germanic mythology and folklore *and* Indian, Persian, Egyptian, Sumero-Babylonian, Palestinian, Greco-Cretan, and Celtic mythology and folklore. There is no place in my approach for thinking in terms of biological categories like the racial concept of the Nazis. The categories that my investigations deal with are social and theoretical ones, which I use to research two different societal forms and their development in history, namely, matriarchies and patriarchies.

Within *that* social and theoretical framework, the "Indo-Germanics" so glorified by the Nazis appear in an unfavorable light upon their entry into history, because in the area from India to Europe *they* were the peoples who—as early patriarchal warrior tribes—invaded the highly developed cultures and civilizations of their predecessors, the matriarchal peoples; and they, through the destructiveness and primitiveness of their own culture, unleashed the archaeologically verifiable, cultureless Dark Ages. The "Indo-Germanics" gradually established their own classical patriarchal societies by means of intellectual and cultural appropriation and simultaneous disavowal. That the so-called Indo-Germanics were the first to spread culture in this region is a legend similar to the one the patriarchal Greeks of antiquity created about themselves.

The same is true of the Teutons, the Germanic tribes that settled on what is now German soil. Except for their arid warrior culture, the Teutons *brought* nothing; instead, they *found* a rich mixed culture that had evolved from the integration of the patriarchal Celts with the matriarchal pre-Celtic population. The Teutons absorbed the Celtic and pre-Celtic myths so extensively that, strictly speaking, there is no such thing as a "Germanic" mythology and folklore as such. At best there is a "Celtic-Germanic" mythology, to which the Germanic tribes contributed—in a further push toward patriarchalization—their cunning, deceitful, cruel, megalomaniacal father-warrior-god Odin-Wotan, who subjugated all other gods just as Zeus had in Greek mythology.

Any such nationalist perspective is fundamentally misguided because it ignores the international diffusion and intermingling of those cultures, as presented here, and attributes to a particular national state—which arose very late in history—extensive prehistoric developmental connections that have nothing at all to do with it. It is even more misguided to reduce extensive social and historical processes to biological categories—regardless of what sort—because the development of the various matriarchies into patriarchies also encompassed the extremely diverse races and peoples on other continents *outside* the Indo-European area.

Given the factual basis of my research perspective, I cannot understand the intent of such defamatory reproaches on the one hand, and heavy-handed sweeping generalizations on the other. I can understand them only as the problem of people who, because of the blind bias of their own prejudices, cannot or will not acknowledge something different or new.

On the Charge of Neobiologism

The accusation of neobiologism likewise maintains that matriarchal research is merely a disguised reworking of the old definitions of the female essence in terms of biological factors. After all, isn't matriarchy preoccupied with eternal motherhood, and isn't the Great Goddess constantly invoked as the embodiment of fertility? Women who pursue such themes today supposedly end up casting themselves in the very role patriarchy has forced upon them for millennia. These critics claim that we women are merely withdrawing into matriarchally idealized maternalness and leaving to the men—now as before—all spheres of public life, all domains in which women have laboriously struggled for representation. That is the thrust of this reproach.

Such criticism contains fundamental misunderstandings about the nature of matriarchal research and the matriarchal spirituality of *today*. The misunderstandings stem from the *former* matriarchal research performed by *men,* which is full of disparaging prejudices concerning women's cultures: matriarchies were supposedly nonintellectual, physically oriented societies that were biased by gloomy thinking caused by the menstrual cycle and incapable of higher intellectual achievement; as such, they allegedly typified the primitiveness of the early Stone Age. That legend about the matriarchy has existed since Bachofen (1861).[4] And it is still perpetuated in official opinion, which has remained unchanged even to this day, despite the diversity and continued development of contemporary matriarchal research (cf. the relevant literature).[5]

These misinterpretations have universal currency only because no one has taken the trouble to examine the evidence or the methods used to evaluate the evidence. Of course it is easier to mouth a cliché than to examine the evidence. Even women perpetuate this hackneyed misinterpretation—and here, too, ignorance and defensiveness go hand in hand.

In my study *Die Göttin und ihr Heros* (The goddess and her hero), I make it clear that the figure of the Great Goddess is not limited to the child bearer; as the Triple goddess she is also the youthful, wild, autonomous goddess, the Amazon, and the old, wise goddess, the master of art, philosophy, and all inventions. Matriarchies were not primitive mother-societies but, in the case of urban societies, highly developed civilizations with a high intellectual and spiritual level. The subsequent patriarchal cultures fed intensively on both the civilization and the intellectuality of the matriarchies and, at the same time, generated the legend of the primitiveness of those cultures to rationalize their conquest and pillage.

But, as creators of culture and leaders of large and small communities, matriarchal women were completely self-sufficient long before the blessings of patriarchal culture. In addition, they were able to do something men could never take from them: to give birth and create new life. Patriarchies reduced women to this single, indispensable function and robbed them of everything else in order to mold them into something that profited and served the strategic purposes of men.

Women continue to suffer from this diminishment and deprivation, and it would be absurd to offer them motherliness *in place of* all the other things—something that always happens with the most beautiful words. But it is equally wrong to strive for everything else *in place of* motherliness. Both attitudes betray the dualistic thinking of patriarchy, which forces women to plan their lives in terms of an either-or and causes a painful internal split within women and among women.

By contrast, I believe we should want *everything*—and no less than *everything*—in order to become the complete people we are. Not only the development of women's creative, intellectual, and political potency but also the development of their creative, motherly potency have a place in such thinking. And that was precisely the thinking in the ancient matriarchies. It is revealed to us in the image of the Triple goddess as the young, warlike Maiden goddess, the motherly Nymph goddess, and the knowing Crone goddess, who directed all things. This goddess did not consist of three incompatible parts but possessed all three capacities simultaneously. She was the unity-in-threeness, the trinity.

In the practice of matriarchal spirituality today, women reexperience the union of all their capacities, which were either denied them (e.g., intellectuality) or imposed on them as an obligation (e.g., motherliness). From the restored union of the various powers of their personality, women gain the courage and the energy to defend themselves against the conditions that seek to dismember them. For to have experienced the complexity of their identity makes women rebel against *all* old and new attempts to diminish them.

Another theoretical argument that reveals the absurdity of the charge of neobiologism as directed against me concerns terminology. Unlike many feminists, I never speak of "feminine" culture, "feminine" history, "feminine" language, "feminine" art, or "feminine" philosophy. Such designations always lead to the question of the precise nature of the feminine aspect of this "feminine" language, philosophy, or art. The question is legitimate, and it embarrasses the proponents of all these "femininities" to have to explain their conception of the feminine. No matter how deft, ingenious, or sophistic their explanations are, those feminists run the risk of imposing new prescriptions and definitions of the feminine, thus opening the back door to the old biological formulas.

I therefore deliberately speak of *matriarchal* aesthetics, art, and spirituality and thus avoid the temptation to redefine women in terms of eternal characteristics. Instead, I focus on a societal form that underwent a historical evolution and suffered a historical demise—a societal form with all its myriad components such as economy, ecology, social structure, culture, and religion; a societal form in the fabric of which women actively and influentially established themselves in many places on earth. Since the concrete manifestations of that societal form were very diverse, I am not compelled to trace everything back to a common denominator like "femininity"; instead, I can attempt a multidimensional explanation of the complex historical development of the matriarchies in terms of complex causes. Mine is an undogmatic, flexible, social-historical approach that fundamentally rejects explanations in terms of rigid, ahistorical concepts like "femininity" or any other archetypes. Matriarchal aesthetics is *always* a matter of history and *never* of biological prescriptions.[6]

ON THE CHARGE OF APOLITICALITY

The application of unsuitable political terms—*rightist, leftist, conservative, reactionary,* or *progressive*—to autonomous systems of feminist thought merely reflects a misinformed, arrogant pigeonholing of independent and original perspectives into the conventional patterns of official politics. These critics do not even notice that those concepts of political orientation do not fit autonomous systems of feminist thought because they defy categorization along the lines of the male-dominated political parties and politics. That is the context in which this reproach usually emerges, namely, the accusation that matriarchal spirituality, or the new women's spirituality in general, is apolitical. When one is unable to lay the criticism of irrationalism, occultism, National Socialism, or neobiologism at the door of matriarchal spirituality, then it must at least be apolitical: the private pleasure of starry-eyed females who withdraw out of frustration—or other reasons—into the safety of their mystical world. The political finger is immediately pointed the moment too many women are seized with this new "apolitical" mania to the detriment of their "true" concerns.

I wonder how others always know what the "true" concerns of women are—be they critics of the male or the female sex. We women should finally be permitted to discover *for ourselves* how multifarious our true concerns are. I also wonder on the basis of whose political beliefs this objection has been raised. Is it based on the prevailing type of politics in which organizations, institutions, and parties are formed to protect the power interests of certain groups? It really makes no great difference whether the conception of politics is a bourgeois one, in which power is enforced from above by parliamentary means, or a Marxist one, in which power is enforced from below with the aid of opposition organizations. In both cases the perspective is hierarchical and the basic attitude is aggressive. In both cases the purpose is to gain power and influence over others by some sort of well-organized means. I call such a political attitude—regardless of its orientation—*patriarchal,* and a conception of politics gained from it is unsuited for judging whether matriarchal spirituality is "political" or not.

Of course, insofar as matriarchal spirituality is nonaggressive and noninstitutional and does not seek to gain power over others, it is apolitical in the sense of conventional male politics—and fortunately so.

But perhaps we can develop a different conception of politics that diverges from the conventional definition in patriarchal societies. Such a different conception would have to contain as its basic objective the changing of inhumane conditions through nonviolent means. The oppression and exploitation of women in patriarchal societies is a condition in urgent need of change, and such change is the aim of a political vision formulated by women. The change must be nonviolent, since violence breeds endless counterviolence, and it is high time to get out of this vicious circle. There are proven forms of nonviolent protest, for example, passive resistance, work stoppages, simply walking out on indefensible conditions, or the "vote of the feet," which women have always made use of—today more than ever before.

And what about the situation of women's spirituality? More and more women are leaving the institutions that have exploited their spiritual capacities in the name of "religion." However, they are not retreating into passive nihilism; instead, they are developing their own spiritual world, a new intellectual world, and, at the same time, a world of new possibilities of expression. They are finding and creating new places to practice that spirituality. And the many institutions that are dependent on the tireless yet resented collaboration of women are finding their withdrawal—the desiccation from below—disturbing and threatening. Is that not politics?

The claim that such an exodus and simultaneous autonomous new beginning are apolitical can be made only by those who think that the spirit, innovation, and most important events of our times manifest themselves solely within existing institutions. Such a claim is made by men with their self-centered view of the world or by women who want to have successful careers in those institutions at any price. Those who have worked within those institutions for a long time—as I have, for example—know from experience how insipid, trivial, and power-political their machinations are.

A NEW POLITICAL CONCEPTION: A NEW POLITICS

Matriarchal spirituality is not an institution in the patriarchal sense but a movement possessing a political essence based on a different conception of politics: it is *a politics that oversteps the system*. The system that is overstepped is the mechanistic, one-sided, hierarchical system of thought and action of patriarchy. Matriarchal spirituality esteems diversity, change, vitality, and a dynamism that admits of no strictures or incrustation. Matriarchal spirituality respects and promotes the union of the psychic interior—which patriarchal politics obscures—and the physical exterior, one's well-being in the natural environment, which patriarchal religions and spiritualism have always obliterated. Matriarchal spirituality negates and neutralizes all types of dualism used by patriarchal politics throughout the millennia to secure domination. It is irrelevant whether it is a dualism that places the intellectual and spiritual above all else and despises the body—particularly the woman's—and controls women through forcible childbearing and unpaid work (as in all conservative patriarchal systems); or a dualism that seeks salvation in materialism or economic determinism and dismisses as superfluous all spiritual expression—a false parallel to the character of patriarchal religions; or the oppressive "opiate of the masses" (as in all patriarchal systems influenced by Marxism). All forms of dualism serve the principle "divide and conquer" and are the antithesis of the radical antiestablishment politics of matriarchal spirituality.[7]

The ethics of matriarchal spirituality is committed to the vital diversity, to the vital process of life itself. When the Goddess is visible and tangible for us in the natural, life-sustaining contexts on this earth, when she stimulates and supports us, when she acts within us as our own best powers, we respond to her with our spiritual love, which refers us not to the hereafter but to our concrete existence in the here and now. The divine is immanent in the here and now, it does not allow us a placating ideology or withdrawal into the otherwordly contemplativeness of cloisters.

Retreat is acceptable only insofar as it is desirable and necessary for personal renewal, for becoming and remaining complete and intact persons amid our confrontations with *this* world. Through continually repeated but temporally limited retreats into meditation, we gain the power to act in thought and deed in *this life:* in our relationships to other people, in our families, in our working world, in our present social context, and in the extended biosphere—in commitment to this concrete goddess. Nothing about our commitment to the Goddess encourages us to flee from the world into a falsely understood mysticism; everything about it moves us to intervene responsibly into the current situation. For we bear collective responsibility for the consequences of treacherous deeds inimical to life—no one from outside relieves us of that responsibility.

The ethics of matriarchal spirituality therefore motivates us to work passionately for the integration and healing of every individual, for justice in human society, and for the restoration of the ecological balance of the biosphere. And our most passionate commitment is to counteract violence and war—regardless of their provenance. Such thinking stems from the recognition of the divine as immanent, as present in this world. Moreover, since all life is sacred, our complete participation is demanded. There is no superhuman being to relieve us of this responsibility, nor is there a superhuman standard to be imposed upon us. We are human and fallible; we do not cause ourselves feelings of guilt or self-contempt. Instead, we try to fulfill to the best of our abilities our responsibility to every living thing—standing in the midst of life, in the midst of human society. A life grounded in the ethos of matriarchal spirituality demands honesty, integrity, courage, and, above all, love.[8]

It follows that the completeness of the individual in matriarchal spirituality cannot be achieved cheaply, for example, by simply glossing over the violent facts of this world such as hunger, oppression, and pollution. Harmony at the price of almost total deafness and blindness is unthinkable. Matriarchal spirituality is the refuge of hope, and hence a constant protest that never acquiesces to the inhumanity and unnaturalness existing today. Through its words and deeds, matriarchal spirituality continually expresses its yearning for completeness, for a gentle and just society, for an environment in equilibrium; and it speaks out against the fragmented, the threatening, the terrible. This matriarchal yearning combats unhealthy reality by constantly revealing its concrete utopia—facets of which have already been achieved—and the "matriarchal aesthetic" to which the concrete utopia owes its form and shape.

At present, the life of the continually and gradually advancing utopia exhibits a rift, or limitation, but it is a conscious and necessary one. In all daily confrontations, whether large or small, it is necessary to endure this painful tension between real inhumanity and lived human, natural utopia. The process of change inherent in matriarchal spirituality is furthered by constantly repeated injury to this newly gained unity with ourselves, with nature, and with other people. Under today's conditions, this deeply and spontaneously experienced pain will always recur. But we must risk the pain and further the difficult task of sustaining a utopia in a hostile reality—not only in the personal but also in the general sense. And we must do so collectively and with increasing numbers of people. Only in this way can we profoundly deepen, extend, intensely experience, and communicate the totalities that unite us. Even though it means more suffering (conscious, oppositional suffering), the growing common interest that arises without coercion and the growing circle of people experiencing this utopia will gradually help us survive the increasing tension inherent in our situation of having to endure the hostile reality around us.

SPIRITUAL REVOLUTION

Matriarchal politics leads to a different sort of revolution that also does not fit into the political categories of right or left. Implicit in the revolution is an open, nonabsolute model of the future that oversteps the prevailing system—not through orthodoxy or strategy but through countless diverse, intangible experiments. Matriarchal politics thus evades control by rightist or leftist political ideologies and causes ideologues considerable uneasiness. Matriarchal politics is the model of the consensus revolution—the complete opposite of the patriarchal model of the conquest revolution.[9]

In conquest revolutions, where conquest comes from below, the end justifies the means: violence is permitted and constantly begets violence. An absolute model of the future, which admits of no variations, is supposed to be carried through as abruptly as possible within one generation. The result is a continuation of the degradation of other people (those who have not yet achieved the "correct consciousness"), the rationalization of their oppression, and disregard for their profound suffering.

The consensus revolution, by contrast, proceeds on the assumption that the necessity of change rests with us and society alike. This means that not only the goal but also the path to it, the continuous process, are valued in order to do justice to that which we have become—whatever we are. All aspects of creating change are valued equally—how we initiate it, how we develop it, and how we conclude it. This requires us to follow circuitous paths with patience, since overt, direct opposition merely revives the old antagonisms and various types of dualism. The consensus revolution also entails a vision of the future, but it is one that can be continually changed in accordance with our experiences. It is a flexible utopia: it has a perspective but does not slavishly adhere to it.

The decisive aspect of the consensus revolution is the absence of a revolutionary leader and an elite cadre, i.e., a select group with the correct vision, the correct utopia, the correct consciousness; they would only re-create the old patriarchal hierarchy, in essence changing nothing. The development of vision, utopia, and consciousness, as well as the associated deeds and actions, takes place collectively in various groups; the one whose experiences are beneficial "leads" temporarily so that the group can concentrate on their vision and its active, political expression. This requires time and space; and instead of an absolute vision of the future, there arises a fabric of visions and actions that fuse into a multifarious consensus in which all feel included. It is a revolution not of violent, unprecedented upheaval but of many patient developmental steps. It also does not require for the well-being of humanity the immediate (or bloody) realization of an absolute utopia; instead, it operates over generations and does not justify any impatience that, for the sake of the attainment of the goal, would make others into semihumans or subhumans.

A just society and peace cannot be achieved by means of violence—either violence from above or violence from below through a conquest revolution. On the contrary, justice and peace develop in the patiently woven, increasingly strong and broad fabric of a consensus revolution. The consensus revolution results in a qualitatively different society, a society supported by the ethic of matriarchal spirituality, the passionateness of its love. It puts an end to the cycle of violence.

Notes

ONE: *Art as Ghetto*

1. Heide Göttner-Abendroth, *Die Göttin und ihr Heros: Die matriarchalen Religionen in Mythos, Märchen, Dichtung* (The goddess and her hero: The matriarchal religions in myth, fairy tale, and poetry) (Munich: Verlag Frauenoffensive, 1980).

2. Oral traditions can be reconstructed by means of comparative research in folklore, ethnology, and archaeology.

3. *Trans. note:* For a clear demonstration of how the patriarchal biases of historians, archaeologists, and mythologists resulted in distorted interpretations of the evidence of the worship of the Great Goddess and the existence of matriarchies, see Merlin Stone, *When God Was a Woman* (New York: Harvest/HBJ, 1976), xvii–xxiv and 156–58.

4. *Trans. note:* Throughout *The Greek Myths I* (New York: Viking Penguin, 1960), Robert Graves—the source for much of the mythological information in this essay—refers to the suppression of the matriarchies by patriarchal invaders. Also see Stone for a convincing argument supported by historical, archaeological, ethnological, and literary evidence that matriarchal societies were in fact the earliest forms of civilization and were later conquered by patriarchal invaders who tried to suppress the worship of the

matriarchal Great Goddess and oppress the powerful matriarchal women (30–61).

5. I am developing this historical perspective in my comprehensive work-in-progress "Theorie des Matriarchats" (Theory of the matriarchy).

6. *Trans. note:* The term *Triple goddess* is from Graves, *Greek Myths I*, 22.

7. Paraphrased from Robert Graves, *Mammon and the Black Goddess* (London: Cassell, 1965), 145ff.; cf. Robert Graves, *The White Goddess: A Historical Grammar of Poetic Myth* (New York: Creative Age Press, 1948), 316–37.

8. Homer, *Iliad* i.603–4.

9. Graves, *Greek Myths I*, 79–82.

10. *Trans. note:* Plato's views on art are found throughout his dialogues. His harsh criticism of the tales told to children by nurses and mothers appear in the *Republic* 377A–378E; and his intention of banishing certain types of poets from his ideal state is expressed in the *Republic* 401B.

11. *Trans. note:* For this characterization of women, see Aristotle, *On the Generation of Animals* 1.2. For his views on the inferiority and primitiveness of women, see *On the Generation of Animals* 2.3; *The History of Animals* 8.1; *Politics* 1.5.

12. Ernst Bloch, *Das Prinzip Hoffnung* (Frankfurt am Main: Suhrkamp, 1959) [English version: Neville Plaice et al., trans., *The Principle of Hope* (Cambridge, Mass.: MIT Press, 1986)] and *Literarische Aufsätze* (Literary essays) (Frankfurt am Main: Suhrkamp, 1965); Walter Benjamin, *Das Kunstwerk im Zeitalter seiner technischen Reproduzierbarkeit. Drei Studien zur Kunstsoziologie* (Frankfurt am Main: Suhrkamp, 1963) [English version: "The Work of Art in the Age of Mechanical Reproduction," in *Illuminations,* trans. Harry Zohn (New York: Schocken Books, 1969)]; Theodor W. Adorno, *Ästhetische Theorie*, ed. Gretel Adorno and Rolf Tiedemann (Frankfurt am Main: Suhrkamp, 1970) [English version: C. Lenhardt, trans., and Gretel Adorno and Rolf Tiedemann, eds., *Aesthetic Theory* (London and Boston: Routledge & Kegan Paul, 1984)] and *Prismen. Kulturkritik und*

Gesellschaft (Frankfurt am Main: Suhrkamp, 1969) [English version: Samuel and Shierry Weber, trans., *Prisms* (London: Spearman, 1967)]; Herbert Marcuse, *Eros and Civilization* (Boston: Beacon Press, 1966).

For a logical analysis of Adorno's aesthetic theory against the backdrop of Marxist aesthetic theory, see Heide Göttner-Abendroth and Joachim Jacobs, *Der logische Bau von Literaturtheorien* (The logical structure of literary theories) (Munich: Fink-Verlag, 1978), chap. 4.

13. Umberto Eco, *The Open Work,* trans. (from the Italian) Anna Concogni, introd. David Robey (Cambridge, Mass.: Harvard University Press, 1989); Max Bense, "Zusammenfassende Grundlegung moderner Ästhetik" (An overview of modern aesthetics), in *Mathematik und Dichtung. Versuche zur Frage einer exakten Literaturwissenschaft,* ed. Helmut Kreuzer and R. Gunzenhäuser (Munich: Nymphenburger Verlagshandlung, 1965/67); J. M. Lotman, *The Structure of the Artistic Text,* trans. (from the Russian) Ronald Vroon (Ann Arbor: Dept. of Slavic Languages and Literatures, University of Michigan, 1977); Jan Mukarovsky, *Studien zur strukturalistischen Ästhetik und Poetik* (Studies on structuralist aesthetics and poetics) (Munich: C. Hanser, 1977); Roman Jakobson, "Linguistik und Poetik," in *Literaturwissenschaft und Linguistik,* ed. Jens F. Ihwe (Frankfurt am Main: Athenäum Fischer Taschenbuchverlag, 1972), 1:99–135 [English version: "Linguistics and Poetics," in *Style in Language,* ed. T. Sebeok (Cambridge, Mass.: MIT Press, 1960), 350–77]; Samuel B. Levin, "Die Analyse des 'komprimierten' Stils in der Poesie" (The analysis of 'condensed' style in poetry), *Zeitschrift für Literaturwissenschaft und Linguistik* 3 (1971): 59–80; Roland Barthes, *Literatur oder Geschichte* (Literature or history) (Frankfurt am Main: Suhrkamp, 1969); Hans Robert Jauss, *Literaturgeschichte als Provokation* (Frankfurt am Main: Suhrkamp, 1970) [English version: "Literary History as Challenge to Literary Theory," in Jauss, *Toward an Aesthetic of Reception,* trans. Timothy Bahti: (Minneapolis: University of Minnesota Press, 1982), 3–45]; Wolfgang Iser, *The Implied Reader: Patterns of Communication in Prose Fiction*

from Bunyan to Beckett (Baltimore: Johns Hopkins University Press, 1974).

For an analysis of the theories of Jakobson and Levin, see Göttner-Abendroth and Jacobs, *Die logische Bau von Literaturtheorien*.

14. Georg Lukács, "Es geht um den Realismus," "Tendenz oder Parteilichkeit?" and "Reportage oder Gestaltung?" in *Marxismus und Literatur. Eine Dokumentation in drei Bänden,* ed. F. J. Raddatz (Hamburg: Rowohlt, 1969), 2:60–86, 139–49, 150–58.

15. Marcuse, *Eros and Civilization.*

16. *Trans. note:* While Freud does of course assign eternal value to patriarchy, the concept of the "primal horde" did not originate with him but with Darwin (in *Primal Law*), as Freud acknowledges in *Totem and Taboo* (1913), in his discussion of the association between the totem animal and the father/husband: "The Darwinian conception of the primal horde does not, of course, allow for the beginning of totemism" (A. A. Brill, ed., trans., introd., *The Basic Writings of Sigmund Freud* [New York: Random House, 1938], 915).

17. Göttner-Abendroth, *Die Göttin und ihr Heros.*

18. Cf., for example, S. J. Schmidt, *Ästhetizität* (Munich: Bayrischer Schulbuch-Verlag, 1971), and *Elemente einer Textpoetik* (Munich: Bayrischer Schulbuch-Verlag, 1974).

19. Silvia Bovenschen, *Die imaginierte Weiblichkeit. Exemplarische Untersuchungen zu kulturgeschichtlichen und literarischen Präsentationsformen des Weiblichen* (Imagined femininity: A concrete study on the cultural-historical and literary representations of the feminine) (Frankfurt: Suhrkamp, 1979).

Trans. note: Also see Silvia Bovenschen, "Is There a Feminine Aesthetic?" in Beth Weckmueller, trans., *New German Critique* 10 (1977): 111–37 (a translation of an article first published in *Aesthetik und Kommunikation* 25 [1976]).

20. Julia Kristeva, *Revolution in Poetic Language,* trans. Margaret Waller, introd. Leon S. Roudies (New York: Columbia University Press, 1984). Luce Irigaray, *Waren, Körper, Sprache. Der verrückte Diskurs der Frauen* (Commodity, body, language: The insane

discourse of women) (Berlin: Merve-Verlag, 1976); *Unbewusstes, Frauen, Psychoanalyse* (The unconscious, women, and psychoanalysis) (Berlin: Merve-Verlag, 1977); and *Speculum of the Other Woman*, trans. Gillian C. Gill (Ithaca, N.Y.: Cornell University Press, 1985).

For a comprehensive critical commentary on Irigaray, see Göttner-Abendroth, "Wissenschaftstheoretische Positionen in der Frauenforschung (Amerika, Frankreich, Deutschland)" (Theoretical positions in women's studies in America, France, and Germany) (in press).

Trans. note: With two exceptions, German translations of the works of Kristeva and Irigaray are cited.

21. *Trans. note:* See "Femininity," in *Sigmund Freud: The Complete Introductory Lectures on Psychoanalysis*, trans. and ed. James Strachey (New York: W. W. Norton, 1966), 576–99, and Jacques Lacan, *The Four Fundamental Concepts of Psychoanalysis*, ed. Jacques-Alain Miller, trans. Alan Sheridan (New York: Norton, 1978).

TWO: *The Dancing Muse*

1. *Trans. note:* The English terms *Maiden, Nymph, Crone,* and *Goddess in Triad* are from Graves, *Greek Myths I,* 92.

2. Descriptions are from Robert Briffault, *The Mothers: A Study of the Origins of Sentiments and Institutions,* 3 vols. (London: Unwin, 1969).

3. *Trans. note:* Graves refers to the contrast between the matriarchal (pre-Hellenic) and the patriarchal (Hellenic) conceptions of death in his discussion of the pre-Hellenic Persephone and Hecate and the Hellenic Hades: "Persephone and Hecate stood for the pre-Hellenic hope of regeneration; but Hades, a Hellenic concept for the ineluctability of death" (*Greek Myths I,* 123).

4. *Trans. note:* See Graves, *Greek Myths I,* 172: "A primitive theory that children were the reincarnations of dead ancestors lingered in the erotic cult of the Mare-goddess."

5. *Trans. note:* See Graves, *Greek Myths I,* 55: "The Muses

('mountain goddesses'), originally a triad (Pausanias: ix. 19.2), are the Triple-goddess in her orgiastic aspect." Graves also refers to the "Triple-Muse of Parnassus" (66).

6. See Graves, *Greek Myths I,* 19, and *The White Goddess,* 316–37.

7. *Trans. note:* As Graves points out, "The Maenads in fact represented the Muses" (*Greek Myths I,* 114).

8. *Trans. note:* For the spiral as a goddess symbol in the earliest known spirals in the history of art, cf. Joseph Campbell, *The Masks of God: Primitive Mythology* (New York: Viking, 1959, 1969), 331.

9. *Trans. note:* For the association of the labyrinth with the underworld and its rendering as a spiral, cf. Campbell, *Primitive Mythology,* 189 and 65. For the association of the labyrinth with the internal organs, specifically the mother's body, from which one is reborn, cf. Campbell, 69, and his source W. F. Jackson Knight, "Maze Symbolism and the Trojan Game," *Antiquity* 6 (December 1932):445–58; 450, n.3.

10. See Janet Bord, *Mazes and Labyrinths of the World* (London: Latimer New Dimensions, 1976). The figures are taken from this work.

11. *Trans. note:* In the patriarchal interpretation, Polyhymnia was considered the Muse of sacred poetry, and Terpsichore the Muse of choral song and dance. See, for example, Thomas Bulfinch, *The Age of Fable or Beauties of Mythology* (Philadelphia: David McKay, 1898), 12.

12. *Trans. note:* In the patriarchal interpretation, Calliope was considered the Muse of epic poetry (cf. Bulfinch, 12).

13. See Graves, *Greek Myths I,* 77, and his sources.

14. *Trans. note:* In patriarchal musicological terms, an octave is an interval (the distance in pitch between two notes) embracing eight diatonic tones, and hence its name. Cf. Willi Apel and Ralph T. Daniel, *The Harvard Brief Dictionary of Music* (New York: Washington Square Press, 1960), 197.

15. See Graves, *Greek Myths I,* 63–66, and his sources.

16. *Trans. note:* In the patriarchal interpretation, Euterpe was considered the Muse of lyric poetry (cf. Bulfinch, 12).

17. *Trans. note:* For a discussion of the annual sacrifice of the hero-king, see Stone, *When God Was a Woman*, 129–52.

18. *Trans. note:* As Graves points out (in *Greek Myths I*, 108) this etymology is suggested by Virgil (*Georgics* 2.380–84).

19. *Trans. note*: The matriarchal ritual sacrifice took place in autumn—in contrast to Graves's opinion that the sacrifice of Dionysus took place in midsummer; he further maintains that the surrogate offerings included bulls, goats, or *stags* (*Greek Myths I*, 108). However, Dionysus is also associated with rams; e.g., in Arcadia he was disguised as a ram (ibid.).

20. *Trans. note*: Friedrich Nietzsche first expounded on the Dionysian revel as the origin of tragedy. The dichotomy between the "wild" and the "tamed" Muse is already implicit in the dichotomy Nietzsche draws between the Dionysian and Apollonian aspects of art. However, he interprets art in patriarchal terms and fails to recognize the matriarchal origins of the Dionysian revel. (See *The Birth of Tragedy and the Genealogy of Morals*, trans. Francis Golfing [New York: Doubleday, 1956; Anchor Books, 1956].)

21. *Trans. note*: I assume Göttner-Abendroth intends *Weltalter* (literally, "age") as a translation of Graves's term *cycle*: "The figure twenty-two . . . probably refers to the twenty-two five-year *lustra* which composed a cycle—the 110-year cycle constituting the reign of a particular line of priestesses" (Graves, *Greek Myths I*, 141).

22. *Trans. note:* By comparing the structure of matriarchal mythology to counterpoint in music, the author means to compare this preexisting framework and the endlessly varied moon dances to the *cantus firmus* (Latin, "fixed melody"), the preexisting, fixed melodies used by medieval composers as the basis for contrapuntal variations. (See Apel and Daniel, *Harvard Brief Dictionary of Music*, 44, and *Funk & Wagnalls New Encyclopedia* [New York: Funk & Wagnalls, 1983], 7:274).

23. See Göttner-Abendroth, *Die Göttin und ihr Heros*, 5–22.

24. For a discussion of magic, see Bronislaw Malinowski, *Magic, Science and Religion, and Other Essays*, introd. Robert Red-

field (Garden City, N.Y.: Doubleday, 1948); and particularly Claude Lévi-Strauss, "The Sorcerer and His Magic" and "The Effectiveness of Symbols," in *Structural Anthropology,* trans. Claire Jacobson and Brooke Grundfest Schoepf (New York: Basic Books, 1976), 1:167–85, 186–205.

25. See Göttner-Abendroth, *Die Göttin und ihr Heros.*

26. This structural scheme was distilled from Graves's detailed investigation of Greek mythology in *The Greek Myths I* and *The Greek Myths II* (New York: Viking Penguin, 1960).

27. *Trans. note:* As Graves maintains, Helius was originally not a god and was subordinate to the Great Goddess, who controlled both the sun and the moon. Cf. *Greek Myths I,* 156: "The Sun's subordination to the Moon, until Apollo usurped Helius's place and made an intellectual deity of him, is a remarkable feature of early Greek myth."

28. *Trans. note:* The term *serpent demiurge* is from Graves, *Greek Myths I,* 28. For a discussion of the Pelasgian creation myth of Eurynome and the fact that fatherhood was unknown to these peoples, see *Greek Myths I,* 28.

29. *Trans. note:* See Göttner-Abendroth, *Die Göttin und ihr Heros,* 33, where she explains that the Minoan culture of Crete absorbed the influences of Sumerian and African cultures (including those of Libya and Egypt) and hence their veneration of the Libyan goddess Neith and the Egyptian figures Isis, Osiris, Horus, and Re/Ra (cf. Graves, *Greek Myths I,* 146, 80, 153).

30. *Trans. note:* The Persian hero Mithra is related to the Indian figure Mitra (cf. Joseph Kaster, *Putnam's Concise Mythological Dictionary* [New York: Putnam Perigee, 1963], 110).

31. *Trans. note:* The English spellings of the names of these goddesses and heroes have been carefully researched. The only questionable spellings are those of Hekuba—which cannot be "Hecuba," since she was not a goddess but a mortal, the wife of Priam—and Kubaba (which Stone spells "Kupapa"). For many, there are alternative spellings, e.g., Inanna/Ininni and Baldr/Balder/Baldur. Besides Graves, Campbell, Bulfinch, Stone, and Kaster, my sources include James G. Frazer, *The Golden Bough: A Study in Magic and Religion,* 3d ed. (London: Macmillan, 1980);

and H. R. Ellis Davidson, *Gods and Myths of Northern Europe* (Baltimore: Penguin, 1968).

32. *Trans. note:* See Göttner-Abendroth, *Die Göttin und ihr Heros* for a discussion of all the goddesses and heroes listed here as well as an analysis of the transformation of these cults under patriarchal influence.

THREE: *Witchcraft/Witch Art*

1. Jana Wisniewski, *Rollenbild der Rollenverschweigerung* (Roll picture of role concealment), exhibition "masculin-feminin" in the Neue Galerie, Graz, 1979; see catalog.

2. Cosey Fanni Tutti, *Life Forms,* exhibition "masculin-feminin" in the Neue Galerie, Graz, 1979; see catalog.

3. Friederike Pezold, *Zorn und Zärtlichkeit* (Rage and tenderness), in the catalog to the exhibition in the Galerie Maeght, Zurich, 1980.

4. Ibid.

5. For Carolee Schneemann's performance *Eye-Body* (1963), see Lucy Lippard, "Quite Contrary: Body, Nature, Ritual in Women's Art," *Chrysalis: A Magazine of Women's Culture* 2 (1977):36.

Trans. note: This paragraph—with the exception of the last sentence—paraphrases Lippard, 36. For a discussion of the serpent goddess of the matriarchy, cf. Stone, *When God Was a Woman,* 198–214.

6. For Ana Mendieta, see Lippard, 37.

Trans. note: This paragraph paraphrases Lippard, 37.

7. Mary Beth Edelson, "Documenting Rituals: What a Modern Day Problem!" *The Blatant Image: A Magazine of Feminist Photography* 1 (1981):74–77.

8. Mary Beth Edelson, *Sexual Rites,* in *Seven Cycles: Public Rituals* (New York: A.I.R., 1980), 16–18; photograph, 18; also in *Chrysalis* 6 (1978):93.

9. Quoted from Mary Beth Edelson, *Chrysalis* 6 (1978):93.

10. Cf. Raquel Tibol, *Frida Kahlo* (Frankfurt am Main: Verlag

Neue Kritik, 1980), which also contains the illustrations described here.

11. *Trans. note:* This painting is titled *My Nurse and I* (1937) and is discussed in much the same terms by Lippard, "Quite Contrary," 35.

12. All quotations and interpretations are from my personal conversations with Anna Fengel.

13. Anna Fengel, *Die unterirdische Göttin* and *Amazonen mit ihren Schlangen und Drachen,* Munich. All paintings of both series are privately owned and were exhibited in the Frauenbuchladen, in Munich.

14. Margarete Petersen, "Ich durchlebe die Karten, die ich male" (I experience the cards I paint), an interview with Luisa Francia (abridged), in Billie Potts, *Ein neues Tarot der Frauen* (A new women's tarot) (Munich: Verlag Frauenoffensive, 1982). Petersen published the reproductions of her paintings herself; they can be ordered from M. Petersen, Gunezrainer Str. 6, im Hof, 8000 München 40, Federal Republic of Germany.

Trans. note: The work cited was originally published in English: Billie Potts, *A New Women's Tarot,* 2d ed. (Woodstock, N.Y.: Elf and Dragons Press, 1978). (An earlier edition was published in 1977 under the title *The Witch's Tarot.*) I have translated the quotation from the German.

15. Lena Vandrey, exhibition *Cycle des amantes imputrescibles,* Atelier Jacob, Paris. Further materials in the form of slides are privately owned. Cf. the article "Lenas Amazonen," *Emma* 12 (1978):56–59 and illustration, 58.

16. Ingeborg Lüscher, exhibition in the Galerie Maeght, Zurich, 1980; cf. catalog. Exhibition in Centre d'art contemporain, Geneva, 1980; cf. catalog. Tarot card collection *Die vier Elemente. Leben und Licht* (The four elements: Life and light), Geneva, 1980; exhibition in the Galerie Dany Keller, Munich, 1982; cf. catalog. The picture "Ingeborg I" (1981) was a photo from that exhibit.

17. My entire commentary is taken from Ulrike Rosenbach, *Videokunst, Foto, Aktion/Performance/Feministischer Kunst* (Video art, photos, actions, performances, feminist art) (Cologne: Ver-

trieb Verlag Walther König, 1982). The figure is reprinted from p. 14.

18. *Trans. note:* Cf. Graves, *Greek Myths I,* 28: "Eurynome ('wide wandering') was the goddess's title as the visible moon; her Sumerian name was Iahu ('exalted dove'), a title which later passed to Jehovah as the Creator." Jehovah, of course, is another name for Yahweh in the Old Testament.

19. *Trans. note:* The author is referring to the *matriarchal,* Pelasgian creation myth of Eurynome, not to the myth in which the Triple goddess (as black-winged Night) created the universe through her universal Eros by laying the egg that hatched Eros, who then set the universe in motion—which is a later, Orphic creation myth (cf. Graves, *Greek Myths I,* 30).

20. *Trans. note:* See Graves, *Greek Myths I,* 72, for his discussion of Aphrodite as the "Goddess of Death-in-Life." The Goddess of Life-in-Death appeared at the winter solstice; the Goddess of Death-in-Life, at the summer solstice (*Greek Myths I,* 165).

21. Cf. Ulrike Rosenbach's practical work with women: *Schule für kreativen Feminismus (Beispiel einer autonomen Kulturarbeit* (School for creative feminism: An example of autonomous cultural work) (1980), which she published herself; it is available from U. Rosenbach, Venloer Str. 21, 5000 Köln 1, Federal Republic of Germany.

22. For Jere Van Syoc, see *Chrysalis* 6 (1978):95.

23. Colette, *Spiegelsaal als Kirche* (A hall of mirrors as a Church) exhibition "masculin-feminin," Neue Galerie, Graz, 1979; cf. catalog.

24. The reproduction of Colette's *Persephone's Bedroom* is from Lippard, "Quite Contrary," 42.

25. *Trans. note:* As Colette herself says, "I create my landscape and then become one with it" (quoted from Lippard, 41).

26. The figures are from Judy Chicago, *Embroidering Our Heritage: The Dinner Party Needlework* (needlework background provided by Susan Hill) (New York: Anchor/Doubleday, 1980). Cf. the video film about the creation of *The Dinner Party.*

27. *Trans. note:* Quoted from *Chrysalis* 6 (1978):96.

28. *Trans. note:* The terminology throughout the discussion of

The Dinner Party is taken directly from Chicago, *Embroidering Our Heritage,* e.g., "Fertile Goddess" (38), "runner" (9), "chalice" (9).

29. *Trans. note:* The wrong photograph must have been published, since the author's description does not quite match Fig. 21.

30. *Trans. note:* Sophia—not "Hagia Sophia"—is the correct name of the place setting. The names (and the spellings) of all place settings are quoted directly from Chicago, *Embroidering Our Heritage.*

31. *Trans. note:* The names are given here in the order in which Chicago discusses them in *Embroidering Our Heritage.*

32. Quoted from Susan Renni and Arlene Raven, "The Dinner Party Project: An Interview with Judy Chicago," *Chrysalis* 4 (1977):93–94.

33. *Trans. note:* Quoted from Renni and Raven, "Dinner Party Project," 100.

34. *Trans. note:* Quoted from Renni and Raven, "Dinner Party Project," 101.

35. Mimi Lobell, *The Goddess Temple* (1975), reproduction in *Chrysalis* 6 (1978):94.

36. *Trans. note:* The term *earthwork* is from Lippard, "Quite Contrary," 39. Lippard defines earthwork as "outdoor sculpture using earth and natural materials, usually gigantic in scale, and often referring back to ancient architecture, earth drawings, and mysterious mounds and barrows."

37. Sigrid Neubert, *Der Park* (The park) (Hamburg: Knaus-Verlag, 1980), and her exhibition *Die Neue Sammlung* (The new collection), Munich, 1982.

38. *Trans. note:* This is a paraphrase of Lippard, "Quite Contrary," 38. Lippard quotes here from Jody Pinto, *Artpark: The Program in Visual Arts* (Lewiston, N.Y.: Artpark, 1976). As Lippard indicates, Pinto calls this series *The Spotted Bundle Enclosures.*

39. *Trans. note:* This paragraph is a paraphrase of Pinto's words as quoted by Lippard, 37–38.

40. Robert Smithson, *Spiral Jetty,* photo from the exhibition in Centre d'art contemporain, Geneva, 1981.

41. For Margaret Hicks, see Lippard, 40—from which the figure was taken.

Trans. note: The author's description of *Hicks' Mandala* is paraphrased from Lippard, 40.

42. For Alice Aycock, see Lippard, 40–41.

43. Mary Beth Edelson, *Woman Rising* (1973–74), from *Seven Cycles: Public Rituals* (New York, 1980), 17–19; photograph, 19.

44. For Mary Fish, *Twenty-Eight Days' Activity* (Doheny State Beach, California, 1974), see Lippard, 46.

Trans. note: The Lippard quotation also contains a quotation from Mary Fish, *Twenty-Eight Days* (Chesterfield, Mo.: self-published, 1976).

45. Mary Beth Edelson, *Drawing Fire Energy Series,* in *Chrysalis* 6 (1978):93. The reproduction of *Pilgrimage to a Neolithic Cave* is from *The Blatant Image* 1 (1981):77.

46. *Trans. note:* Quoted from Edelson, *Seven Cycles,* 6. More precisely, it is from Lippard's introduction ("Fire and Stone: Politics and Ritual"), and the entire passage reads: "Mary Beth Edelson's work arises from Feminism's double strength. Like the Great Goddess to whom she has dedicated her art, she has (at least) two aspects—political rage and life-giving affirmation. The two merge in an individual identification with the collective ego: 'Women exploring who "we are" and not who "I am," ' as she puts it."

47. The performance *Mourning Our Lost Herstory,* in the exhibit *Your 5,000 Years Are Up!* (1977); the performance and earthwork *Memorials to 9,000,000 Women Burned as Witches in the Christian Era* (1977); the performance and earthwork *Fire Flights in Deep Space* (1978); the performance *Where Is Our Fire?* (1977/79); and the performance *Creation Begins with a Green Light: Ritual on the Earth* (1980) are from Edelson, *Seven Cycles.* Illustrations are taken from 4 and 57.

48. *Trans. note:* Quoted from Edelson, *Seven Cycles,* 34.

49. *Trans. note:* I have supplied the direct quotation (Lippard, "Quite Contrary," 39).

50. Mary Beth Edelson, as quoted by Lippard, 39.

Trans. note: I have supplied the quotation, replacing the author's paraphrase of it.

51. "Dreams, Signs and Images—An Interview," an interview with Mary Beth Edelson by Louise Moore, Los Angeles, 1979.

Trans. note: The English original could not be located, and the passage does not appear in any of the 1979 issues of *Chrysalis*. It could be from a self-published pamphlet or an article in an unindexed journal. I therefore translated it from the German.

52. Cf. the musical historical investigations of Eva Rieger, *Frau, Musik und Männerherrschaft* (Woman, music, and male domination) (Frankfurt: Ullstein, 1981).

53. Meri Franco-Lao, *Hexen-Musik* (Witch music) (Munich: Frauenoffensive, 1979).

Trans. note: Because an English translation of the Italian original, *Musica strega: per la ricerca di una dimensione femminile nella musica* (Roma: Edizioni delle donne, 1977), could not be located, I translated from the German.

54. *Mooncircles,* songs written, composed, and arranged by Kay Gardner, *Urana Records,* 1975.

55. *Trans. note:* Quoted from the album notes by Kirsten Grimstad (reprinted in an advertisement in *Chrysalis* 6 [1978]:99)

56. *Trans. note:* As Grimstad points out in the album notes, Plutarch attributed the invention of the mixolydian mode to Sappho (*Chrysalis* 6 [1978]:99).

57. *Trans. note:* "Lunamuse" is the correct spelling of the piece, as indicated in Grimstad's album notes quoted in *Chrysalis.*

58. *Alte Hexenlieder. Lieder-Zyklus* (Ancient witch music: A song cycle), ed. Gisela Meussling, with music by Inge Latz and illustrations by Petra Kaster (Bonn, 1982). The authors published the work themselves; it may be ordered from G. Meussling, Friedrich-Breuer-Str. 77, 5300 Bonn 3, Federal Republic of Germany.

59. From Franco-Lao, *Hexen-Musik.*

60. In Adrienne Rich, *The Fact of a Doorframe: Poems Selected and New, 1950–1984* (New York: W. W. Norton, 1985), 256.

61. In Adrienne Rich, *Poems Selected and New, 1950–1974* (New York: W. W. Norton, 1975), 109–10.

62. In Rich, *Poems Selected and New, 1950–1974,* 231–32.

63. In Barbara Starrett, *I Dream in Female: The Metaphors of Evolution and the Metaphors of Power* (Gloucester, Mass.: Cassandra, 1976).

64. Anne Waldmann, *Fast Speaking Woman and Other Chants*

(San Francisco: City Lights, 1975); reprinted in *Helping the Dreamer: New & Selected Poems, 1966–1988* (Minneapolis: Coffee House Press, 1989), 36–58.

65. *Trans. note:* Cf. Waldman's footnote to the poem: " 'Fast Speaking Woman' is indebted to the Mazatec Indian shamaness, Maria Sabina, in Mexico guiding persons in magic mushroom ceremony & is a reworking & coincidence of the same for all wandering spirits" (*Helping the Dreamer,* 58).

66. From Verena Stefan, *Mit Füssen und Flügeln* (With feet and wings) (Munich: Verlag Frauenoffensive, 1980).

67. From Heide Göttner-Abendroth, *landschaften aus der gegenwelt. gedichte* (landscapes from the counterworld: poems) edition hagia (Munich, 1982). This self-published book may be ordered from Frauenliteraturvertrieb, Schlossstrasse 94, 6000 Frankfurt am Main 90, Federal Republic of Germany.

68. *Trans. note:* Elsewhere the author interprets these as *four* individual festivals.

69. Robin Morgan, "The Network of the Imaginary Mother," in *Lady of the Beasts* (New York: Random House, 1976), 61–88.

70. From Morgan, *Lady of the Beasts,* 83.

71. From Morgan, *Lady of the Beasts,* 83.

72. From Morgan, *Lady of the Beasts,* 88.

FOUR: *The Lunisolar Drama*

1. For this topic, cf. Göttner-Abendroth, "Urania. Zeit und Raum der Sterne (zum Weltbild matriarchaler Völker im Spiegel der modernen Physik)" (Urania: Time and place of the stars [on the worldview of matriarchal peoples as mirrored in modern physics]), *Feministische Studien* 1 (1982).

2. For a treatment of the concept "matriarchal spirituality," see Göttner-Abendroth, "Du Gaia bist Ich (matriarchale Religionen, früher und heute)" (You, Gaea, am I [matriarchal religions of the past and present]), *Religion heute* 3 (Sept. 1981):22–34.

3. Zsuzsanna Budapest, *The Feminist Book of Lights and Shadows* (Venice, Calif.: Luna Publications, 1976). For elementary rituals for concrete purposes, see Luisa Francia, *Berühre Wega, kehr'*

zur Erde zurück (Touch Vega and return to earth) (Munich: Verlag Frauenoffensive, 1982).

4. *Trans. note:* For the myth of Kore and Demeter, see Graves, *Greek Myths I,* 89–96.

5. Cf. Göttner-Abendroth, *Die Göttin und ihr Heros.*

6. Starhawk (Miriam Simos), *The Spiral Dance: A Rebirth of the Ancient Religion of the Great Goddess* (San Francisco: Harper and Row, 1979).

7. Quoted from Starhawk, *The Spiral Dance,* 216.

8. For a discussion of the lunar calendar, see Anne Kent Rush, *Moon, Moon* (Berkeley and New York: Moon Books/Random House, 1976).

9. *Trans. note:* The author means to establish a parallel between the four-month time of transition and the time it takes a woman's body to recover from childbirth. Because she complicates her own argument by stating that recovery from childbirth requires about *three* months, I took the liberty of stating that it takes about *four* months for the woman's body to recover.

10. *Trans. note:* As Graves indicates, the pre-Hellenic, Pelasgian year consisted of thirteen months (*Greek Myths I,* 138). Graves also speculates that the three heads of Hecate (lion, dog, and mare) was a reference to the tripartite year (124–25).

11. *Trans. note:* In the American liturgical year, this feast is simply called Candlemas. The Christian festival of Candlemas celebrates the purification of Mary; the original pagan festival celebrated the lengthening days. (Cf. *Funk & Wagnalls New Encyclopedia* 5:251 and *Webster's New Universal Unabridged Dictionary,* ed. Jean L. McKechnie, 2d ed. [New York: Simon & Schuster, 1983], 263.)

12. For a discussion of the tarot cards, see the excursus at the end of this essay.

13. *Trans. note:* Old High German *Ostara,* modern German *Ostern,* Old English *Eastre,* and modern English *Easter* derive from the word *Eostre,* (the Northumbrian spelling of *Eastre*), the name of the goddess celebrated at the vernal equinox (*Oxford English Dictionary* [Oxford: Oxford University Press, 1933] 3:18–19). To distinguish between the pre-Christian (and the new matriarchal)

festival and the Christian festival, the author uses *Ostara* for the former and *Ostern* for the latter. I follow her lead by using *Eastre* for the Pre-Christian (and the new matriarchal) festival and *Easter* for the Christian feast.

14. *Trans. note:* The author provides no source for or explanation of the statement that the directions east and west, the sides right and left, and architectonic arrangements were switched. Concerning architecture, however, she could be referring to the fact that the ancient Egyptian concept of space did not correspond to that of European high civilizations. (See Rudolf Pfefferkorn, *Stilkunde des Abendlandes. Architektur,* Humboldt Taschenbuch, no. 101 [Berlin, Munich: Verlag Lebendiges Wissen, 1961], 7.)

15. *Trans. note:* Walpurgis Night, the eve of May Day, is when witches were said to gather on Brocken Peak, in the Harz Mountains of Germany; it was later Christianized as the feast of Saint Walpurgis, an English missionary to Germany in the eighth century (Cf. *Webster's New Universal Unabridged Dictionary,* 2058, and *Wahrig Deutsches Wörterbuch,* ed. Ursula Hermann and Gerhard Wahrig [N.p.: Mosaik Verlag, 1980], 4100.)

16. *Trans. note:* Actually May Day has been Christianized: In Roman Catholic ritual in the United States (in which I participated as a child) and in the Catholic areas of Germany (in a ritual described to me by a German colleague), a statue of the Virgin Mary is crowned the "Queen of the May" by a young girl on May 1.

17. *Trans. note:* For this etymology, cf., among others, *Funk and Wagnalls Standard Dictionary of Folklore, Mythology and Legend,* ed. Maria Leach (San Francisco: Harper & Row, 1972), 652.

18. *Trans. note:* In the Christian liturgical year, the Assumption is celebrated on August 15.

19. *Trans. note:* The *OED* supports the author's etymology of *Halloween.* According to the *OED,* the English word *halloween* is derived from *allhallow-even* ("eve of all saints"), which in turn derives from *allhallows* ("all saints")—a Celtic term. "In the old Celtic calendar the year began on 1st November, so that the last evening of October was 'old-year's night,' the night of all the witches, which the Church transformed into the Eve of All Saints" (5:43).

20. *Trans. note:* According to *Wahrig,* the festival is called *Perchten*—not *Perchta,* as the author indicates. However, the procession is led by Frau Perchta/Berchta, a figure similar to Frau Holle (2813).

21. *Trans. note:* Some clarification is in order here. All Saints Day is November 1, the day *after* Halloween, so the author probably meant to refer to both All Souls Day (October 31) and All Saints Day (November 1). Moreover, Saint Martin's feast day (*Martinsfest* or Martinmas) is November 11, not November 1, as the author implies (*Wahrig,* 2471, and *Webster's,* 1105). However, this does not undercut her argument that the procession of Frau Holle was turned into the procession of Saint Martin, since all Christian holidays tend to fall near the original pagan festival—if not on the precise date—and intentionally so.

22. *Trans. note:* Unlike the modern German word *Weihnachten* ("nights of commemoration"), the English word *Christmas* obviously in no way reflects the pagan origins of the holiday. According to *Wahrig,* the German *Weihnachten* derives from Middle High German *wihe(n)naht(en),* meaning "holy nights" (4140).

What the author identifies as a Celtic term—*Modronight*—is actually an Anglicized form of the Celtic *Modraniht* ("the night of the mothers"), a pagan festival that falls on what is now Christmas Eve and was associated with childbirth (H. R. Ellis Davidson, *Gods and Myths of Northern Europe,* 113, and her source, the Venerable Bede, *De Temporum Ratione,* 13

23. *Trans. note:* This is a controversial etymology. While many standard works do not connect *Jule*/Yule with Old Norse *jól* as meaning "wheel," Shipley does give some credence to the connection between Yule and *jól* meaning "wheel" (Joseph T. Shipley, *Dictionary of Word Origins* [New York: The Philosophical Library, 1945], 898).

24. For an introduction to tarot, see Robert Wang, *The Golden Dawn Tarot* (New York: Samuel Weiser, 1978); Paul Huson, *The Devil's Picture Book* (London: Abacus, 1972); Billie Potts, *A New Women's Tarot,* 2d ed. (Woodstock, N.Y.: Elf and Dragons Press, 1978) [earlier edition published in 1977 under title *The Witch's*

Tarot; and Luisa Francia, *Hexentarot* (Witch's tarot) (Munich: Verlag New Age, 1981.

25. *Trans. note:* The "harvest thanksgiving feast" of the autumnal equinox is not to be confused with the American Thanksgiving, which occurs not at the autumnal equinox but on the fourth Thursday of November.

26. *Trans. note:* Contrary to the German text, it is not the Goddess of Death-in-Life but the Goddess of Life-in-Death who appears at the winter solstice. Cf. chap. 3, n. 20.

27. *Trans. note:* This is of course an allusion to Friedrich Nietzsche's "Umwertung aller Werte" ("revaluation of all values") which Göttner-Abendroth renders as "Umwertung der Werte" ("revaluation of values"). "Umwertung aller Werte" was Nietzsche's intended title for the work published from his notes in 1901 by his sister *Die Wille zur Macht* (The will to power). See Walter Kaufmann, "Friedrich Nietzsche," vol. 5, *The Encyclopedia of Philosophy,* ed. Paul Edwards (New York: Macmillan & The Free Press, 1967; 1972), 510. The translation "revaluation of all values" is from Kaufmann. It seems a more precise translation in terms of Nietzsche's moral theory and, more important, in terms of Göttner-Abendroth's conception of matriarchal versus patriarchal values than Francis Golffing's "transvaluation of all values" in *Friedrich Nietzsche: The Birth of Tragedy and the Genealogy of Morals* (New York: Doubleday & Company, 1956; Anchor Books, 1956), 296.

AFTERWORD

1. For a critique of science, see the introduction to my book *Die Göttin und ihr Heros* and my essay "Erato. Strophen der Liebe" (Erato: strophes of love), *Feministische Studien* 2 (1983).

2. *Trans. note:* The linguistic problems involved in describing matriarchal art and spirituality are clearly reflected in the facts that earlier in the book the author herself speaks of "matriarchal *religions*" and that she has also published a work on "matriarchal *religions.*"

3. Cf. my essay "Du Gaia bist Ich" (You, Gaea, am I), in *Feminismus. Inspektion der Herrenkultur*, 1983. *Trans. note:* Since in an earlier reference the author gives the date of the essay as 1981, this must be a reprinted version.

4. *Trans. note:* See Johann Jakob Bachofen, *Das Mutterrecht. Eine Untersuchung über die Gynaikokratie der alten Welt nach ihrer religiösen und rechtlichen Natur* (Mother right: a study on the 'Gynecocracy' of the ancient world according to its religious and legal nature) (Stuttgart: Krais & Hoffman, 1861). For a translation of excerpts from this work, see Ralph Mannheim, trans., *Myth, Religion, and Mother Right* (Princeton: Princeton University Press, 1967).

5. *Trans. note:* The following works by women (that predate Göttner-Abendroth's study) reflect a positive view of early matriarchies: Jane E. Harrison, *Prolegomena to the Study of Greek Religion*, 3d ed. (Cambridge: Cambridge University Press, 1922); Jacquetta Hawkes, *Dawn of the Gods* (London: Chatto and Windus, 1958); Kathleen Kenyon, *Archaeology in the Holy Land* (Tonbridge: Ernest Benn, 1960); Sybelle von Cles-Reden, *The Realm of the Great Goddess* (London: Thames and Hudson, 1961); Rivkah Harris, "Naditu Women of Sippar I & II," *Journal of Cuneiform Studies* 15 (1962):117–20 and 16 (1962):1–12; Margaret Murray, *The Genesis of Religion* (London: Routledge & Kegan Paul, 1963); Jacquette Hawkes, *Prehistory: History of Mankind, Cultural and Scientific Development*, vol. 1, pt. 1 (New York: Mentor, 1965), and *The First Great Civilizations* (London: Hutchinson, 1973); Merlin Stone, *When God Was a Woman* (New York: Harvest/HBJ, 1976); Froma I. Zeitlin, "The Dynamics of Misogyny: Myth and Mythmaking in the *Oresteia*," *Arethusa* 11 (1978):149–84; Charlene Spretnak, *Lost Goddesses of Early Greece: A Collection of Pre-Hellenic Myths* (Berkeley: Moon Books, 1978; Boston: Beacon Press, 1981); Margot Adler, *Drawing Down the Moon: Witches, Druids, Goddess-Worshippers, and Other Pagans in America Today* (New York: Viking Press, 1979; Boston: Beacon Press, 1981).

More recent relevant works that postdate the author's study include Marija Gimbutas, *Goddesses and Gods of Old Europe, 7000 to 35000 B.C.: Myths, Legends and Cult Images* (Berkeley: University of California Press, 1982); Jean Shinoda Bolen, *The Goddesses in Everywoman* (Los Angeles: J. P. Tarcher, 1982); Monica Sjöö and Barbara Mor, *The Great Cosmic Mother: Rediscovering the Religion of the Earth* (San Francisco: Harper & Row, 1987); Elinor W. Gadon, *The Once and Future Goddess: A Symbol for Our Time* (New York: Harper & Row, 1989); Margaret Ehrenberg, *Women in Prehistory* (Norman, Okla.: University of Oklahoma Press, 1990); Patricia Monaghan, *The Book of Goddesses and Heroines* (St. Paul, Minn.: Llewellyn, 1981; new and enlarged edition, New York: E. P. Dutton, 1991).

Scholars who doubt or have attempted to disprove the existence of early matriarchies include, among others, William Blake Tyrrell, *Amazons: A Study in Athenian Mythmaking* (Baltimore and London: Johns Hopkins University Press, 1984); Joan Bamberger, "The Myth of Matriarchy: Why Men Rule in Primitive Society," in *Woman, Culture, and Society,* ed. Michelle Zimbalist Rosaldo and Louise Lamphere (Stanford: Stanford University Press, 1970), 263–80; and Gerda Lerner, *The Creation of Patriarchy* (New York and Oxford: Oxford University Press, 1986.

For an excellent bibliography of matriarchal research, see Charlene Spretnak, ed., *The Politics of Women's Spirituality: Essays on the Rise of Spiritual Power within the Feminist Movement* (Garden City, N.Y.: Anchor Books, 1982), 581–90.

6. This complex description and explanation of the development of the matriarchal form of society requires a comprehensive scientific investigation, on which I am now working. Of course, the present collection of essays—which merely attempts to contribute a new perspective to art and spirituality of women today—is not a scientific treatise on the history of matriarchy.

7. Cf. Spretnak, ed., *Politics of Women's Spirituality.*

8. Starhawk (Miriam Simos), *Dreaming the Dark: Magic, Sex, and Politics,* 2d ed. (Boston: Beacon Press, 1988), and "Ethics and Justice in Goddess Religion," *Anima* 7 (Fall 1980):61–68.

9. Cf. Dorothy Riddle, "Politics, Spirituality, and Models of Change," in *Politics of Women's Spirituality,* ed. Spretnak, 373–81.

Trans. note: The terms *conquest revolution* and *consensus revolution* are Spretnak's.